Routledge Revivals

Marshal Pilsudski

First published in 1939, *Marshal Pilsudski* presents a comprehensive biographical history of Józef Klemens Piłsudski (1867-1935). He was a Polish statesman who served as the Chief of State (1918–1922) and first Marshal of Poland (from 1920). He was viewed as the father of the Second Polish Republic, which was re-established in 1918.

This book discusses various facets of his life such as birth and parentage (1867- 1877); life in Wilno (1875- 1885); undergraduate life (1885-1887); Pilsudski as P.P.S. agitator; Pilsudski in the Great War (1914); Pilsudski and the New Poland; Pilsudski and Parliament; the Polish crisis (1922); the Pilsudski question; constitutional friction (1928); Pilsudski in Madeira and Poland and his last triumphs. This is an important historical reference work for scholars and researchers of Polish history, history of World War I, European history and Military history.

Marshal Pilsudski

W. F. Reddaway

First published in 1939
by George Routledge & Sons Ltd.

This edition first published in 2024 by Routledge
4 Park Square, Milton Park, Abingdon, Oxon, OX14 4RN

and by Routledge
605 Third Avenue, New York, NY 10017

Routledge is an imprint of the Taylor & Francis Group, an informa business

© W. F. Reddaway, 1939

All rights reserved. No part of this book may be reprinted or reproduced or utilised in any form or by any electronic, mechanical, or other means, now known or hereafter invented, including photocopying and recording, or in any information storage or retrieval system, without permission in writing from the publishers.

Publisher's Note
The publisher has gone to great lengths to ensure the quality of this reprint but points out that some imperfections in the original copies may be apparent.

Disclaimer
The publisher has made every effort to trace copyright holders and welcomes correspondence from those they have been unable to contact.

A Library of Congress record exists under LCCN: 39021584

ISBN: 978-1-032-94112-7 (hbk)
ISBN: 978-1-003-56901-5 (ebk)
ISBN: 978-1-032-94113-4 (pbk)

Book DOI 10.4324/9781003569015

W. F. Reddaway

MARSHAL PILSUDSKI

Illustrated

LONDON
GEORGE ROUTLEDGE & SONS LTD.
Broadway House: 68–74 Carter Lane, E.C.

First published 1939

Printed in Great Britain by T. and A. CONSTABLE LTD
at the University Press, Edinburgh

To
MY POLISH FRIENDS

CONTENTS

	PAGE
PREFACE	xi
INTRODUCTION	1

CHAPTER
I.	BIRTH AND PARENTAGE (1867–1877)	5
II.	LIFE IN WILNO (1875–1885)	10
III.	UNDERGRADUATE LIFE (1885–1887)	16
IV.	SIBERIA (1887–1892)	19
V.	THE POLISH SOCIALIST PARTY (P.P.S.)	23
VI.	PILSUDSKI AS P.P.S. AGITATOR (1893–1900)	27
VII.	PILSUDSKI IN PRISON (1900–1901)	35
VIII.	WORK FOR THE P.P.S. IN EUROPE AND JAPAN (1902–1905)	41
IX.	PILSUDSKI AND THE MILITANTS (1905–1908)	47
X.	BEZDANY (26 SEPTEMBER, 1908)	52
XI.	PILSUDSKI AND THE RIFLEMEN (1908–1914)	59
XII.	PILSUDSKI IN THE GREAT WAR (1914)	69
XIII.	PILSUDSKI AND THE LEGIONS (1915–1916)	76
XIV.	PILSUDSKI AND "INDEPENDENT POLAND" (1917)	83
XV.	PILSUDSKI A PRISONER (JULY, 1917–NOVEMBER, 1918)	93
XVI.	THE RESTORATION OF POLAND (NOVEMBER 1918)	101
XVII.	PILSUDSKI AND THE NEW POLAND (DECEMBER, 1918–FEBRUARY, 1919)	110

CONTENTS

CHAPTER		PAGE
XVIII.	Pilsudski and Parliament (1919)	116
XIX.	Wilno and the Ukraine (1919)	121
XX.	The Russo-Polish War (1920)	126
XXI.	The Decisive Phase (August–October, 1920)	135
XXII.	Pilsudski and Poland (1920–1921)	143
XXIII.	Poland in 1922	153
XXIV.	The Polish Crisis (1922)	159
XXV.	The Polish Presidency (December, 1922)	167
XXVI.	Pilsudski's Retirement (1923)	174
XXVII.	Pilsudski at Sulejowek (August, 1923)	180
XXVIII.	Pilsudski in 1924	191
XXIX.	The Pilsudski Question (1925)	204
XXX.	Pilsudski and the Government (1926)	212
XXXI.	The "Events of May" (1926)	227
XXXII.	The Pilsudski Régime (June, 1926–1927)	236
XXXIII.	Constitutional Friction (1928)	249
XXXIV.	Régime v. Seym (1929)	258
XXXV.	Pilsudski's Triumph (1930)	272
XXXVI.	Pilsudski in Madeira and Poland (1931)	285
XXXVII.	Pilsudski in 1932–1933	295
XXXVIII.	Pilsudski's Last Triumphs (1933–1935)	303
XXXIX.	The Final Scenes (1935)	311
XL.	The Standpoint of 1939	317
Index		322

LIST OF ILLUSTRATIONS

"Pilsudski within the Framework of the March Constitution" . . . . . *Frontispiece*	
Caricature by Captain Z. Czermanski	FACING PAGE
The Marshal on "Kasztanka"	1
Pilsudski's Father and Mother	4
Pilsudski as a Schoolboy and as a Prisoner .	16
Pilsudski as a Socialist Agitator . . .	30
"A certain Pilsudski"	36
Pilsudski as "Commandant" of the Legions .	76
Roman Dmowski and Ignatius Daszynski . .	106
Pilsudski with General Rydz-Smigly . . .	130
Stanislas Wojciechowski and Gen. Skladkowski .	170
Pilsudski and his Family in 1928 . . .	250
The Patience-Table	262
Pilsudski, aged	288

MAPS

I. Russia in 1914	1
II. Pilsudski's Share in the Great War and Wars of 1919-20	72
III. Reborn Poland, 1939	152

PREFACE

MARSHAL PILSUDSKI was born in December 1867 and died in May 1935. Had he perished at fifty, in a German prison, he might have been remembered as a foolhardy rebel. On the eve of the Armistice he was set free. Within eight hundred days, he had shaped reborn Poland and driven Lenin's armies out of Europe. Then, during his last fourteen years, he so wrought that, both to the Poles and to the outside world, Pilsudski stood and stands for Poland. His biographer, therefore, during three-quarters of his hero's life, must chiefly concern himself with his inheritance, his character and his training for the final stage. From November 1918, he must attempt to trace the impact of the man upon his country, and, through Poland, upon the world. His task is harder because during the term of Pilsudski's adult life the ideas, the communications and the boundaries of Europe underwent revolution.

In writing of Poland, moreover, an Englishman is handicapped at every turn. He treats of Slavs, that is, of men whose thoughts and acts are not easily comprehended by the West. What western nation could find satisfaction in fulfilling a destiny of suffering for the benefit of mankind? Historically and geographically, Poland has been peculiarly remote from Britain. It has been joined to her only by the slenderest bonds of trade and intercourse, and devoted to an alien form of faith. English notions of Poland have usually come from Germans—a race filled with conscientious contempt for their eastern neighbours. Many untravelled Britons, moreover, suffer from the accident

PREFACE

that Slavonic nomenclature seems to them too grotesque for serious people. "Bombardment of P-r-z-e-m-y-s-l," spelt out the old gentleman; "would that be a printer's error? or have the letters got mixed up by the bombardment?"

Pilsudski, again, baffles the Briton because of his manifold unlikeness to our accustomed conception of a Pole. Chivalry, oratory and courtesy, indeed, were his birthright, and he shows a Polish capacity for swiftly-varying moods. But attributes often declared by Poles to mark their race—prodigality, superficiality, indolence, exaggerated respect for what comes from abroad, inconstancy, unpunctuality—of these Pilsudski had nothing. His frank and outspoken realism in estimating his own powers and achievements, moreover, jars against one of our strongest conventions. Which of our calumniated heroes could declare that, when he stood before his Maker, he would entreat Him not to send our nation more great men? Much of his biography, too, cannot yet be adequately written. Many years must pass before the historian can deal fully with the domestic life of one who was by nature a devoted son, brother, husband and father, or can measure accurately his achievement as a statesman. The fourfold personality which he claimed —joyous child, affable lordling, sage and commander—may always defy analysis. My hope must be that the dispassionate use of what is already public, particularly his own words, may result in a true outline of one who in talents, ideals and force ranks high among modern men and who receives widespread worship from a great and fertile nation.

The English reader of 1939 will find an admirable introduction to modern Poland in Prof. R. Dyboski's *Poland* (1933). Polish history from 1914 is fully outlined in R. Machray's *The Poland of Pilsudski* (1936). Lord d'Abernon treats of the *Eighteenth Decisive Battle of the World*. The

PREFACE

brief biography, *Pilsudski, Marshal of Poland*, by E. J. Patterson and the translation of portions of the Marshal's autobiographical works, with connecting historical notes, by D. R. Gillie, should be of service. Articles and interviews in contemporary English newspapers, notably *The Times*, and Sir E. J. Russell's *Poland Revisited* (1937) appear to deserve the respect paid to them by Polish historians. The *Slavonic Review*, the writings of C. Smogorzewski, the *Polish Handbook* and the publications of the Birmingham Slavonic Department fill many gaps. E. J. Harrison's *Lithuania* (1922), like the works of D'Etchegoyen and Korostowetz, is a trenchant *advocatus diaboli*, and Prof. Bruce Boswell's *Poland and the Poles* and Baedeker's *Russia* are most helpful for pre-War Poland.

My own indebtedness must be expressed first and foremost to works published at Warsaw in Polish, especially to the ten-volume edition of Pilsudski's *Collected Writings* (1937) and, for the years 1867–1908, to the two solid and well-documented volumes of Pobog-Malinowski (1935). On the years 1914–1935, Gen. F. Slawoj-Skladkowski's works offer valuable and delightful fragments. H. Cepnik's shorter eulogy, approved by three Ministers (1936), reproduces useful documents, and J. K. Malicki's comprehensive work on *Pilsudski and the Seym* (1936) treats a difficult topic on liberal lines. As an editor of the forthcoming *Cambridge History of Poland*, I have profited by the general tenor of several contributions to that work. Dmowski's *Polish Policy* (1925), two volumes of investigations in and after 1933 by K. Wrzos, and the newly-published works of Mlle C. Illakowicz, Wl. Baranowski, and ex-Premier Sliwinski (in *Niepodleglosc*, 1938) have been of great though very diverse service. The vivid caricatures of the ex-Legionary Z. Czermanski are immensely illuminating and human.

PREFACE

A few special references are made in footnotes and in the Index.

Permission to print extracts from *The Comedy of Poland* and from *Wings over Poland*, published respectively by Messrs. Allen and Unwin and by Appleton-Century, has been kindly given. With regret, diacritical signs and all non-essential names have been omitted. A few imitated pronunciations will be found in the Index.

For invaluable help and criticism, my grateful thanks are due to Mlle Illakowicz, to Mr. J. Tomaszewski of the Polish Embassy in London, and to Dr. H. Wereszycki of the Pilsudski Institute in Warsaw.

Mr. A. P. Goudy, Mr. T. M. Ragg, and Mr. G. F. N. Reddaway have lightened some of the heaviest labours.

W. F. REDDAWAY.

KING'S COLLEGE, CAMBRIDGE,
February 1939.

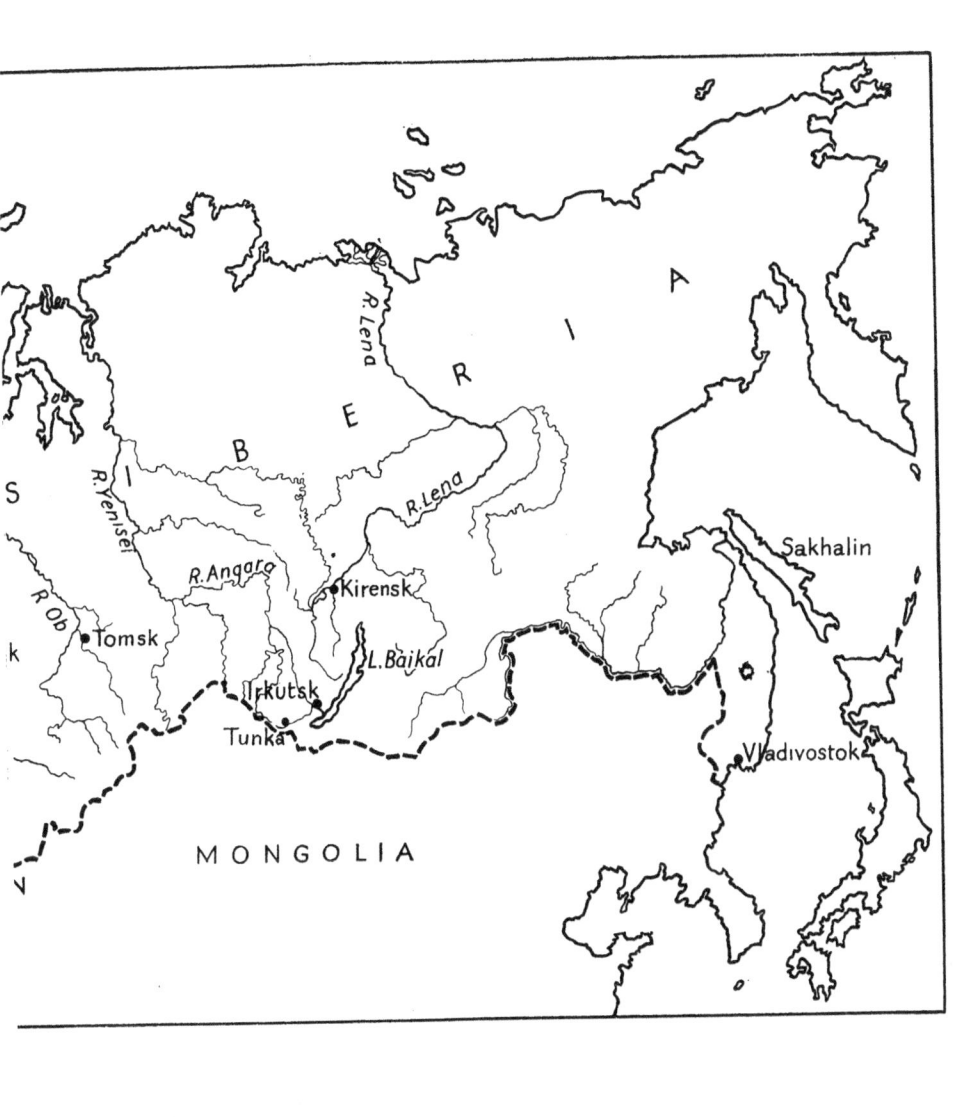

The Marshal on "Kasztanka."

INTRODUCTION

NO State-founder in modern times has been more highly honoured by his people than Pilsudski by the Poles. In 1938, a retired university teacher was sentenced to a substantial term of imprisonment for insulting the Polish people. When reviewing a pamphlet for a Wilno newspaper, he had quoted the words of "a certain comedian (*cabotin*)", and the words were those of Pilsudski. "The late Marshal Pilsudski", held the Court of Appeal, "is honoured by the people; he spent his whole life in their service; he won for them what they value most—the independence of Poland. Of that people he is the symbol. To insult him, therefore, wounds their holiest feelings, and is tantamount to insulting the people."

This verdict was pronounced by men who had lately witnessed, on 12 May, perhaps the most elaborate tribute ever paid by any nation on the anniversary of a statesman's death. In gratitude for the gifts of union and freedom, the Poles then honoured his death-day with observances which in England might combine both the Armistice and the abdication of the King. A month before, their parliament had made liability to five years' imprisonment the penalty for belittling his name. To appreciate their action, we must recall the condition of their country in his early days, and realise the change from 1871 and even from 1914.

The year 1939 finds a Polish State of some 35,000,000 subjects solidly established over 150,000 square miles of eastern Europe. About two-thirds are racially Polish.

Twenty years earlier, the fortunes of the nation and the region alike were obscure, and the future, as now appears, depended on one man. But almost half a century earlier still, when in 1871 the new German Empire had emerged from the Prussian war with France, the Polish question seemed to have vanished in a wholly different Europe. Historic Poland, undermined in the seventeenth century, partitioned in the eighteenth, denied reconstitution after the Napoleonic wars, had sunk into a large tract ruled by Russia and lesser tracts ruled by Germany and Austria. The struggles of her sons, in 1830 and in 1863, had failed to throw off the Russian yoke, and Europe appeared to be so simply and so firmly organized that their descendants might well abandon hope.

For most Poles of the 'seventies, the outstanding political fact was that the "Congress Kingdom" of Poland, sanctioned by the Vienna Congress in 1815, had become the Vistula provinces of Russia. These were a kind of bastion thrust into the German lands by an empire which spread smoothly from the Baltic to the Pacific and from the Arctic to the Black Sea and to China. Poland, as most non-Russians still called it, was a bastion cut off from Europe by unusual restrictions upon travel, and so largely deprived of roadways and waterways as to make invasion difficult. Memories of a past when Poland had been the equal or superior of her neighbours Prussia, Austria and Russia, survived in their tacit understanding that a common interest bade them keep her down. Russians and Prussians at least strove to replace the Polish language by their own.

Through the half-century which preceded the Great War, moreover, that part of eastern Europe which comprises Poland was organized on lines far simpler than those dictated by regard to race. Where now some nine states

INTRODUCTION

function, small fractions of three empires then sufficed. Estonians, Letts and Lithuanians were subjects of Russia; Danzigers, of Germany; Czechs and Slovaks, of Austria-Hungary; Ruthenes, of the two eastern empires; and Poles alone, of all three. A Polish dream of national independence was, therefore, far wilder than today. The destiny of the smaller peoples, it seemed, must be incorporation in great empires; and Polish resurgence would be a threefold violation of historic law. The Germans and the Italians, indeed, had lately asserted their national rights by force of arms. They, however, were peoples far more numerous and wealthy than the Poles. The houses of Savoy and Hohenzollern had endowed them with strong native kingdoms and they were aided by great allies. Their examples might rather deter than incite a Polish student of history who should calculate the chances of imitation. In the last decades of the nineteenth century, only the very bold or the very romantic could hope for a Polish revival.

The regeneration of Poland was in great measure the work of one rare man—Marshal Pilsudski. Perhaps no recorded scene in the Marshal's life presents him more vividly than his interview, in mid-October 1919, with ten young American airmen who had volunteered to fight for Poland against the Bolshevists. As 1st Lieutenant K. M. Murray wrote:

"The Marshal received them courteously but with very few words. They represented a branch of the service wholly alien to him. Stocky, with heavy shoulders and muscular legs, he was a cavalry officer of the old school through and through; taciturn, cold, powerful, and as hard as granite, [with] sharp eyes deep-set beneath their heavy brows.

"When Major Fauntleroy had formally offered the

Squadron's services, and Captain Bacinski (*sic*) had carefully interpreted his words, the Marshal turned first and looked at him, then frowned and set his jaws together with a click.

"'Poland is able to fight her own battles', he said at last. [His] heavy mustaches moved but little as he spoke."

The Major, however, showed that the scheme was well thought out, and "the Marshal listened with kindling interest as Captain Bacinski put into Polish the words that Fauntleroy had used. And at the end they spoke together rapidly, the Marshal interrogating, the Captain nodding a strong assent. Pilsudski finally arose and faced the pilots.

"'You will, I fear, have great difficulties with our language; our aviation equipment is at present almost nil; you will meet with difficult obstacles at every turn. If you still feel that you can successfully undertake the cause of Poland, Captain Bacinski will assign you to a service unit!' He snapped his heels together, saluted and left the room.

"Every one relaxed suddenly from the rigid stiffness of their return salute. Captain Bacinski smiled gently. 'He is a man of iron—' he said, watching the pilots.

"'He is a fighting man!', said Cooper, mopping his brow."

Unconquerable will, indeed, above all else marked Pilsudski throughout his life. It often triumphed over sickness, and always, as in 1919, determined him never to submit or yield. The Americans also saw something of that inscrutability which a quarter of a century of conspiracy had taught him. His fire, his lofty vision and his charm, no brief collective interview could reveal.

Pilsudski's Father and Mother, in pictures hung beside his bed at Sulejowek. His father, he said, gave him ability; his mother, character.

Chapter I

BIRTH AND PARENTAGE (1867–1877)

JOSEPH PILSUDSKI (1867–1935) was the fourth child, second son and namesake of a Polish gentleman, whose pedigree comprised legendary chieftains of early Lithuania. The family name, Pilsudski, appears to derive from the Lithuanian language, and to convey something of the sense of "Castle". What is certain is that, for some 250 years before Joseph's birth, his ancestors had been members of the ruling class, often serving the State and receiving rewards in land. A full century before he saw the light, one of them had won the approval of a Polish king for a plan to create a port upon the Baltic, but Russia and Prussia forbade the enterprise.

His father, intermarrying as usual with Lithuanian families like his own, espoused Maria Billewicz, the heiress of Zulovo, a large estate some forty miles from Wilno, in the direction of St. Petersburg (Leningrad). There, on 5 December, 1867, their second son, Joseph, was born.

In later life, Pilsudski often spoke of himself as "a canny Lithuanian", and criticized severely many shortcomings of the Poles. These utterances, and the unhappy ambiguity of the adjective "Lithuanian", may suggest that he stood to Poland in a relationship like that of his hero, the Corsican Napoleon, to France. There is, indeed, a Lithuanian race, with little, save neighbourhood, in common with the Poles. Since the Great War, a "Lithuanian" is, primarily, a citizen of the State of Lithuania—a small Baltic republic, speaking a non-Slavonic language resembling that of its kinsfolk and neighbours, the Letts of Latvia. During a part of the Middle Ages, Lithuania had been a vast dominion stretching almost from the Baltic to the Black Sea, and, of course, comprising many races. In the days of the Pilsudskis, however, that is, in the sixteenth, seventeenth and eighteenth centuries, a Lithuanian was a denizen of a wide Grand Duchy, politically federated with Poland, and inhabited both by Slavs and non-Slavs, by Latins, Greeks and Jews, with Poles in general as a ruling race.

Since no one knows their origin, it is possible that in prehistoric times Pilsudski's forebears were partly or wholly non-Polish. To their mutual relationship with Poland, however, we may well apply words used in 1863 by an Englishman [1] confronted with the theory that the Polish nobility were Tartars oppressing a Slavonian peasantry, "with which," as he scornfully observed, "it has nothing in common except language, religion, national customs and traditions, history and a residence in the same country for upwards of a thousand years".

The Pilsudski family, indeed, had been so long in Lithuania, that the countryside had had time to influence them as it had influenced the indigenous Lithuanians. If Joseph lacked some of the characteristics of the southern, or lowland, Poles, he certainly possessed some of those ascribed by the *savant* to the indigenous population of Lithuania. Stoicism, adaptability, love of nature, dignity, tenacity, good faith—these were both his and theirs. But in other—and perhaps deeper—traits, his character resembled theirs as little as his grey eyes and black hair resembled their blue-eyed fairness. Oriental passivity, religious fervour, lack of originality and of driving-power—such Lithuanian characteristics mark the very opposite of Pilsudski. To

[1] Sutherland Edwards, *Polish Captivity*, i. 137.

him the indigenous Lithuanians, whose language he never knew, were kinsmen as little as the Letts or Estonians to the German squires and barons who had been their tyrants since the Middle Ages.

Pilsudski's recent ancestors, indeed, were among those Poles who clung to their western faith and their Polish mother-tongue and culture with passionate devotion. This was heightened by their repugnance to the Muscovites who had ravished their Lithuanian homeland from Poland in 1795. When possible, they rose in rebellion. The result was that, as the nineteenth century advanced and nationalism everywhere grew stronger, the Russian government strove more and more to make Lithuania Russian. Garrisons, civil and judicial officers, and, wherever feasible, the Greek confession were thrust upon the country. As a bid for the support of the peasants, moreover, government harried the landowners, deciding every disputed point against them, and encouraging Labour to confront them with impossible demands. At the same time some 700,000 peasants became freeholders, and many squires could not obtain the services without which their land was worthless.

All Russian Poland, and Lithuania most of all, was dominated during Pilsudski's childhood and early manhood by the catastrophe of 1863. Then, in the so-called Insurrection of January, the impetuous Poles, who had seen Russia vanquished in the Crimean War, endeavoured to protect the remnants of their liberties by an ill-organized appeal to arms. A thousand fights, it is calculated, were fought, but Bismarck kept the ring, and no foreign Power could interfere. Against a great military Power, mere valiant volunteers could not prevail. Some 20,000 irregulars faced 400,000 regulars arrayed by Russia.

Many Poles, Pilsudski's parents among them, came, therefore, to regard the January insurrection as a blunder. It was followed by the abolition of every vestige of Polish liberty, and by the outrages which earned for Governor Muraviev his sobriquet of "the Hangman". The temper of the Russian dignitaries was illustrated by their lesser acts of tyranny—in one place the townsmen forced to kneel when they appeared, in another, to shave off their moustaches, while one ruffian hanged four workmen for showing him inadequate respect. For a whole generation at least, the spirit of the Poles was broken. During two generations, an independent Poland seemed to the world more remote and visionary than an independent Abyssinia today.

Any young squire born in Lithuania in 1867 must rank the downfall of "January" among the formative influences of his character. Joseph Pilsudski also owed much to direct heredity, especially to his mother. His father, who in some mysterious way escaped punishment for his share in the rebellion, was a man of restless energy and unquenchable enthusiasm. Some of his domains were covered with experimental buildings, his yeast factory at Zulovo being an especially notorious innovation. Passionately musical, he lost his life through deliberately hazarding it to attend a concert. Such a father doubtless contributed to the inventiveness, the high resolve and the loathing of tsardom which characterized his son.

Joseph, however, both consciously and unconsciously, owed more to the mother whom he adored and at whose feet his heart is buried. The birth of twelve children, the loss of the Pilsudski fortune, the social and political pressure of the Muscovites, the disease which crippled her for years before her death—all were powerless to shake her romantic patriotism. Her last sufferings were soothed by readings from the Polish poets. She refused to let a Russian cross her threshold, taught her children the forbidden literature of their country, and so impressed her personality upon her son that, in after years, he solved his hardest problems by enquiring, What would my Mother advise? "Only he deserves to be called a man who has strong convictions and acts on them, heedless of consequences"—such was his mother's doctrine, and, through him, it changed the history of Europe. Her death, when he was sixteen, formed the greatest sorrow of his whole career.

Chapter II

LIFE IN WILNO (1875–1885)

IN 1875, when Joseph was seven years old, a destructive fire at Zulovo caused the Pilsudski family to migrate to Wilno for the greater part of every succeeding year. There they occupied a series of large flats and educated the children from their diminished income.

The migration to Wilno formed an outstanding landmark in Pilsudski's life, and, through him, in the history of all north-eastern Europe. If today the city and its district form a Polish promontory thrust deep into a sea of alien states, it is in no small measure due to the fact that in 1875 a lad of seven found in that Lithuanian metropolis his cherished home. The wooded hills embosoming its countless cupolas and towers, the rushing deep-set rivers, the crowded streets and lanes, narrow and winding as in the Middle Ages, for ever echoing the crash of peasants' carts, the throng of men of diverse faith and ornament and race, the general atmosphere of history and of travel—all this could not but stamp itself upon a far duller soul than his.

A country-bred youngster must have found the town life enchanting beyond his dreams, for a finer countryside than that of his birthplace lay close at hand, while in Wilno companionship and adventure were his in plenty for the asking. Clear streams, sandy river-beaches, relics of old fortresses, mysterious caverns which fancy could people with dragons—these were now added to the joys of the open air in summer, and in winter, when wolves might invade the outskirts, of unfailing ice and snow. Thus Wilno became for Pilsudski his incarnate Polish fatherland, never to be renounced.

A city of mixed race and faith also taught him that tolerance which adorned his whole career. Daily he beheld the crowd of devout Latins kneeling or chanting in the highway before that picture of the Virgin whose medallion he carried until his death. Almost within their hearing swelled the deep-throated liturgies of the Greeks. Latins and Greeks alike worshipped on the very verge of the great Hebrew warren, whose religion made much of Wilno a dead city on the last day of every Christian week. His family dwelt successively in many houses, but never far from the vast colony of Jews, and Jews could never afterwards appear to him as mere intruders without human rights.

Every day spent in Wilno, on the other hand, deepened his longing to avenge her upon the tsardom. There the Muscovite oppression of which his kinsfolk had told him became a manifold torment hourly afflicting the city and his private life. No one could view what the Russians styled "Vilna" without observing the disastrous evidences of their attempt to russify every aspect of their conquest.

The Latin churches had been the most conspicuous sufferers. Muscovy, indeed, in many respects came into being as a Church rather than as a State. Even in 1905, when the crew of a Russian warship mutinied and ran amok, the ringleader addressed them as "Ye Orthodox". From the days of Peter the Great (1689–1725), however, the State had bridled and exploited the Church, making it in the nineteenth century a mere agent of aggressive nationalism. The formula "One tsar, one faith, one language" signified that the border peoples, such as Letts or Poles, within the Russian empire were at least to admit the primacy of the Greek (or Orthodox) Church. In their chief places—Riga, Reval, Helsingfors—conspicuous exotic cathedrals were built to dominate, where possible, the city. For some years Warsaw groaned under one of these, "as though a Mohammedan mosque had been set up in the middle of Trafalgar Square".

In Wilno the last and the most hideous of the series waited for the Romanov tercentenary in 1913. Before 1875, however, many Wilno churches had been seized for Orthodox use, often with a measure of reconstruction in the Russian manner. "Paunchy spires" jarred against the classical or gothic temples. The historic castle and some gates were razed to the ground: the Polish university was closed. Statues of Catherine II, whom every Pole hated as the destroyer of his country, and, later, of "Hangman" Muraviev, affronted the Wilno streets.

As the seat of a "government" or province, Wilno received a Russian hierarchy of civil servants and judicial officers, to whom, as to the officers of the garrison, the Poles must pay due deference. Above all, as young Pilsudski thought, education was made completely Russian. To attend school he must wear uniform, which at least gave him the opportunity to escape a Russian ceremony by pleading that he had no trousers. He must obey Russian masters, who sometimes sneered at Poland, and refrain from speaking Polish on penalty of detention in the school "gaol". All this made, as he said, a hell of what should have been among the better parts of an almost idyllic boyhood.

Country-bred, living alternately in town and country, and surrounded by a pleasant family circle, "Joe"[1] none the less enjoyed much of his childhood to the full. Money he held in lifelong contempt, but he could not but be happier

[1] In Polish, "Ziuk," a N.E. borderland abbreviation for Józiùk, the local vernacular for the formal Józek (Joseph).

LIFE IN WILNO

for living in modest comfort. From tender years he showed himself quick, bright and interested, and in Wilno he developed early. In 1880, that is, in his thirteenth year, he produced a manuscript newspaper, *The Zulovo Pigeon*,[1] recording, in a surprisingly mature hand, such facts as that France had 968,300 regulars, or that in Warsaw a studious schoolboy had shot himself. His contributions in prose show that he was attracted by history, especially by that of Poland, and that he gave promise of writing well, while his rhymed fables and other verses may be thought to indicate ambition and powers of observation, not without the possibility of encouraging his tendency towards self-esteem. This may well have been strengthened by what seemed to be the special favour of fortune in many of his ventures, making "Joe's luck" proverbial among his friends.

Two years later, in 1882, his elder but slower-paced brother, Bronislas, his partner throughout their schooldays, joined him in forming the "League", a secret circle for reading forbidden books and discussing freely the world questions which ever interest youth. "If a man were not a Socialist at twenty, I should not think much of his heart," a shrewd king once declared, "and if he remained one at forty, I should not think much of his head." Pilsudski's evolution was of that order. The forefront of his schooldays, however, was filled with despairing struggles against that Muscovite miasma which tainted the Wilno air. One of his Russian schoolmasters appeared to him in every evil dream throughout his life.

Pilsudski's deepest feelings were outraged both by the Muscovite sacrilege in Poland and by his own impotence to chastise it. But he reacted with an impishness that never left him, and that never gave more joy than to his school-

[1] Reproduced in part in *Illustr. Kuryer Codzienny* (19-viii-1935).

mates. To keep a Polish festival he would send to school transparent pleas of illness. Church parades for Russian festivals caused his unobtrusive disappearance, or failing this his refusal to kiss the cross when offered by a Russian priest. Thrice at least he was punished for failing to salute Russian dignitaries, or for speaking Polish in the cloakroom, and despite his successes with his books, he was threatened with expulsion, which automatically closed the door to every profession.

A few Polish boys, it was clear, could not alone defy the tsardom, save in their hearts. Pilsudski's adolescent judgment endorsed the command of his dying mother, "Live for vengeance, but eschew provocation." He found little solace in the League discussions, which he had outgrown, and turned to solitary reading, especially about France in 1789. The French, he argued immaturely, had deposed their tyrants, while the Poles had failed. The French, then, must be better people than the Poles. Perhaps the Russians with their formidable revolutionary society of the "People's Will" might follow the French example. If so, should the Poles embrace the home-grown Russian revolution? More than twenty years must pass before that question found a final answer in his mind.

The year 1884 brought a threefold change into Pilsudski's life. He then applied himself with great fervour to his books and became an outstanding scholar. His mother's death broke up the family and left a void in his heart which no man or woman could ever fill. And at this time, under Russian influence, he became a Socialist. Intellectually, indeed, Wilno lay in some respects nearer to St. Petersburg than to Warsaw. Since the downfall of 1863, the romanticism of the Poles had largely given place to a new realism. The leaders of thought urged their fellow-Poles to look facts in the face, to admit that an independent Poland was impossible, and to content themselves with a quiet life and with intellectual and material progress. Socialism, in their eyes, was a universal rather than a national ideal.

Russian Socialism, on the other hand, did not demand from Pilsudski the abhorrent sacrifice of his nationality. It gave him, as he declares, a guiding thread, replacing the social ideals of his boyhood. While criticizing *bourgeois* society, as all Socialism must, it added an anarchistic ideal of self-governing communes, and a glorification of the Russian people, who had retained their communal village system long after the adoption of individual tenure in the West. While some young Poles in Wilno, dazzled by this view of Russia, learned to despise their own nation, Pilsudski accepted only the criticism of the Polish *bourgeoisie*, and became, as he confessed in 1903, "a very superficial Socialist".

CHAPTER III

UNDERGRADUATE LIFE (1885-1887)

MEANWHILE, after eight years, his schooldays were drawing to a close. After his seventeenth birthday, he decided to enter the university of Kharkov, in the Ukraine, some 700 miles south-eastward from his home, and travelled thither in August, 1885. It is not without interest to observe that in his qualifying examination he excelled in history and geography, and did well in divinity, Latin, Greek and mathematics. With Polish, Russian and German in addition to the classical languages, and with the prospect of acquiring French and English in the near future, his linguistic endowment at least reached the exacting standard of the educated Slav. He was now to study medicine.

His academical year in Kharkov proved him a good student, especially of inorganic chemistry. In other respects he met with disappointment. Excepting those who were russified, the young Poles at Kharkov seemed to him unawakened and apathetic, and Polish books were few. The "People's Will" had been suppressed, and in Russia reaction triumphed. The Warsaw Socialist organization was brought to trial. Pilsudski, whose Kharkov days had been enlivened by a share in some disturbances in March, 1886, which were punished by six days' confinement, felt that organization in Poland itself had become the crying need. At the beginning of the summer, he returned to Wilno, with the intention of spending his second year in the nearer university of Dorpat (Tartu), to which many Poles

Piłsudski as a schoolboy at Wilno, and, in his 20th year, as a prisoner.

resorted. Meanwhile he formed a circle of the Wilno youth, his old schoolfellows now including some students from St. Petersburg. His editorial zeal found vent in a hectographed journal, and he hoped to work out plans for the salvation of the country. These were carried no further than a mutual pledge to oppose the brutal attacks of the Russian government on the national civilization in Lithuania. The studies of the group, however, went on, and some contact with the Wilno working-men was effected. Pilsudski at this time read part of Karl Marx's *Capital*, though its abstract logic and the doctrine that goods dominated over man proved uncongenial. Soon, however, he found himself caught up in the far more dangerous student movement which centred in St. Petersburg.

The triumphant aggressive of the tsardom against the "People's Will" had provoked a desperate counter-attack by a terrorist section among the students of the capital, Lenin's elder brother among them. Bronislas Pilsudski was connected with the group through some of its members from Wilno, but he was not initiated into their deepest secret. This was none other than the extirpation of Alexander III, when he attended a memorial service to his murdered father. Bombs were to be made for this purpose, and since these might prove too weak to kill, they were to be charged with poison. In January, 1887, the St. Petersburg conspirators sought chemicals, revolvers and funds from their Wilno friends. The emissaries received help from Bronislas, and, at his request, some courtesies from Joseph. In mid-March, when all was ripe, arrests were made, and the weakness of some of the conspirators brought full disclosure. The Pilsudski brothers were arrested, and, on 2 April, Joseph found himself in the fortress of St. Peter and St. Paul, on a charge of treason.

Further investigation, however, failed to produce any proof of guilt, and he was released. Fifteen prisoners, including Bronislas, were tried, and on 29 April, the third day of the trial, Joseph was called as a witness. He replied to more than sixty questions, always briefly and without incriminating himself or the accused. If he was to be believed, he had entertained a stranger for a day and two nights in his uncle's flat at Wilno without knowing his business or even his name, and had sent off a telegram at the request of another stranger without understanding its contents. These were, "Sister has left, meet her", and the destination was Bronislas' address in St. Petersburg. The message should have been sent off next day, but Joseph forgot it for more than three weeks and then despatched it. Such was his story.

Evidence, however, mattered little, since it was political expediency that must prevail. The Court sentenced all fifteen to death, but recommended them to ask the Tsar for mercy. Five, Lenin's brother among them, were executed; the rest, condemned to imprisonment for various terms. Bronislas, an opponent of terrorism, who had been made guilty against his will, received fifteen years' hard labour in Siberia. On 20 April, 1887, the Minister of Justice had decreed that Joseph should be detained in Eastern Siberia for five years.

Chapter IV

SIBERIA (1887–1892)

THE dreadful name "Siberia" comprised punishments of the most varied grades. Hard labour in the mines might signify a lingering death by torture. Preventive detention in a town or village for a term of years was very much what chance and the exile contrived to make it. The government trusted to distance and their local agents to keep the offender harmless. The agents had no desire to increase their labours by unnecessary zeal, and were not immune from the kindly Russian feeling for the unfortunate. Many political exiles lived like officers billeted in a remote region. If active-minded, they could explore the neighbourhood, read, write, pay visits, hold discussions and even help the administration. Not a few remained in Siberia as colonists. Let an exile despair, however, and sloth and perhaps drink would destroy his manhood in Siberia as in many other scenes of isolation.

Joseph Pilsudski spent the summer months of 1887, his twentieth year, in journeying slowly from St. Petersburg almost to the southern end of Lake Baikal. Train to Nijni Novgorod, steamer down the Volga and up the Kama to Perm, train across the Urals to Tiumen, steamer down the Irtuish to the Ob, and up the Ob to Tomsk, thence, as a noble, by carriage to Irkutsk, with intervals in dirty gaols —such was the itinerary. His party, some twenty strong, was, as he confessed, a mutinous party, and was therefore treated with exceptional severity. Its progress was punctuated by disputes with the local officials, usually ending in a harmless "protocol", signed by both sides. At the city of Irkutsk, after their 3000-mile journey, Pilsudski and twelve other men, with three women, must wait until ice should convert the river Lena into a northern road. Weeks of idleness bred quarrels with the Governor of the prison. The prisoners declared a strike; the Governor answered by the strict enforcement of prison law; they smashed their cell doors and refused to obey him. On this, soldiers tried to beat them into compliance, using the butt freely.

When the battered Pilsudski, who had lost several teeth, regained consciousness, he felt himself choked by his helplessness and passion. After a quarter of a century, he still remembered how his indignation at the outrage on his dignity would hardly suffer him to breathe. Yet the prisoners, missing three of their number, formally declared a hunger strike and persisted in it for three days. It was crowned with victory, and they became privileged persons with whom the authorities did not dare to interfere. Later, however, they were sentenced to six months' imprisonment on a charge of "armed resistance", which they, though totally unarmed, contemptuously refused to deny. The chief fruit of the "Irkutsk mutiny" was its effect upon Pilsudski. "For some time", he declared, "I could not look calmly at a soldier or a uniform. My fists clenched themselves, and, when I shut my eyes, I sometimes saw that savage onslaught of a host of armed soldiers on a handful of unarmed men huddled in a corner."

In mid-December, 1887, after two months of Irkutsk gaol, Pilsudski, with other prisoners, set out in sledges down the Lena, travelling at the rate of more than sixty miles a day. On the eleventh day he reached Kirensk, with its post-office, district treasury and hospital, a country place lying on an island in the river. Kirensk was destined to be his home for the next two and a half years. As his journey thither had proved, only a slender thread linked Kirensk with civilization. Winter extended over some three-quarters of the year, and the sole artificial light was that of torches. These conditions he fought by constant activity—by gymnastics, long walks, wood-cutting, hunting, study of the natives and so forth. His sentence by the Senate to six months' imprisonment proved his salvation, for it brought him into the prison hospital, where he became a clerk. In this capacity he had to deal with *dossiers*, one of which persisted in returning, enlarged, from various destinations. He therefore despatched it to Vladivostok, to him the equivalent of Timbuctoo, and there it remained in peace.

In September, 1888, Pilsudski petitioned the Minister of the Interior to transfer him to the island of Sakhalin, where Bronislas was serving his sentence. The request to be conveyed some 2000 miles at the public expense in order to associate with a "dangerous criminal" argues a certain confidence on Pilsudski's part in the benevolence of the government. It was not granted, but, in the summer of 1890, the efforts of his friends procured his removal on grounds of health to Tunka, a Buriat village some 130 miles south-west of Irkutsk.

Tunka had much that Kirensk lacked—romantic scenery, a milder climate, more interesting native races, and, above all, the society of many Polish exiles. Here for the first time he could hire a room of his own. Careless of comfort, he lived largely on bread and milk, hunted, sometimes on skis, read much in Russian, but without undue reverence, and often talked politics with his fellow-Poles. His Socialism deepened, for he could see no other panacea for the labouring masses, but he still resented the undue stress on economic motives which he discerned in Marx. Economics, none the less, strengthened his demand for Polish independence, since the russification of the country closed the doors to educated aspirants for office and drove many of them overseas. At Tunka, in the last two years of exile, Pilsudski learned from an old rebel much of the technique of rebellion, and many of the watchwords of 1863. At the same time he became convinced that Polish independence and Polish Socialism were inseparable. Polish independence, however, was for him an ideal far more sacred than was any scheme of policy or school of thought.

Early in 1892, in his twenty-fifth year, the term of his exile was fulfilled. The Irkutsk police gave him a clean sheet as regards misconduct, but recorded the vehemence of his character. From the government he received permission to return, but subject to supervision by the secret police, while, for five years, Twer, Nijni Novgorod and all university towns were closed to him. For the first time in his life he must have rejoiced at the suppression of the university of Wilno. Quitting Irkutsk in May, he journeyed straightway to his beloved city, intent on changing Polish Socialism from an international basis to a national. To his joy he found that, during his five years' absence, this change had already been prepared for. In November, representatives of many Socialist groups met in Paris, and united to form the Polish Socialist Party, usually styled the P.P.S. At the same time, however, different views of the destiny of Poland were giving rise to another great party, that of the National Democrats, described in 1925 as comprising the larger landowners, many of the educated, " and what there is of 'big business' in Polish hands."—(Dyboski). Ere long its leader, Roman Dmowski, was to become the bitter opponent of the man who more and more came to personify the P.P.S.—Joseph Pilsudski.

Chapter V

THE POLISH SOCIALIST PARTY (P.P.S.)

FOR some sixteen years (1892–1908), until he had turned forty, Pilsudski's biography is largely the history of the P.P.S. In the service of the party he developed his character and powers, passed through his strangest adventures, and made some at least of his closest friends. A generation later, the doctrinal differences between the contemporary schools of Socialism have ceased to rouse our passion. During the early manhood of Pilsudski, however, they and the life of a conspirator and propagandist sharpened and toughened him into the force that was revealed when the time for active warfare arrived. Small as was the change that the exertions of these years could make in Poland, they were of high importance for the change that they made in him.

The strong and eager young man who returned from Siberia plunged swiftly into his life's work as he then conceived it. In Wilno he found only a sister, who failed to recognize the bearded stranger at first sight. The family was with his father on their estate,[1] but Joseph was in no mood for holidays. After greeting his relatives, he soon returned to Wilno, among whose cosmopolitan inhabitants he hoped to find a breath of revolution. By degrees, however, the sad truth came home to him which was to trouble him for more than twenty years. The Polish people as a whole did not desire revolution. Had they unanimously embraced the cause of independence they might have numbered one

[1] In Western Lithuania N.E. of Tilsit.

in twenty-five of the subjects of their three imperial rulers. But in 1892 Polish unanimity was almost unthinkable.

Posen, Warsaw and Cracow were severed by cleavages of opinion, tradition and interest. These were far too deep and wide to be bridged by reverence for the great Polish poets and men of letters, by hatred for the German and the Muscovite, by faith in the ultimate triumph of justice, or by romantic memories of the Polish past. A great majority of Polish-speaking men throughout the world might well have subscribed to the verdict of an impartial foreigner, "the national history of Poland closes with the rising of 1863".

In Galicia, a backward province of some seven million inhabitants, Catholic Austria employed Poles in the administration, and offered them the prospect of constitutional progress within the Austrian empire. Prussia was conscious that, in great areas of her eastern provinces, Germanism was overshadowed by the Catholic Slavonic mass, and, for political reasons, she took harsh measures of Germanization. These roused the Roman Church to lead resistance, and increased the racial consciousness among the Poles. In the German parliament, and in the financial sphere, Poles and Germans were in conflict. But from this to a movement by prosperous communities to throw in their lot with the Russian Poles in some hopeless rising for an almost unimaginable independence, the distance was astronomical.

The Russian Poles, moreover, had no mind to change their state. "The Provinces on the Vistula", as they were now officially styled, contained some nine million people, of whom about two-thirds were Poles. The great majority lived by agriculture, and thought more of crops and household economics than of politics and history. Among those whose views were wider, most accepted the new teaching of "Realities, not romance", and, as the most capable population within the Russian empire, they were enjoying a vast protected market for their manufactures.

Among them, it is true, dwelt many Jews, both old-time Polish Jews and Jews driven thither from the sheltered provinces of Russia. These comprised a larger proportion of literates than the Poles, and many men and women with that flexibility of mind which offers scope to the agitator. Thus the Jews in Russian Poland produced many revolutionaries, but few who could think that the first object of revolution must be Polish independence. The Jewish League, or *Bund*, might form a valuable ally of the P.P.S. against the tsardom, but, as the organ of an international people, it could hardly embrace a strictly national Polish cause. Still more dangerous were those Polish aristocrats who held the ideal of harmonious co-operation with the brother Slavonic people, and sought the well-being of the Polish people within the framework of the Russian empire. These disavowed both the ideals for which Pilsudski strove —social reconstruction and Polish independence.

In such circumstances, and faced by an active Russian government which made many arrests, the Polish Socialists turned rather to endless discussion than to a new campaign. When Pilsudski, with his cry of "Romantic plans, practical execution", flung himself into the movement, it was indeed at a low ebb. Three weak organizations, however, united at Paris into the Foreign League of Polish Socialists, and the growth of industrialism and town life at home was increasing the number of actual and potential Socialists among the workmen. A Polish Socialist paper—the *Dawn* (*Przedswit*)—was published in London, and there were innumerable demands for smuggling this and other revolutionary literature across the frontier and into the people's homes. In the ruthlessness of its democratic and Socialist programme, moreover, the Paris meeting had left nothing to be desired. Complete equality and enfranchisement of men and women, the eight-hour day, the gradual socialization of land, of instruments of production and of means of communication, were prominent amid a host of corresponding resolutions.

For some six months Piłsudski studied law at Wilno, only to turn from its mass of definitions to a more fruitful and exciting life. He acted as the Wilno correspondent of *Dawn*, describing life under the Russians in Lithuania as like that of an ownerless dog. Early in 1893 he devoted himself to the service of the P.P.S.—a service which might well create what appeared in 1920 " his ingrained proclivity to the secret and the indirect " (Lord d'Abernon).

Chapter VI

PILSUDSKI AS P.P.S. AGITATOR (1893-1900)

THE apostle of the P.P.S., which had arisen from the Paris resolutions, was Stanislas Mendelson, who journeyed to Warsaw, Wilno, Riga and St. Petersburg, with a view to establishing and co-ordinating its branches. Wilno, where Pilsudski and others held a study circle, found itself promoted to be the "Lithuanian section". Some four years later, it still had little contact with the masses and it absorbed barely thirty copies of the *Workman* (*Robotnik*), the party organ. Such were the beginnings of the P.P.S. in Pilsudski's own city.

As in every sphere which he entered throughout his life, Pilsudski soon made his mark in the P.P.S. He had the strength which comes from a lofty but simple ideal in which he passionately believed. For Polish freedom and independence, he maintained, man might well be content to die, but no one would die for ten farthings' higher wages. Within a month of Mendelson's visit, Pilsudski protested in *Dawn* against the severity of his attacks upon patriots who were opposed to Socialism. During the summer a secret congress of the party was held near Wilno, and delegates were sent to the International Socialist Congress at Zurich. Pilsudski was not among them, but in October, as a delegate from the Lithuanian section, he obeyed the summons of Wojciechowski, later a Co-operative champion, whose principles were as lofty as his stature, to the Workmen's Committee of the P.P.S. The Committee placed him on its central executive and proceeded to draw up an elaborate organization for propaganda.

Within eight months, in May, 1894, Pilsudski could report that the P.P.S. was extending its influence to several secondary towns. It had dared to join in the Warsaw celebrations of the popular uprising of 17 April, 1794, celebrations which resulted in the imprisonment and deportation of nearly 150 people. Besides Wojciechowski, several men of outstanding ability had joined the party. Prominent among them was Pilsudski's fellow-Lithuanian, Sulkiewicz, a master of the art of circulating illegal literature and of enabling prisoners to escape. "Comrade Victor", as Pilsudski was styled among the party, toiled indefatigably to keep these highly individualized members in line, and to centralize and stimulate the various branches. His journeys carried him through the length and breadth of Russian Poland, and to the chief towns in western and southern Russia where Polish colonies were to be found.

At the same time, by becoming editor of the *Workman*, he took up a burden which was to weigh upon him for some six years. The P.P.S. was bound to depend upon its literature for propaganda, and the most effective literature must be a news-sheet. To publish periodical exhortations, libels and revelations was at once to make converts and to prove the impotence of the government to prevent the publication.

From July, 1894, the *Workman* frequently appeared. Pilsudski, it is said, hoped that he might reach five numbers, the record for such a publication. In fact, he himself produced more than seven times that quantity. At first the paper was brought out near Wilno, later in Wilno and eventually in Lodz. The two editors, for Wojciechowski was his colleague, with infinite labour, themselves set up and struck off the whole edition, which rose gradually from 1200 to 1800 copies. It was then packed into suitcases, conveyed by rail to various destinations, and smuggled by night to points within reach of the subscribers—to be read in secret by groups of working-men. Its influence in extolling the idea of Polish independence and in proving that Poles could outwit the government was incalculable.

The toil of the men who were editor, contributor, printer and distributor in one was only equalled by their success. "I had not only to accomplish work for which I was untrained," declared Pilsudski later, "I had also to form a new vocabulary, a new party style, for our political thoughts and designs did not fit the old formulae of Socialism." To pour the new wine of Polish independence into the old bottles, much diplomacy was needed, but this the later man of iron proved able to provide. Moreover, in *Dawn* and in the *Workman* he showed himself a first-rate journalist, incisive, humorous and not averse from scandal.

The record of the three government students who robbed the Ostra Brama chapel and pleaded that they were driven to this by hunger—a plea which led to enquiry into the menu of their government boarding-house, when it was discovered that the provisions were supplied at exorbitant rates by the official responsible for education—such revelations stripped off the mantle of benevolence, majesty and omnipotence from the Tsar's administration. How such a newspaper as the *Workman* could be produced in Russia, remained for years a problem which the tsardom failed to solve—to the delight of its readers, and to the encouragement of new anti-government volunteers. Pilsudski mocked at the perplexities of the police and provided them with various false clues, ostentatiously disproving, however, their hypothesis that the *Workman* must be brought in from abroad.

Pilsudski's realism and sense of humour, indeed, were strongly marked during his labours as editor and organizing secretary of the P.P.S. When the police had arrested a comrade and placed their official seals upon the doors of his flat, it was Pilsudski who pointed out that by slipping in from the back they could conspire there under the protection of the official seals. His life and conversation were conspicuously clean, and his calm courage such that in his presence hunted conspirators felt safe. That courage and that influence he upheld by never drawing upon them save in necessity. "Seek no peril, and fear none" might well have been his advice. His serene and confident bearing must have saved him a thousand times from suspicion and arrest. In 1894 and the five years which followed, 289 of the P.P.S. were sentenced.

Although the *Workman* came from Wilno, the bulk of conspirative literature was at this time supplied from London. No. 7 Beaumont Square, Mile End, formed the headquarters of the Foreign League of Polish Socialists, and such men as Ignatius Moscicki, the later President of the Republic, resorted thither from time to time. The house formed a kind of laboratory of Socialism and capital of revolutionary Poland, linked by secret channels with half the capitals of Europe. A well-known photograph of 1896 shows Pilsudski as the bearded and forceful centre of a group of six leading residents, Moscicki among them. The great triumph of the Beaumont Square directorate came in that year, when the International Socialist Congress in London voted for an independent Poland.

The historic mission of Polish Socialism, argued Pilsudski, was to save Poland for the West. The Muscovite was threatening to drag her down to his own Oriental level. His system of brutality and plunder was ruining the country. In Wilno in 1893, when the people tried to save a church from being closed, men had been massacred and women violated as a prelude to wholesale condemnations by the

Pilsudski (centre) as a Socialist agitator in London, 1895. On the left, I. Moscicki (Polish President, 1926-).

courts. The taxes were so heavy as to compel the exploitation of the workmen and a rise in the cost of living, while the influx of worthless Russians drove the Poles across the Atlantic. An armed rising, he declared, was Poland's sole resource. Although her gaolers might purchase the support of the landowners and Roman clergy, the P.P.S. was growing, and education, organization and confidence would in time bring victory.

Such was the burden of Pilsudski's articles. They were supplemented, on occasion, by proclamations to the Polish people which he drew up. In August, 1897, Warsaw received the Tsar, Nicholas II, with an enthusiasm which was only heightened by hopes of benefits to come. Pilsudski replied by calling upon "comrades and workmen" to spurn this demonstration by the possessive classes. "Although today", he wrote, "we do not greet the Tsar with bombs or weapons, both he and his new Polish satellites know well that in us they have a resolute foe." We will work, he declared, for the day when the streets of Warsaw shall resound with cries of "Death to despots! Down with slavery! Long live the free Polish people!"

No less outspoken, and seemingly no less barren, was Pilsudski's protest against the desecration of Wilno by a statue of "Hangman" Muraviev. On the other hand, when Warsaw prepared to honour with a statue the great poet Mickiewicz, Pilsudski, his fellow-Lithuanian, called on the people to attend in multitudes, and to make the ceremony an anti-government demonstration. The result was that the intended programme was much reduced, that the police arranged for the workmen to receive their pay at the hour fixed for the unveiling, and that only a few hundred attended. The moral effect of a vigorous and determined opposition was, none the less, considerable. It shattered the illusion of Polish unanimity for collaboration with the government. It raised a standard round which the adventurous few could rally. It brought into the country a flood of illegal literature, for other societies, such as the Jewish *Bund*, could not be outdistanced by the P.P.S.

Pilsudski himself produced more writings than his strictly journalistic work and his voluminous and pregnant official correspondence. Among them, perhaps the most notable was the introduction which he wrote in London in 1898 to the stolen memorandum of a Governor-General of Warsaw. This, with its demonstration that, failing further reform, the Polish peasants would be captured by the revolution, and with the sceptical annotations of the officials, caused an immense sensation and inflicted a severe check on the russophil policy of the Conservatives.

With the pen, it may be added, Pilsudski was bold and trenchant, but never wild. He hated violence in actions short of war, and at this time he both preached and practised moderation in the use of words. Energy under restraint marked the editor no less than the champion of revolution. When his friend and colleague Wojciechowski seemed to assert in a pamphlet that independent Poland would be Socialist, Pilsudski objected that the statement was risky, uncalled for and premature. As Socialists, he maintained, they might work for a Socialist Poland, but a statement that they could dispense with the Polish *bourgeoisie* should not be included in their programme.

From 1893 to 1900, Pilsudski toiled without ceasing to build up the P.P.S. and to supply Russian Poland with illegal literature. At the end of that time, he could calculate that some 250,000-300,000 copies of uncensored publications reached the people every year. About one-third of these came from the P.P.S. That party had a highly practical constitution, designed to give the maximum of unity without risking disaster, if at some point the police broke in. The leaders were known only by nicknames, which were often changed. No addresses were ever written down, and the art of spy-dodging was brought to perfection. A general meeting of the initiated belonging to the highest grade was held every year, but in general a committee of six formed the administration. These communicated with the local committees and supervised the agitators who went from place to place.

Polish students at Russian universities provided many recruits and no small fraction of the slender funds. Although under Pilsudski and Wojciechowski the income was almost quadrupled in four years, it amounted in 1899 to less than £1400. In the same period the number of strikes was trebled, reaching 67, and the demands of labour for less inhuman treatment rose. May Day became ever a more important demonstration, raising the fame of the P.P.S. Meanwhile, the party negotiated for alliance with parallel movements in other countries, notably in Russia, and not without success. While Pilsudski ruled, however, the P.P.S. would help them and accept their help only so long as it retained complete freedom of action and the ideal of Polish independence was accepted.

In 1897, a difficult question was settled by including the Lithuanian proletariat in the P.P.S. with the exception of those whose language was Lithuanian. Efforts were made to solve the difficult problem of the Jews, by printing a Yiddish publication in London; and to appeal to the peasants, by devising a journal for their special use. This wide-ranging activity, however, was hampered by constant lack of funds. The workmen-members contributed hardly anything to the party chest. In October, 1896, Pilsudski complained that they were up to the ears in debt, and that Wojciechowski—"the positivist who loves to freeze my romantic plans and projects"—was unable to afford warm clothing.

The year 1899 brought a threefold change in Pilsudski's life. First, Wojciechowski married and quitted Poland. In consequence, a six months' interval separated No. 30 of the *Workman* from its successor. Then, in July, Pilsudski himself entered into wedlock. His bride was a well-known revolutionary, daughter of a Wilno doctor and divorced wife of a Polish engineer in Russian service. Pilsudski espoused her in the Protestant church of a Lithuanian village, declaring himself to be a merchant resident in Lapy. His wife, a lady famous for her beauty, was robust enough to carry, on occasion, more than four stone of illegal literature under her clothing. No children were born to them, but her little daughter, whom Pilsudski dearly loved, lived with them until her untimely death in 1906.

Before the new year, a third change was gradually effected. This was the transference of the Pilsudski household, which contained the brain and soul of the P.P.S., from remote and insecure Wilno to the straggling town of Lodz, the Birmingham or Manchester of Russian Poland, nearly ninety miles beyond Warsaw. There, in a first-floor flat over a haberdasher's, the Joseph Pilsudskis made their home, and set up the secret press. In Lodz, the police had not yet risen above the ordinary Russian level of inefficiency. No one noticed the advent of another business man or lawyer, as Pilsudski seemed to be, and from Lodz that proletariat which formed the basis of the P.P.S. might easily be reached by propaganda.

Chapter VII

PILSUDSKI IN PRISON (1900–1901)

BETWEEN June, 1899, and New Year's Day, five numbers of the *Workman* saw the light. Two additional publications appeared in January, and in due course all was ready for another *Workman*. Then, at 3 a.m. on 20 February, 1900, the Pilsudskis and their press were seized by the police. "Only three pages remained unfilled, and my article on the suppression of the newspaper duty in Austria was written"—so the editor lamented. "Thanks to the uncommonly energetic and intelligent activity of the chief of the provincial *gendarmerie*, and the due co-operation of the police in the investigation . . . a certain Pilsudski, living under the name of Dombrowski", and his press, with much revolutionary literature, had been captured. Thus boasted the official report. In fact, the government agents lighted upon Pilsudski in the belief that his quarters were those of Malinowski, a revolutionary friend who had ordered paper to be sent there. Surprised in his bed, Pilsudski could destroy nothing, not even his forged passport or the seal of a Wilno church. He whispered to his wife to conceal her name for the sake of their relations, and spun out the police search so that he might go to gaol by daylight.

For several weeks, while the P.P.S. strove to recover from the blow, and the government pursued its investigations, Pilsudski occupied a cell at Lodz, which reminded him of the worst Siberian prisons. In April, while the missing number of the *Workman* was being prepared in London, he was removed to the Warsaw Citadel, and confined in that Tenth Pavilion from which no prisoner could hope to escape. Yet his mood on entry, as he records, was cheerful, for he was treading in the footsteps of many Polish martyrs, and he burned with curiosity to see the famous place.

The Russian chief officer received him with distinguished courtesy. With a smile and an apology, he declared that they must search his clothes, but waived this on Pilsudski's assurance that he had already been searched four times. "Only," he added, "please be so good as to take off your tie." The order amazed and amused Pilsudski, and, three years later, he still failed to understand it. An English gaol-bird, shuffling into the Governor's presence while holding up his trousers with the hand, could have informed him of the danger of leaving any kind of rope with desperate men. The official went on to give him permission to import even liquor from the town, taking a kind of parole against excess. Pilsudski assured him that solitude did not conduce to drinking—a doubtful generalization, but one supported in his own case by his conspicuous abstinence when in Siberia.

With mutual courtesies they parted, and Pilsudski was escorted to a dismal and dirty cell. This vital moment—the first contact between a helpless man and the semblance of his tomb—drew from the prisoner a memorable revelation of his mind. The smell of decay transported him to a remote inn kept by a Lithuanian Jew, looking like a goat being slaughtered with a blunted knife, in which he had once taken shelter. So strong was the illusion that, when the prison orderly brought in his dinner, he mentally gave him the Jew's daughter's name. Only the man's action in extracting a spoon from the pocket of his filthy trousers broke the spell.

For some eight months, that is until mid-December,

"*A certain Pilsudski*" *photographed by the Russian police in* 1900.

1900, the Tenth Pavilion was Pilsudski's home. To a man of his self-command and spiritual force, prison offered an exciting challenge to defy its power by making himself a new creature. In such conditions, he held, time ceases, values change, trifles become momentous, and man must so refashion his desires as to enjoy what his environment provides. To him the Tenth Pavilion was commended by many merits. Prison life was a national inheritance which almost every eminent Pole passed through. In the Tenth Pavilion discipline was polonized, that is to say, abolished. The warders left the prisoners to themselves, and the prisoners spent much time in tunnelling and in communication.

The unwonted freedom to arrange the dilapidated furniture as he pleased gave Pilsudski rare delight. In such a hostel, he felt, he could give full play to his vivid imagination and shape for himself a dream-world in which to live. At the same time he did not eschew thoughts of escape, in which almost all prisoners indulge, nor work, deliberately undertaken as mental exercise. It was in prison that he studied English, with the result that he could never afterwards pronounce the words aright.

In the meantime, the efforts of the P.P.S. to set him free seemed hopeless without a change of prison. A friendly Russian warder with a Polish wife served as the necessary channel of communication. His favourite method was to leave his match-box on the prisoner's table. When the prisoner had taken out the message from his friends which it contained, and had inserted his own reply, the warder would discover the loss of his box and come back to reclaim it. By this channel Pilsudski received instructions to pretend to be insane, since madmen could not be treated in the prison hospital.

To the great grief of the unsuspecting warder, he displayed only too faithfully the symptoms of mania which a mental specialist prescribed. To simulate fury at the sight of a Russian uniform was easy, to reject all food that might have been poisoned was more difficult. For a time he accepted only eggs, then clamoured for sealed-up chocolate of a special brand. The performance, though flawless, was exhausting, for a single slip would enable the prison doctors to detect the cheat. After a few months, indeed, his strength was plainly failing, and his friends were forced to try a last resort.

They appealed to the Siberian head of a Warsaw mental hospital to make an independent examination of an unfortunate Polish "relative" of theirs, whose case the prison doctors could not understand. The charitable man consented, refusing to take a fee, and his name secured the necessary permission. A military doctor accompanied him, but Pilsudski's fury at the sight of uniform brought about his withdrawal. The *tête-à-tête* at once revealed the truth, but the visitor succumbed to Pilsudski's charm, and for an hour they talked about Siberia. That hour, declared the doctor, was among the most pleasant of his life. He then reported that the prisoner was incurable without a change of scene.

The new scene proved to be St. Petersburg, where Pilsudski was placed at the disposal of the Governor-General. He was, quite naturally, assigned to the political offenders' section of the asylum dedicated to St. Nicholas the Worker of Miracles. The Russian capital, however, sheltered many Poles, including the head of the hospital and a strong section of the P.P.S. If these men needed urging to contrive Pilsudski's escape, the head of the hospital was there to remind them that for his own sake his connivance must have limits, while the Warsaw leader, Sulkiewicz, was giving his whole time to the problem of release.

During the first months of 1901, Pilsudski, who could now abate the most inconvenient symptoms of his disease, entertained himself in part with the problems of chess. In later days the legend ran that he was no player, but won by willing his opponent to make suicidal moves. In point of fact, he passionately loved the game, and now contrived a board by placing matches on the cover of the cell Bible, with a secret set of chessmen fashioned as best he could. As spring drew near, he was sustained by the gradual evolution of a hazardous but not impossible plan of escape. This was based on the success with which the P.P.S. had introduced into the staff of the hospital a young Polish doctor, who was prepared to sacrifice his career to the revolutionary cause. He, it was agreed, when his turn came to take charge, should have Pilsudski brought, for a thorough examination, to his own room. Thence doctor and disguised prisoner could walk out together, to find members of the P.P.S. waiting either to take them to a hiding-place or to give battle in case they were pursued.

The chance came on 14 May, 1901, when the government had provided a fête on the parade-ground as an antidote to Socialist propaganda. The orderlies were delighted with the special leave which their new superior freely gave, and the porter respectfully opened the gate when a stranger with a bushy beard, spectacles and a cap much too large for him, accompanied the doctor into the town. The P.P.S. men were, in fact, waiting at another gate, but two cab-rides brought the fugitives to the rendezvous, and all was well. Some three hours passed before the servants broke open the doctor's door, and no clue to the line of flight could be discovered.

Two days later, the police of all Russia were summoned to search for the missing men. But Pilsudski, calling for a time-table, had found that a train to Reval might be caught on the 14th, and thither, disguised as a customs officer, he departed. Riga, the point originally selected, came next, and then Kiev, where he helped to prepare a new number of the *Workman*. In the marshy region west of Kiev he met his wife, who had been released on bail after eleven months in prison. Thence they were smuggled into Austrian territory, where they lay in safety. After a few weeks they reached London, and spent some time at the P.P.S. headquarters in Leytonstone. Pilsudski's health, however, had suffered from his long adventures. In 1899, nervous exhaustion and arthritis threatened, and now tuberculosis was feared. Too poor to take the doctor's prescription of Switzerland, he returned to Cracow, and in the neighbouring mountains fully regained his health.

Chapter VIII

WORK FOR THE P.P.S. IN EUROPE AND
JAPAN (1902-1905)

HEALTH with Pilsudski meant capacity for party work, and the P.P.S. stood in dire need of him. To pick up all the threads, he made once more for London and spent four months upon the task. Christmas he celebrated by the sea, as the guest of Wojciechowski. He was planning a forward movement in Russian Poland, to be effected by his usual instruments—centralization and the press—when the news of fresh arrests necessitated the presence in Russia of a leader. Wojciechowski's wife was ill and Pilsudski undertook the mission. Papers were duly forged, and on 21 April, 1902, he crossed the Russian frontier.

His entry into Russia within a year of his renowned escape must rank among the bravest actions of even Pilsudski's life. The frontier itself was guarded as perhaps no other in the world. The actual boundary of the Tsar's dominions was lined, by day and night alike, with riflemen placed, in the daytime, from two hundred to six hundred yards apart. Their duty was to see that no one crossed save through a customs station. A mile or so inland, every road was occupied by a mobile party, whose duty was to ride in quest of persons or goods present without due right. The third barrier consisted in a zone some seventy miles wide, subject to the special scrutiny of the so-called Green Police.

Smuggling, it is true, had developed to a like perfection, and Sulkiewicz, himself a customs officer, boasted that a piano could be smuggled in. On more than one occasion, Pilsudski characteristically turned the Tsar's weapons against himself by donning the cap of an official in the customs. In 1902, however, his portrait and description had been circulated throughout the Russian empire, and, if denounced, he could not escape a terrible term of imprisonment. Besides the many offences which he had committed, he stood indicted for complicity in the murder of a spy, a crime of which he would never have incurred the guilt.

Pilsudski's tour of Russian Poland, however, was undisturbed. The slackening of the P.P.S. which he discovered impelled him towards a new organization in five circles which could be supervised from Cracow. There, though with frequent journeys into Russia, he took up his meagre abode, and struggled for years with poverty, with the defects of his colleagues, and with the formidable onslaughts of the police. After a year, he had at least established the P.P.S. in every considerable town, but the competition with Social Democracy was severe.

The Austrian authorities, on the other hand, treated him with marked politeness, as a refugee gentleman at war with Russia. Although there was much to dishearten the keen party member, he felt that a rising against Russia was beginning to be discussed as a possibility. In *Strife (Walka)*, which he made the organ of the P.P.S. in Lithuania, he urged resistance to the Russian advance. An all-Polish party of thinking men and women, stressing their party life and substituting mass tactics for individual—such became his ideal. "The brain of the party", he wrote to a friend, "is reduced to literally one person, your humble servant." "You cannot imagine", he added, "how lonely I feel"—for, excepting his wife, there was no one with whom he could discuss his teeming plans. But he continued to move from branch to branch and from conference to conference, always centralizing, co-ordinating, providing for instruction, and steering the Polish movement clear of commitments to movements in other lands.

At the close of 1903, the P.P.S. had about 500 full members in Warsaw, and about as many outside. Associates outnumbered this *élite* by five or six to one. The normal income had risen to somewhat more than £2000, of which teeming Lodz contributed some £3. Yet the P.P.S. was unquestionably the foremost of the revolutionary parties, equal in numbers and influence to all the rest combined. Such figures made it clear to the most "romantic" of conspirators that, unless the conditions changed, it would be fantastic, nay criminal, to strike for independence.

In 1904, however, the struggle between Russia and Japan suddenly held out fresh hopes. In intellect and in mobility, the Russians proved inferior to the Japanese, and their defeats on land were only surpassed by their defeats at sea. A novel public opinion turned against the government, and in several regions revolution seemed to be at hand. The Tsar's brother was slaughtered by the son of a Warsaw Pole: there were disturbances in the army and in the fleet: strikers were numbered by millions: in October, 1905, the tsardom attempted to buy domestic peace by issuing a constitution: peasant revolts were widespread: in December, the workers held four-fifths of Moscow. Although the army, in the main, proved loyal, and the *bourgeoisie* rallied to the Tsar, enough had happened to show that the State had been in danger.

Among the Poles, the war evoked mixed feelings. Some joined in the loyal demonstrations which the outbreak of hostilities brought forth. Others, like the P.P.S., sympathized with the small nation against the great. Few save the P.P.S., however, hoped that the time had come for action, basing their calculation on the fact that Poles were liable to be called up, and that rebellion might cost less lives than war.

Even in the P.P.S., Pilsudski's far-reaching ideals were not widely shared. He, almost alone, thought in terms not of a party but of the Polish nation as a whole, for whose good he was prepared to sacrifice his life as an example to the rest. When war seemed imminent, he held that the time for an exemplary movement had arrived. His fevered advocacy of this view, however, met with no response. He wrote a manifesto for the *Workman*, but, to his horror, found that the then editor had committed the paper to a policy of indifference to quarrels between *bourgeois* States. The P.P.S., indeed, joined the Socialists of neighbouring non-Russian peoples in proclaiming a resistance which did not take place, and Pilsudski vainly arranged for conferences with possible rebels, particularly with the Finns. Hampered in his anti-Russian efforts by lack of funds, he turned to the Japanese minister at Vienna within a few days of the outbreak of war. Various schemes for aiding Japan were mooted, that of Pilsudski, an insurrection with Japanese aid and championship of Poland at the peace. As the outcome of various negotiations, he was deputed to journey by way of America to Japan and to effect a Polish-Japanese alliance.

Early in July, 1904, therefore, Pilsudski reached Tokio, only to find the National Democrat, Roman Dmowski, already on the spot. Pilsudski argued that a Polish rising would help Japan; Dmowski, that it would do her harm, since Russia would crush it and then transfer her army of occupation from Poland to the Far East. Such a divergence, which a meeting of nine hours failed to remove, was fatal to Polish collaboration with Japan. Pilsudski could only claim that he had secured that the P.P.S. should instruct Polish conscripts to surrender and that the Japanese should grant such prisoners separate treatment. The Russians, however, skilfully mobilized Poles chiefly from rural districts outside the orbit of the P.P.S.

The autumn of 1904 found Pilsudski once again in Austrian Poland, racking his brains for some effective plan of opposition. "I cannot remember", he wrote, twenty-five years later, "how many sleepless nights I passed in walking about my room, smoking cigarette after cigarette, and drinking an inordinate amount of tea." War, however, makes even those outside its sphere less indisposed to violence, and the Poles found themselves more nearly threatened by the mobilization. He was therefore able to convince the P.P.S. that an armed demonstration against the conscription should be made in Warsaw, and, if possible, in other towns. His own part was the supply of arms for what he always reckoned one of the choicest landmarks in his life—the first armed challenge to the tsardom since 1863.

On Sunday, 13 November, 1904, the congregation pouring from high mass into a Warsaw square (Plac Grzybowski) was greeted by a crowd of students and workmen, who unfurled banners and led a procession singing revolutionary songs. Some shots drove off the police, but cavalry dispersed the demonstrators. At a cost of about fifty killed and wounded, the capital was disturbed for several hours. The plan was not to Pilsudski's taste, but the demonstration limited the Polish mobilization and proved that Poles were still ready to die for their country. On the other hand, it shocked the *bourgeois* and impelled the National Democrats towards collaboration with Russia.

Upon Pilsudski, the chequered year 1904 produced a clear and lasting effect which differed from its influence upon the Polish masses. From an attitude of indifference the masses were forced towards active co-operation either with the revolutionaries or with the government. Soon the P.P.S. and its allies found their numbers multiplied tenfold. Such growth lent weight to strikes, but left the government almost unaffected. In any armed uprising, the participation of an untrained mass increased the likelihood of defeat and the certainty of slaughter. At the same time, growth in numbers inflamed the eagerness of the uninstructed for quick results, thereby hampering and endangering the leaders. Pilsudski, on the other hand, suffered no rebuffs to turn him from the path towards an armed Poland ready to win her independence with the sword. The first stage, and that no small one, was to educate the boldest elements in the nation, and to organize them into an army, centralized and disciplined, yet secret. To create the framework of such an army was the destiny of the P.P.S., and it began by forming small groups of militants to make demonstrations.

The P.P.S., however, now comprised younger men, who took a different view. Pilsudski was always influential and respected, but in 1905 he ceased to be all-powerful. In January, the general strike had seemed to show that the P.P.S. was the "moral dictator" of the nation. The police massacre of workmen in St. Petersburg, known as "Bloody Sunday", had given the cue to demonstrations in Poland embracing every class. Leadership, however, was lacking, and, in February, a great though secret conference of the P.P.S. was held in Warsaw. Its object was in reality to agree on an ideal for the whole movement. Although Pilsudski was elected to the executive, it was as the colleague of younger men of a Left-wing universalist type, and with a programme which included terrorism and mass demonstrations. As the result, Slawek and Prystor set to work to create a Militant Organization which should cow the government by acts of terror.

Chapter IX

PILSUDSKI AND THE MILITANTS (1905-1908)

THANKS to the Warsaw Congress, Pilsudski's life from 1905 to 1908 was largely coloured by the series of outrages which constituted the war of the P.P.S. against the tsardom. Instead of almost casual and often futile attacks upon statues and bridges, the government was faced with sudden onslaughts by trained and desperate men upon banks, post-offices, policemen, and any vulnerable agent or institution. "The cruelty of the government", declared the leaders of the Militants, "has brought the masses to such a point that the mere sight of a policeman calls forth the desire to kill him." Weary of passive and hopeless suffering, they proposed to train and arm companies to avenge their wrongs. Groups of students went through courses of technical instruction, and the Japanese provided in Paris a school of bomb-construction.

Poles, it is said, fight best in groups and share with the Russians a spirit of self-dedication rarely found in the conspirators of the West. This was exactly the mentality for Militant success. Success and failure, indeed, alternated, but the skill with which the police introduced their own agents into the movement tended to check its wide diffusion. During May, vast strikes in Warsaw and other towns appealed to the people more than did isolated assassination. Other popular demonstrations followed, government replying with a memorable orgy of murder on Friday, 23 June, 1905. The P.P.S. found itself quite unable to control the masses of the population, and Pilsudski was hampered in his strenuous labours for the cause of independence by inability to control the P.P.S. He was able, however, to combat successfully those who wished to rise forthwith, while Russia was convulsed with revolution. Poland, he urged, must always choose a line of action for herself.

The prospect of any change immediately raised questions of what the change should be. The boundaries of 1772 would be too great, and those of 1815 too small, for the capacity of the Polish people. In February, 1906, a congress of the P.P.S. showed that the younger section desired a federal union with Russia, and regarded the Militants as a terrorist police force, while Pilsudski and the older men looked on them as a training-school for the future independent nation. Whereas Pilsudski frankly denounced mere homicide, and declared that they were combatants, not executioners, the Militants themselves had been clamouring for action and for independence of the central Committee. The outcome was that neither view completely triumphed. The Militants, whom Slawek organized in groups of five, accomplished several *coups* which added to their cash resources, but which, even during the Russian revolution, held out small hopes of victory.

In 1905, none the less, the tsardom made not a few concessions. The Poles received the right to open schools, to form societies and to change from the Orthodox or Greek confession. When the October constitution was proclaimed, however, Pilsudski distrusted its permanence, and wisely declined to announce his own presence in Russia with a view to receiving a lawful passport. The planless and sporadic character of the revolutionary uprisings in the winter proved that they were not inspired by him. At the congress of February, 1906, by sheer force of will and intellect, he regained for a moment his old ascendancy.

PILSUDSKI AND THE MILITANTS

The triumph of his speech was heightened when a card with the words "Don't applaud this", which the Left passed from hand to hand, reached the Chairman, who read it to the meeting. The younger men, however, retained their majority, and the columns of the *Workman* were closed to their opponents.

Determined that his followers should learn to fight, Pilsudski had formed at Cracow a kind of military academy of revolution. A deep, though self-taught, student of war, he gave lectures on organization and tactics, while professional instructors taught sabotage, the manufacture and use of bombs, map-making, anatomy, field fortification and the like. This was part of a plan for gradually militarizing the nation by a number of similar educational centres.

Time and P.P.S. unity, however, were both lacking. Government had yet another weapon, and, provoked by the outrages of the Militants, as Pilsudski believed, it was employed. This was the *pogrom*, of which the West now heard—a local massacre of Russian Jews. Early in September, a *pogrom* took place at Siedlce, some fifty miles east of Warsaw. A week later, it is said, a Warsaw *pogrom* would have been effected, had not the P.P.S. detected and published the plans. Faced by massacre wherever the Russians chose to incite it, the Militants were cowed into inactivity.

It might have been foretold that sudden and widespread assassination of the police would expose the civil population to reprisals, and that many would then turn against the P.P.S. Such reprisals as the *pogrom*, however, though unworthy of any government, terrified the people as a whole. A train robbery, though it brought in more than £5000 without any Militant loss, only increased the general fear of consequences. The Russians, moreover, were now dispersing their army throughout Poland, thus menacing the countryside. In these circumstances the party congress of November, 1906, assembled at Vienna.

The outcome of this Vienna Congress was a schism in the P.P.S. The assembly served as a battle-ground for the devotees of words against the doers of deeds, for the *doctrinaires* against Pilsudski. The disaffected indicted the Committee on such charges as failure to punish a Russian officer, beloved by his men, for torturing his prisoners by hanging them thrice over and cutting them down when still alive. Long and confused debates left one fact clear—that the majority would not allow the Militants the freedom of action which these deemed indispensable. After an indecisive first vote, twenty-eight delegates passed an adverse resolution, which Pilsudski and some eleven others regarded as making their own further collaboration impossible. Refusing to remain in a mere talking-shop, they appealed to the P.P.S. against its delegates, and formed at Cracow the so-called Revolutionary Fraction of the party to continue the work of the Militants. Thus, to the initial discomfiture of both, the men who believed in striving for Polish independence by creating an armed force, and those who trusted propaganda to produce a social revolution, went different ways, the latter largely towards Communism.

The next year, 1907, must rank among the darkest of Pilsudski's life. He was struggling, with but indifferent success, to build up a revolutionary Polish army, and to reconvert the P.P.S., of which the Fraction still regarded themselves as members. The government, on the other hand, was endeavouring, by concession and by attack, to extirpate the revolutionary forces, which themselves were engaged in bloody mutual strife. To harass the government, to gratify the zeal of the Militants, and to gain funds for the work, a series of individual exploits must be attempted. Some of these, notably the raid upon a Warsaw post-office, were brilliantly successful, but some failed. Pilsudski could claim that the mass of the population gained experience of fighting, and that the Militants became true artists at their work. The scores of executions, moreover, produced not a few conspicuous martyrs, who faced their judges and their executioners with inspiring firmness. Secession, none the less, was followed by decline. Disunion went so far that the P.P.S. at Lodz, with some 12,000 members, was dissolved, while actions on the scale of those of 1906 became impossible.

Chapter X

BEZDANY (26 September, 1908)

DESPITE the unstinted sacrifice of his best years, Pilsudski in 1907 had good reason for bitter, if transient, despair. He was not blind to the facts that even a united Polish nation could do little against Russia, and that only a small fraction of one Polish party shared his own ideas. In his fortieth year, he declared to an intimate that for him the high road had been succeeded by a mere track, and the track by a mountain path, where nightfall might overtake a victim whose strength was gone. Characteristically, however, he preferred a desperate enterprise to tame surrender. No less characteristically, he joined like-minded men and women in a new society, the League of Military Action (Z.W.C.).

One successful "military action" against the government might give the new organization the 300,000 roubles (some £50,000 today) which would suffice for a long campaign. A siege of the State bank at Kiev, however, proved impracticable, and some less carefully guarded government war-chest must be found. From this simple political situation, and, not least, from Pilsudski's innate thirst for battle, came the exploit of Bezdany in the autumn of 1908.

Of this, though Pilsudski himself long afterwards emphasized the extraordinary intelligence and self-control which it required, modern Poland speaks but seldom. Even the well-informed Mr. Gillie places the scene upon the Niemen, some forty miles away. One of the most outspoken critics of Polish affairs, reproducing information supplied by a French lady passenger in the Bezdany train, has published the following narrative of the event:

"In 1905, a train coming from Russia (*sic*) was travelling peacefully between Vilna and Grodno (*sic*), when it was forced to stop rather abruptly in the open country on account of some trees that had been thrown across the line; at the same moment armed men of by no means reassuring aspect rushed to the carriage doors. They requested the travellers to hand their leader their jewels, valuables, and money. This act of violence was directed against Russians only; the foreigners were not robbed, or if by chance any of them were subjected to this indignity it was by accident. Then, after having conscientiously emptied the luggage van, which, it was said, contained large sums of money, the modern highwaymen allowed the train to proceed."

The real facts of the seizure of Russian funds on their way by rail to St. Petersburg throw an invaluable light on the history and character of Pilsudski. The outrage was no light-hearted foray, but a deliberate act of "war". It was mooted at Kiev, almost a year before it was carried out. Suggested by Pilsudski, it was accepted by Prystor, a sturdy son of Wilno and a veteran Militant, who had spent five years in a Russian prison and who became to Pilsudski like a second self. These two, having travelled four hundred miles to their own northern city, selected Bezdany, a rural station about eighteen miles along the main line from Warsaw to the Russian capital, and the second halting-place for the mail-train after leaving Wilno. The treasure, they calculated, could be seized on the eve of the Russian Easter, twelve days later than the Easter of the West. As it proved, nine months' unceasing labour were indispensable to prepare for an action lasting barely three-quarters of an hour.

The selection of Bezdany itself was soon made. Although a local government officer, a Russian "land captain", lived there, it was in the main a small aggregate of peasants' *chalets*, with unfrequented country tracks traversing the surrounding forests. Not far from the railway station ran a broad river, whose current would carry a boat to Wilno in a few hours. The necessary score of armed men could therefore approach Bezdany inconspicuously by road or rail, and leave it inconspicuously by road or river. The sandy soil and almost unpeopled forest offered swift and safe concealment for the booty. To the Militants, moreover, Wilno was virgin soil, while the Russian government was far less efficient than near Warsaw. For a score of men to snatch away a large fortune in cash from State keeping, and to vanish without trace, was none the less an exploit which demanded the most careful preparation.

As always with Pilsudski, action was the outcome of dispassionate and exhaustive thought. Where one failure would mean the ruin of the nascent League, nothing must be unprepared or left to chance. Every aspect of the *terrain* must be studied; every habit of the enemy, ascertained; men, funds, tools and vehicles, duly assembled; bases and hiding-places, made secure. Early in the campaign, it was discovered that, however little the government might expect an armed raid, it had no illusions with regard to its own officials. Widespread enquiries into the transport of the precious packages proved that most of the subordinate agents knew nothing of their contents or distribution. Only long observation of railway movements by the young Lithuanian revolutionary, Alexandra Szczerbinska, and by Madame Prystor, showed that the richest booty might be expected from the train which left Wilno on Saturday afternoon with a guard of some half-dozen soldiers.

A Saturday, moreover, had a double advantage for the work. As, owing to the Sabbath, it was not a market day in Wilno, few peasants would be on the road, while in the early hours of Sunday the returning Militants would be lost in the streams of churchgoers who filled the Wilno streets. Bezdany and Saturday being thus fixed points, the leaders could next proceed to pick their men, to accumulate munitions, and to find the hiding-places without which men and munitions would be of no avail.

The choice of men could be fastidious, for, all told, their number did not exceed nineteen. To ensure secrecy, only a handful of the leaders were allowed to know the plan. Although money was scarce, as usual, Alexandra Szczerbinska was installed in a secluded dwelling close to the river and the town of Wilno, where bombs and rifles, dynamite and other "agricultural machinery" could arrive by rail and be kept safe.

All through the spring and summer of 1908 the preparatory work went on. The government, by increasing its severity against the revolutionaries further south, was unconsciously drawing away its forces from Bezdany. But a Militant attempt to gain funds by bombing a mail-van failed, and it became necessary to sell the secret stores of arms in Vienna and Berlin. Even so, a hundred accidents —bad weather, unforeseen movements of troops, the arrest or illness of a key-man, fire, explosion, discovery—might at any moment frustrate the enterprise. The autumn rains would in any case make transport impossible. Only at the end of August could Pilsudski reveal to a small conclave of leaders in Wilno the final details of his plan, and fix its execution for Saturday, 19 September.

MARSHAL PILSUDSKI

The interval was filled with endless study, reconnaissance and drill. Six of the nineteen Militants, it was arranged, should travel to Bezdany by the train itself, speaking only Russian or Yiddish, and each carrying some parcel wrapped in a Jewish newspaper. Their leader was Slawek, later the Premier and, in 1938, the Marshal or Speaker of the Polish Seym or Lower House. No captain-general was appointed, for among veterans like Slawek Pilsudski was a novice, but in action as in debate his moral force secured the prevalence of his will. He took command of the four who were to seize the booty, while six gave battle to the escort and eight dealt with the railwaymen and passengers, the carriage-driver standing by for the retreat.

On Friday, 18 September, Pilsudski assembled the conspirators in Wilno, explained to everyone his part, and divided their cash resources into equal shares. He himself and Alexandra Szczerbinska made no claim, trusting that Wilno or the booty would supply their needs. Next day the train drew up at Bezdany, bringing Slawek and his men from further south. Rifles in hand, they leaped to the ground on the side remote from observation, but no explosion gave them the signal for attack. At the next station they again stood to arms, for Bezdany had never been mentioned to them by name, but again they must re-embark. The fiasco had been caused by failure to transport tools and dynamite from Wilno in the time prescribed. Pilsudski decreed a week's delay, and his undaunted colleagues laughed off their disappointment. The respite was of course seized upon for further study of the scene of action.

When Friday, 25 September, came, Pilsudski again addressed his men, and frankly stated that lack of cash made further delay impossible. Again the roubles were divided into equal shares. Next day, arms and provisions were served out, and the eighteen-mile journey from Wilno achieved in time for a short rest before the hour of action. Then, quitting the shelter of the woods in tiny groups, a dozen men disposed themselves in the gathering dusk about the quiet station. One Militant pretended to be drunk; another, with a four-pound bomb under his coat, flirted passionately with a Jewess. Pilsudski and two others prepared acetylene lamps near the spot at which the postal wagon would draw up, and placed the explosives in position.

Meanwhile, Slawek and his five comrades were seated by couples in the Wilno train, which stopped as usual at Bezdany. Within the next few minutes, Pilsudski's plan had proved almost perfectly successful. One soldier lay dead, another was wounded, the rest had run away. The railwaymen on the train and station were subdued, the signals blocked, the telegraph and telephone put out of action. A mob of passengers and others, some forty strong, were being tended in the station building by the Militants, who gave them fair words and cigarettes, threatening the mutinous with a packet of herrings, which they took for an enormous bomb, and even light-heartedly shooting at the station clock.

Meanwhile, Pilsudski and his three colleagues, one, Prystor, a future Premier, toiled feverishly at the hard task of discovering and appropriating the spoil. Two clerks, frightened by Pilsudski, who threatened them with an imaginary bomb, opened the door of the postal wagon from within. A third, in mortal fear, turned on the electric light and pointed to a heap of mail-bags. An immense treasure lay at Pilsudski's feet, but to separate the grain from the chaff in half an hour proved impossible. Letters with misleading endorsements, packages of notes withdrawn from circulation, masses of bills of exchange, silver too heavy to be removed—all this mocked the Militants on every side. They shattered cases with dynamite, only to find others within. These they hacked open with axes, but then iron coffers defied them. Pilsudski, cool amid the chaos, announced the ever-shortening remnants of their time, while, despite the adverse signals, other trains drew near and lit up the scene with their unwelcome lights. Thus when, at 11.15 p.m., Pilsudski ordered the action to be broken off, the choicest treasures still remained untouched.

Nearly eleven hours of adventurous retreat followed. Carrying their booty in sacks, Pilsudski and his colleagues laid a false trail away from Wilno with complete success, then doubled and rejoined their waiting carriage unobserved. After toiling through the forest and crossing streams, one Militant donned an officer's uniform, and Pilsudski the head-dress of a judge's clerk. Thus at last they flung themselves into their Wilno hiding-place, where Szczerbinska watched for their arrival. There they examined the spoil, of which some five-sixths proved worthless. The remainder, however, amounted to just over 200,000 roubles, in value exceeding 33,000 modern pounds. After burying all save the most precious securities and notes, Pilsudski and Szczerbinska made their way to southern Russia, whence Pilsudski departed to seek rest in the Austrian mountains.

Soon all the chief conspirators had reached safety by various routes. By accident, however, the identity of some was discovered, and, a year later, five received heavy sentences. Swirski, one of the five, became Pilsudski's adjutant when Poland was reborn. Pilsudski's part in the affair appears to have remained unknown. The Russian government, it is said, did not deign to stop the "expropriated" banknotes, and thus the League of Military Action could once again buy munitions, maintain dependents and bribe officials.

Chapter XI

PILSUDSKI AND THE RIFLEMEN (1908-1914)

BETWEEN the Bezdany episode and the outbreak of the Great War, almost six years intervened, carrying Pilsudski through the middle forties. During this period, the development of the Polish people and of the European situation combined to make his life difficult and his course uncertain. As the organizer of the P.P.S., he had enjoyed, amid countless hazards and discomforts, that prime need of his existence, abundant, purposeful and strenuous work. From 1914 onwards, with two brief intervals, that demand was destined never to slacken.

In 1908, however, it became clear that the Militants could not hope for real success against Russia. The tsardom, supported by the middle classes, was rallying from the shock of defeat by Japan, and the economic interest of the Poles demanded that Russia should be peaceful and progressive. She now possessed an all-Russian parliament, in which the Polish representatives, led by Dmowski, pursued a policy of buying favour to their country at the price of loyalty to the Tsar. In Germany, the hereditary enemy of the Slavs, which was now threatening to break the spirit of the Polish minority in her eastern provinces, Dmowski and his colleagues saw the inexorable foe of Polish nationality. There the immemorial struggle between Teuton and Slav was now producing a systematic effort to supplant some Poles by Germans and to Germanize those who remained.

Russia, in the recent past, had been no less hostile.

But Russia was less efficient and methodical, while her Poles formed a far larger body than those in Germany. The Russians, moreover, being Slavs, must sympathize with some at least of Poland's aims, especially their resistance to the Germans. Russia might swiftly change towards liberty, and free Russia could live in fraternal union with Poland. Such hopes inspired the policy of the Polish National Democrats, who, since the October Constitution of 1905, found representation in the Russian parliament. Later, indeed, Pilsudski was inspired to predict that Germany would conquer Russia and would then succumb to France. At this time, however, little save the vast and growing German power could catch the eye in Europe. But for his inbred hatred of the Muscovite, Pilsudski himself could hardly have determined to take the German side in any quarrel.

At this time, however, the relations between Austria and Russia were becoming increasingly strained. Both Powers were impelled towards a forward policy in the Balkans. There Austria attempted to win new prestige for her empire, endangered by the rising nationalism of its constituent parts, while Russia, checked in the Far East, sought solace in her hegemony of the Slavonic world. The Bosnian crisis of 1908, thanks to German support, brought Austria Balkan gains without equivalent for Russia, and both empires took thought for a future struggle. For Austria to conciliate the Poles was obvious wisdom, and Pilsudski as an exiled foe of Russia might well be patronized. In consequence, he was enabled by successive stages to become towards Austria something like a tribal chieftain in alliance with a great neighbouring Power.

In 1908, although hampered by a weakness of the heart, he began to take a controlling interest in the League of

Military Action which Sosnkowski had organized in Lemberg (Lwow). This led to his emancipation from every party tie, and to his self-dedication to the task of creating a Polish army. To make himself a worthy leader, he studied deeply in the history of war and insurrection, accumulating and digesting the knowledge which he was soon both to publish and to make the guide of his campaigns.

In 1910, he was able to convert what had been a tolerated irregularity into a League of Riflemen which the government encouraged. Henceforward the Riflemen wore uniform and were drilled with obsolete government rifles. Their military instruction became as wide as Pilsudski could make it, and went far beyond mere drill. He published successively sets of lectures on Practical Tasks of Revolution in Russian Poland, insisting upon perfect obedience to the officers' commands, on the History of the Militant Organization of the P.P.S., and on the Military Geography of the Kingdom of Poland. Before the close of 1910, he had added a drastic review of a new work on musketry, and a weighty article on Reforms of the Russian Army.

In 1911, he wrote vivid and valuable reminiscences of the Prison Mutiny in Irkutsk, followed, early in March, by a letter from his Italian health resort to his "uncle", a well-known painter and man of letters.

This is long, graceful and tender, and it tells of similar letters received from Bronislas Pilsudski, then likely to settle in Austrian Poland. It throws light on one source of the writer's lectures on Russia—the intimate conversation of a fellow-Lithuanian who had served as a Russian general through the war against Japan. "People", he declares, "readily become pessimists, more readily than optimists, especially we Poles." In May, a notable lecture on Crises of Battles proved that Pilsudski had reflected deeply on the wars between Britain and the Boers and between Russia and Japan. He argued that in modern campaigns, with battles far more prolonged but less costly to the combatants than of old, morale was all-important.

Meanwhile, signs were not wanting that the League of Riflemen embodied a contagious idea. The Austrian Poles of the Right formed Teams of Riflemen, having the same methods and objects as the League. The movement for drilling Poles spread from Cracow and Lwow to smaller places, embracing the gymnastic societies of Polish tradition. By 1912, some 300 such troops, with nearly 20,000 members, existed in Austrian Poland. Poles outside the country, in France, Belgium, Switzerland and overseas, caught and connected the notions of drill and independence. The Balkan War of 1912 between four smaller Powers and Turkey, breaking the long peace of continental Europe, and hinting at a vaster struggle, stimulated military effort. A Polish Military Treasury and a Temporary Committee of the Confederated Parties of Independence were among its firstfruits. The Committee could serve the Polish cause through the fiery Socialist Daszynski and other representatives in the provincial and central Austrian assemblies, and during the negotiations for the Balkan peace.

Of all this activity, the ex-secretary of the P.P.S. and the new lecturer on military topics was the soul. Joseph Haller, an officer of the reserve, drilled troops, but Pilsudski both inspired and organized the army. "He literally lives in the train between Lemberg (Lwow) and Cracow, or on the line to the smaller Galician towns", wrote a contemporary. "He attends reviews of riflemen, orders manœuvres, gives lectures, readings, addresses. On all sides he kindles those whom he meets, and infects them with a sense of his inflexible and all-absorbing will."

PILSUDSKI AND THE RIFLEMEN

Lecturing in February, 1912, on the Eve of the Russian Revolution of 1905, Pilsudski described how, after 1863, the Poles used to say that enlightened Europe would not tolerate such a monster of reaction as Russia, but they threw the whole burden on the shoulders of the Russian people. Now, every day, he laboured to prevent a repetition of the same mistake. The moral factor of revolution, he maintained in a lecture in May, grows with amazing speed, since in quiet times the social forces which produce it are still at work. The technical factor follows a different evolution. We must see that it is not neglected.

Signs appear in his correspondence that what was to prove the most difficult complication of the Polish situation was not wholly overlooked—their hatred of the Prussians. Pilsudski and his associates, the later generals Sosnkowski, Kukiel, Sikorski and others less well known to fame, armed Poles to fight for Austria, although they knew that, in all likelihood, they would be fighting for the Prussians against the Poles of Russia. Those who were Austrian subjects had no alternative except to fight the same enemies, but as conscripts in the Austrian ranks.

The dilemma illustrates the terrible position of the Poles, and in part explains why the National Democrats attempted to procure rewards for their fellow-countrymen by fighting for the Slavs against the Germans. Austria, however, gave an immediate recognition, which Prussia and Russia must refuse, and Pilsudski clutched at the reality of an armed nucleus of independent Poland. For its growth he must trust the future. "Present events", he declared in effect on 5 October, 1912, when Balkan events presaged a European upheaval, "raise our hopes that the moment for action is near, and that the League of Military Action may take the field in Russian Poland. I can only appeal to the revolutionary conscience of the individual to take up the dangerous work of preparation there. I call for volunteers for at least six months, and urge all to be cool and vigilant, to use the present wave of feeling for gaining men and money, to redouble their efforts to spread military education, and to report even the smallest evidence as to Russian preparations for war."

A fortnight later, Bulgaria, Serbia, Montenegro and Greece attacked the Turks, but the Great Powers continued to look on. On 13 October, Pilsudski welcomed the German Social Democrats of Austria, saying that to them the P.P.S. stood nearer than to other parties, and that they had hospitably received its members when the police of all Europe were in pursuit. Poland, he declared, was exhausted by revolutionary struggles, but with their help he hoped for the triumph of freedom. In December, he lectured on the Mobilization of an Insurrection, showing how favourably the Poles had been placed when they rose in 1830. Mutual confidence, ruthlessness, secrecy, disposability and conscientiousness in trifles—these, he said, were the essentials, and the third and last were particularly necessary for Poles.

Early in 1913, a Wilno Democrat published an account of an intimate talk with Pilsudski, whom he found in a modest student's lodging, immersed in his military studies. Energy, sincerity and rare moderation in the statement of his views seemed to be his outstanding characteristics. To these another keen-eyed observer would add *bonhomie*, even to a love of gentle teasing. Few men in Europe, Pilsudski declared, knew as much of the Boer and Russo-Japanese wars as he did. The existing tension between Austria and Russia had nothing to do with Poland, and Austria did not intend to raise the Polish question. Therefore he thought it inexpedient to move in Russian Poland until war began. Then, however, the Poles could not look on inactive, and only as allies of Austria could they intervene. This was to demand that Russian Poles should, like himself, break with the tsardom.

The verdict that the Poles must fight for Austria against Russia naturally provoked the National Democrat to a vigorous debate. Pilsudski granted that the gain would fall to the Germans, but maintained that, when war had exhausted the combatants, Poland would come by her own. The Leagues, he argued, could furnish 20,000 instructors, and, as the Russians had planned to evacuate Poland, and Austria could not occupy the whole of it, they would have the necessary scope. Arms would certainly be found. All the Powers would be brought in, and although the technical skill of the Germans would account for Russia, he expected the resources of France and England to prevail.

Russian Poland, he granted, was technically and morally unprepared for war, and he would therefore prefer it to be postponed. But the Russian Poles lived in such oppression that he did not doubt that they would fight against the government. Was he sure of Austrian victory? the visitor enquired. "All action involves risk," replied Pilsudski. "There are chances, but ultimately all will depend upon the Poles themselves. I can only say that we shall do what we regard as our duty." "You are training all your young men for war alone," declared the other. "Failing war, what will become of them?" "Many," replied Pilsudski slowly, "will be completely wasted. The loss will be great. But it is hard." On this the National Democrat sadly took his leave of the determined man.

On 1 June, 1913, Pilsudski rendered an account at Cracow to the officers of the Riflemen. Lack of funds, as he showed, was crippling the Polish forces, especially in respect of uniforms and arms. The outlook, as he declared next month, was stormy, for the authorities seemed likely to deprive them of their rifles. During the last two years, Austria had encouraged her enemies by the weakness of her policy, and it was difficult to keep up the hope of Polish-Austrian collaboration. He himself had been obliged to abandon the Lemberg (Lwow) manœuvres. He was so weary of governmental uncertainty and interference, that he sometimes thought of abandoning the whole enterprise, and of turning to the policy of reforming and transforming Russia. At the moment he was occupied with preparations for a summer school, 200 strong, chiefly from Russian Poland.

Soon afterwards, however, he entered into fierce controversy with the National Democrats. They had represented the Riflemen's movement as the work of the famous Colonel Redl, who had killed himself when unmasked as a Russian spy. To the Riflemen themselves he declared that they were Poland's only hope, that they must keep the social place which they had won, and must command the respect even of their opponents and of the future foe. Their conduct must show respect for their uniform, and, when in uniform, politics must be laid aside. Now that the expectation of war which had swelled their numbers was over, they must continue to show the strength of will which assured victory in the near future. Meanwhile, he was engaged in enriching the history of war by an elaborate account of the outbreak of the insurrection of 1863.

The dawn of 1914 found Pilsudski, at the age of forty-six, immersed in preparations for a future war. Despite the anti-climax of the previous year, he was inspecting Polish forces both in Austria and in other countries, writing articles, superintending manœuvres and prompting military education. "From 1904 onwards", he maintained before an audience in Paris, "we have witnessed a series of revolutions and conflicts in which armed force has proved decisive. Today only the sword has weight in the scales of the fate of nations."

In a series of articles for the *Rifleman* (*Strzelec*) of which Rydz-Smigly, later the beloved second Marshal of Poland, acted as publisher, Pilsudski expounded the lessons of the recent Balkan War and of the last autumn manœuvres. A characteristic detail was his insistence on the importance of marching. Commanders and umpires were directed always to begin their discussions by criticizing the march itself, even if it was mere locomotion. In a further article, he investigated the gigantic expenditure of ammunition by a modern army. Thus, when the Great War came, he had made himself a military expert of rare qualifications, as well as a leader whose personal influence was unsurpassed.

On the very eve of war, however, the accustomed party strife was embittered by the wildest and most painful of accusations. Pilsudski's admirers believe that his enemies endeavoured by every method—insinuation, falsehood, slander, outright denunciation—to turn the American Poles against him and thus cut off his supplies. The statement that the Riflemen owed their origin to Redl was followed by a visit from American delegates, who in Europe expressed their approval of the organization, but reported adversely after their return. Hence it came about that the last of Pilsudski's writings before the actual clash of arms was a protest, "More about the American Delegates", against this most deadly blow. The protest, besides disposing of the charge of falsification of accounts, revealed the facts that more had been done by Austria in her non-Polish than in her Polish provinces to encourage shooting, that the disparity might be due to Polish party strife, and that Pilsudski, in achieving unity of command, had hoped that military co-operation might appease the dissensions among the Poles.

Criticism of his refusal to buy arms in large quantities he ascribed to "our cherished Polish *naïveté*, combined with ignorance of military technique". Since Poles were subjects of three States, each with a different type of armament, and the conditions of the future struggle were unknown, it was highly inexpedient, he urged, for a Polish army to commit itself to what might prove to be a weapon which they could not use in war.

Chapter XII

PILSUDSKI IN THE GREAT WAR (1914)

THE murder of the Austrian Heir-Apparent at Serajevo (28 June, 1914) degraded the burning questions of peace-time to the level of bygone squabbles. In peace, the Poles had failed to agree on the question whether they should themselves take the initiative or leave Austria to give the cue. When war seemed certain, Pilsudski brushed aside the opponents of immediate action. His view was always that Polish independence must first be asserted by a national army and then accepted by foreign Powers. Abandoning his projected summer school at Cracow, he called upon his forces to appear in arms on 29 and 30 July. Austria fixed on 31 July, and by 2 August both sections of the Riflemen had rallied to Pilsudski. Next day he formed a mixed company of 144 persons fitted for officers' rank. He took the White Eagle as the army ensign and proclaimed a National Government at Warsaw. Some 4000 men had placed themselves at his disposal, but Austria, as of old, was neither speculative nor in a hurry, and, without her, they could not be armed. The National Government, which appointed him Commandant, was a figment of Pilsudski's brain.

On the historic 6 August, therefore, Pilsudski set out to invade Russia with a mere three companies, among them only one equipped with modern rifles. Two days later, he crossed the Russian frontier as the Commander-in-Chief of the Polish army, and for a fortnight he remained supreme and independent. The whole adventure might well seem a grotesque piece of folly, and he expected death or glory. To his lieutenant, Sosnkowski, he predicted death. It is recorded that the first cavalry detachment of the invaders numbered eight men and three horses, the rest carrying saddles for the mounts that they designed to seize in Russia. Though ill-equipped, however, the troops were gay and bold, determined from the first to prove that Poles could out-soldier Austrians. Kielce, some seventy miles from Cracow, was the goal of the first advance, and the Polish foot reached it before the Austrian horse. They had more than once fought against the Russians on their way—an adventure which the Austrians prudently declined.

A fortnight had sufficed to prove that Pilsudski could raise and lead a band of hardy soldiers, but it had by no means convinced the government that Austria would be the stronger for an independent Polish army. The Russian Poles showed no disposition to enlist in such a force. Pilsudski punctiliously asserted his independence, and, in Kielce, occupied the Russian Governor's palace, leaving to the Austrian and German commanders quarters inferior to his own. It was natural for the War Office to demand that Poles who were Austrian subjects should be included in the existing Austrian army. Pilsudski, however, clung to the principle that Polish blood should only be shed for Poland, and demanded that recruits of Polish blood should be assigned to his command.

After ten days at Kielce, he could announce that a National Chief Committee (N.K.N.) of the Galician Poles at Cracow, had agreed with the Austro-Hungarian monarchy that Polish Legions should be formed for war with Russia, and that having consulted the secret National Government at Warsaw, he had consented to organize a great army on those lines. The existing Legionaries would form the *cadres*. A fortnight later, nearly 5000 of them swore allegiance to the Austro-Hungarian emperor. The time seemed ripe for Austria to court the Russian Poles by proclaiming a Polish kingdom. In a triple monarchy, however, Hungary might have become less important than in the dual, and the manifesto creating an Austria-Hungary-Poland always remained unsigned.

Pilsudski's immediate object, however, was to use such recognition as had been granted for the creation of a real Polish army. Within the shortest possible time, men must be recruited, equipped and furnished with the necessary supply and other services. Then their secret self-distrust must be dispelled by victory in Russian Poland over Russians. At Kielce, in August and September, 1914, Pilsudski passed the happiest moments of the war, since he was then most independent. Much had to be done, and his amazing energy produced a visible achievement every day. Workshops were set up, baggage-trains created, the numerous sick, chiefly of dysentery, evacuated, and good relations with the population of Poles and Jews established. The Commandant created a far-flung screen of scouts, including many women, and even chose the field on which he hoped to give the Russians battle. Since the Polish rifles were inferior, he determined to utilize the woods for the encounter.

For all his independent spirit, however, the leader of a few thousand men was bound to conform to the general course of the campaign. This ran in favour of the enemy. The Austro-German offensive was soon checked, and the right wing driven back. Lwow fell, and the National Democrats declined to fight against Russia. Both the Central Powers and the local population magnified the Russian peril, and Pilsudski, longing for the test of battle, was confronted with the duty of retreat. To march south and across the Vistula into Galicia seemed to him the depth of humiliation, but he could only resolve to seek the post of rearguard and to assume the supreme task of fighting a pursuing army.

Pilsudski's defiant spirit and his determination not to weary his men by insisting on every possible precaution were favoured by fortune, and the bold tactics of his Riflemen upon the Vistula brought them self-confidence and rising fame. The Commandant himself, however, fell a victim to influenza, and Sosnkowski, his officers and Dr. Rouppert prevailed on him to return to Cracow. Thus ended his first fight. Looking back upon it after four campaigns, he perceived mistakes, but claimed that his boldness in decision and action had won respect for himself and for his men.

In October, the Austrians made a second offensive northwards towards Warsaw. Pilsudski endeavoured to cooperate by summoning the Warsaw Poles to attack the Russian rear. In the offensive, with six battalions of infantry and a squadron of cavalry, he played a useful part, holding positions near Demblin, despite severe bombardment with guns from the fortress. "Shall the Polish guard", asked the Commandant, "be inferior to the guard from Moscow?" The Austrian army, however, chose to retreat towards the south-west, abandoning Poland to the Russians. Czechs and Poles in its ranks almost came to blows as their units jostled in the flight. Cracow appeared to be doomed, but Pilsudski determined to give battle to the south of it, on the last strip of the fatherland remaining free.

Quitting the main army, he led his Poles through wooded country and across ploughed fields to Cracow, braving many dangers from the advancing Russian columns. Both Commandant and soldiers took the keenest pleasure in the

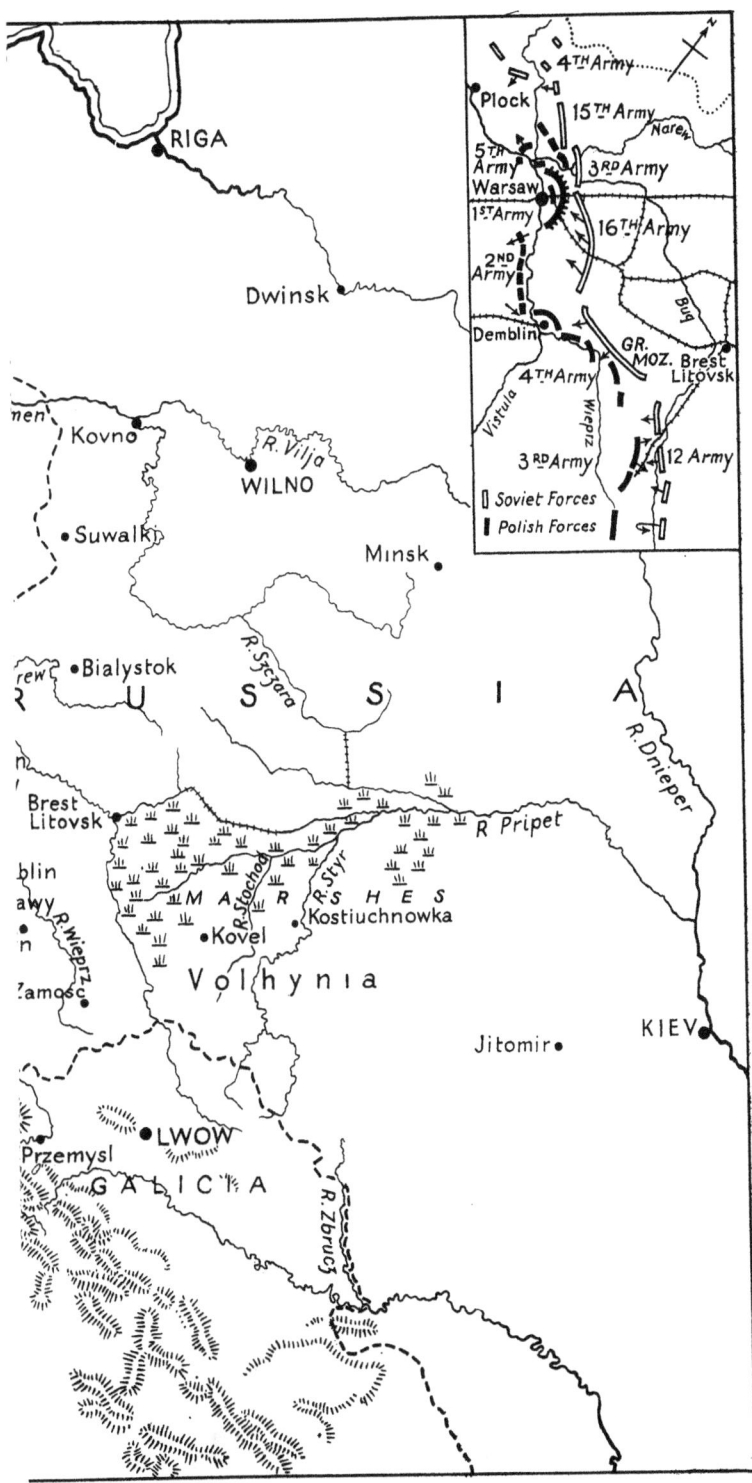

adventurous march, executed on Polish soil and against Austrian orders. Pilsudski has described his own feelings, methods and progress in military education, as danger succeeded danger on the way. Now it was a subordinate who reproved him for hazarding his own life, now a decision taken, not after careful calculation, but in virtue of the almost unconscious self-detachment of a sound idea, now an instinct that the column was marching apathetically, courageously or with eager expectation. His weak heart had stood the strain of three days' marching almost without sleep.

Late in November, after leaving his men for conferences with the N.K.N., he rejoined them for three weeks to the south-east of Cracow. Here, in broken country, he and his small command played a part in the confused manoeuvring and fighting which ended in the Russian retreat beyond the Dunajec. Warfare of this kind, with its almost unlimited scope for individual resourcefulness and courage, was Pilsudski's delight, and his account of the "battle of Limanova", written some three years later, affords much insight into his disposition. After the failure of two Austrian offensives, the Russians seemed irresistible, and Pilsudski's mind was full of the final scene in which he and his Legionaries should make their name immortal by perishing on the last strip of Polish soil. He listened to the sound of heavy shells in flight, so slow that the eye sought instinctively for the missile, and so pitiless that it seemed to say, "I bring certain death, but slowly, that I may see you turn pale before you die". Thus heavy guns mock the soldier, while field guns excite him with feverish clamour.

Valour on either side roused Pilsudski's unstinted admiration. He contrived to find a Russian uniform for a brave prisoner whose mufti would have earned him a firing-squad. Nothing pleased him more than the complaints of the doctors that his Legionaries escaped from hospital to rejoin, or the boast of one lad that his head was hard enough to defy the three bullets which had struck it. He recorded with pride that one of his lieutenants, wishing to cross the Vistula, plunged into it with his men, and all swam over with weapons in their hands. The wounded, with triumph in their faces, refused to groan. Later, indeed, some hearts and characters broke down, and strong men became cowards. When they formed the rearguard, however, he was proud of his men, for he could do with them what he would. In their young eyes he saw innocence and also unflinching will. Even for the most venturesome service there was never any lack of volunteers. They could even assimilate foreigners who strayed among them. Their Commandant declared that, while a soldier's long brotherhood with death makes him indifferent to property, whether his own or another's, his absence from home endears to him domestic life, and that a good soldier develops the best in his soul—reverence for himself and his honour.

On the march, it was the mirth and song of these Polish volunteers that marked them out. Pilsudski recorded that, in a countryside where the people spoke of the Russians as "our army", like all soldiers, they cast eyes and hands upon the fowls and geese, the horses and provisions, that they encountered. Yet when, in almost every village, the women came to complain, they shyly muttered, "Such a merry army". Into the desolate borderlands they imported jollity and life.

The complex relationships between Poles and Russians brought both humorous and poignant results. Now it was a wounded Lithuanian prisoner whose relatives had been Pilsudski's schoolfellows, now a squadron of Russian cavalry who failed to resist the Legionaries because they heard them swearing furiously in Russian. The "man of iron" of later days reveals that on occasion he was at heart as terrified as the rest, but did his duty by appearing calm. In 1918, he still regarded the Davoust of 1806 as a great military figure with whom he could not compare himself. And "the prettiest of all his fights", when, on 6 December, he failed to dislodge the Russians, convinced him that, since false premises encourage boldness, they may be the greatest boon in war.

From the field of Limanova, after victory on 12 December, Pilsudski went to Vienna for conference with the N.K.N. There, at a banquet, one of his officers criticized his speech as derogatory to the service. Pilsudski struck the table and called him to attention, saying that if he wished to criticize his superior officer he must take off his uniform. Soldiers, he declared, must give blind obedience. He was only a colonel, but he led his men and gained their confidence. Let others do the same. He returned to the front three days before December closed, happy in having inflicted great losses upon the Russians.

Chapter XIII

PILSUDSKI AND THE LEGIONS (1915-1916)

THE year 1915 continued what the autumn of 1914 had begun—the creation of a small but heroic Polish army. When the Sixth of August came, Pilsudski could only greet his men as Poland's vanguard. They were her vanguard, he claimed, however, not in arms alone, but in the moral sphere, since they knew how, when necessary, to risk their all. Thanks in a small degree to their exertions, the theatre of war had vastly changed. Pilsudski and his famous First Brigade, after a period of rest, had taken post east of Cracow on the Nida, and had shared in the long-drawn pursuit of the Russians after the German triumph in May at Gorlice, some seventy miles to the south. This allowed him to make contact at Lublin with the insurgent leaders of Russian Poland.

Since the previous autumn, the Polish Military Organization (P.O.W.) offered an escape from the galling overlordship of the austrophil N.K.N. Before midsummer, the Russians had been driven from Lwow: on 4 August, they evacuated Warsaw: Kovno was soon to fall: a million Poles, it was said, were deported into Russia from the eastern borderlands. While no one could be certain that the Russians would not return, their lack of technical equipment at least promised delay, and therefore the Central Powers must provide for the occupation of Russian Poland. Polish public opinion thus gained a new importance, and the leader of the Polish Legions became a man of weight. On 15 August, after further victories in the field, he went to Warsaw, which thenceforth was in German hands.

Pilsudski, as "Commandant" of the Legions, in the front line trenches during the Great War.

THE LEGIONS

The political situation was, if possible, more complex and difficult than before. Italy had entered the war, and it seemed possible that Russia would make a separate peace. Russian Poland remained cowardly and inert, while Austria was simply using the N.K.N. and the Legions as cards in her own hand. The attitude of his superiors in the N.K.N. towards Pilsudski was clearly expressed in a secret report on his fitness to receive a decoration in November, 1915. Admitting his talent and distinguished service, this declared that the First Brigade formed by him differed completely in spirit from the Second and Third, formed by the N.K.N. Pilsudski and his Brigade were ready at any moment to discard Austria in favour of their own nationalist aspirations. Since Pilsudski's ideas were fantastic and contrary to the Austrian interest, the N.K.N. had from the first done its best to stifle his influence.

The indictment was not unfounded, and the confession was certainly true. It was not surprising that at Warsaw Pilsudski exerted himself to make his own instrument, the P.O.W., the supreme recruiting and organizing agency among the Russian Poles. Postponing his own resignation, he suspended the reinforcement of the Legions, and endeavoured to build up a secret national Polish army on both sides of the Russian lines. To this end his officers assigned a great part of their pay.

Meanwhile, Pilsudski and the First Brigade continued to serve the Central Powers. In September, when Wilno was in German hands, they began an autumn campaign in the dreary marshes and forests of northern Volhynia. They were joined by the Second Brigade, which, as the stern struggle went on, imbibed their spirit. That spirit proved more and more discordant with the spirit of their Austrian colleagues. Soon, at headquarters, Poles and Austrians dined at separate tables. In mid-December, the First Brigade was withdrawn from the front for a well-earned rest.

Early in March, 1916, an attack of influenza compelled Pilsudski to quit his resting Brigade and to spend some weeks near Lwow. Thence he journeyed to Vienna, Cracow and Lublin, for secret talks on politics. Russian Poland, of course, now formed a topic for keen discussion between the Central Powers, and to influence them was far more important for Pilsudski than to fight the evicted Russians. Austria and Germany were at one in desiring to recruit extensively in Poland, where a million possible conscripts had been left behind, but, to do this, they must end the sovereignty of Russia, and annex or emancipate the country. Even a client Polish State, however, would gravely threaten the Germanization of the Prussian Poles which Bismarck had begun.

For the time being, therefore, the able German Governor, von Beseler, was established in Warsaw, while the Austrians administered about one-third of Russian Poland from Lublin. Pilsudski, for his part, had created a Council of Colonels, to negotiate with Austria for concessions to the Legions, and to demand a declaration by the Central Powers in favour of Polish independence. He meanwhile was with his men behind the Styr. Early in July, Brusilov's Russians broke the Austrian front some fifty miles to the south, and launched a fierce attack upon the Poles at Kostiuchnowka. After three days, having lost more than half their officers and almost half their men, the Poles conformed to the general movement of retreat, proud to be always the last to quit the field. They then occupied fortified lines upon the Stochod, whence, at the end of July, Pilsudski sent in his resignation.

THE LEGIONS

On the second anniversary of 6 August, his men gave him a sword of honour, and he established the Faithful Service Order. The fate of Poland, he declared, still hung in the balance. The honour of the Polish soldier must at all hazards be maintained. But only the future could determine whether they were to remain soldiers without a fatherland, leaving behind them only "the brief wailing of a woman, and the long converse of their kinsmen through the night". At the end of August, while his resignation remained unaccepted, all the Legionary officers sent a memorial to the N.K.N. They demanded to be made a Polish army, fighting under a provisional Polish government for Polish independence.

A month later, when it was clear that Brusilov's offensive was at an end, Pilsudski's resignation was accepted. While he discussed politics in the neighbourhood of Cracow, where he received a gold medal and an address with 50,000 signatures, the Legionaries on the Stochod were seething with disaffection, and masses of them resigned. Von Beseler assured the Central Powers that to enlist Poles they must establish a Polish State, though he warned them against Pilsudski and his friends. On 5 November, 1916, both Emperors joined in proclaiming a Polish State. The new Poland, they said, was to be free, happy, rejoicing in its own national life, and linked with both their powers. On this, Pilsudski advised his successor, Rydz-Smigly, to withdraw the resignations, and they were withdrawn. The First Brigade, none the less, was broken up, and the Legions, while mutinous Saxons and Bavarians were decimated, were removed elsewhere.

However qualified and vague, the public approval by Germany and Austria of a Polish national State must remain a landmark on the road to Polish independence.

The fact that the Central Powers needed the Poles, moreover, gave the Poles a valid basis for further negotiations. When, within four days of the first proclamation, a second invited them to enlist, but declared that for the present the alien occupation must continue, they made it clear that without a Polish State there would be no Polish army. In a letter of 6 November to the Rector of the University of Warsaw, who had been consulted by the German government, Pilsudski had argued that the Polish subjects of Russia could not join foreign armies. If in war-time, however, his own government ordered him to clean boots or to join an army of Sinhalese, he would promptly obey. His view prevailed, since it was supported by the need for fresh recruits, and by the evidence that, without some change, Poles would not fill the ranks. In mid-December, he came to Warsaw and accepted the Army portfolio from the new Temporary Council of State. His object was to create a large Polish army, which should obey none but a Polish government. If possible, he would base it on the P.O.W., which did not, like the Legions, owe allegiance to Austria.

At this juncture Pilsudski spoke with revealing freedom to a comrade [1] whose report seems faithfully and vividly to portray the conversation. "You judge rightly", he said, "that Austria is done for. The same is still more true of the gentlemen of the National Chief Committee (N.K.N.)." No longer, he declared, would he endure their work behind his back against him, and their attempts to sell cheaply and without authorization what only the people could rightly grant. The opportunity to gain foreign help by making use of his own person might not recur, and he hoped to convince the Germans that they would gain from the establishment of a Polish army on the Russian

[1] Wl. Baranowski: *Rozmowy z Pilsudskim*, p. 40.

frontier. At the same time they might put pressure on the Austrians to recognize the Legions as the basis of the new army. If he only spoke the word, the P.O.W. would submit to the Temporary Polish Government, from which he expected little. But, in return for the establishment of a Polish army on a Legionary basis, he was ready to give it recognition. Unfortunately, he had little hope of united Polish action, for Poles had a deep-rooted distrust of their power to accomplish anything without a foreign crutch.

When Pilsudski used this simile, he was wont to drive it home with gestures. Take away the crutch, he went on, and the whole collapses. This passivity of slaves is quick to change into willing lackey service for titles or other rewards. The energy spent on serving the Central Powers or the Allies might make an independent Poland. "Who can tell how long the war will last, and what chances we shall have?" The Legions had shown that the Polish soldier knew how to shed his blood for the highest end, but to continue in such conditions was impossible. Hence another compromise, this time with the Germans, was necessary—on the clear condition of the widest possible recruiting for a Polish army under a Polish government. "If I succeed, I will return to the army, for above all I am a soldier. But if not——!"

If logic and frankness could have won the day, Pilsudski's memorandum of 26 December, 1916, to von Beseler would have succeeded. The problem was, as he portrayed it, that of establishing a large and well-trained army in the minimum of time. This was difficult because, for more than eighty years, Poland had had no army of her own, and, while the individual soldier might be popular, the army as a whole was not. Whereas elsewhere the warrior who came back from the field was a hero, in Poland he returned to his family cursing the foreign force in which he had been compelled to perform a distasteful and degrading service. Above all, the Poles distrusted bureaucracy and preferred unaided action, while the art of governing them lay in exciting their goodwill. At the moment they were politically disunited, some looking to the Central Powers, others fearing the vengeance of the returning Russians (for few could suppose that Russia would accept defeat). But all disliked the exactions of the armies of occupation, succeeding as they did to governors who had treated the Poles as enemies, and whose rule the Poles had deemed illegal.

From this analysis, Pilsudski concluded that the Poles could only be conciliated and ruled by Poles. The first step should be to utilize the popularity which the Legions had gained by their conformity to Polish tradition, their independence of the government, and their rediscovery of Polish native strength. This could best be done by linking them with the Council of State, by proclaiming the intention to expand them without limit, by using the Legionaries as the *cadres* of the new army, and their most popular leaders as its commanders, and by dispersing them over the countryside as natural centres of recruiting.

Chapter XIV

PILSUDSKI AND "INDEPENDENT POLAND"
(1917)

DURING the first half of the New Year, Pilsudski strove to turn the German fiction of an independent Poland into a fact. Early in January, to a newspaper correspondent, he stressed first and foremost the inexorable hostility between groups of Polish politicians. If this "our hall-mark" could be made more faint, the necessary unity would become possible. When asked if the general conviction were well based that the Germans proclaimed Polish independence above all to gain a Polish allied army, he returned a truly characteristic answer. "A Polish army is as necessary to the Germans as to us. This fact above all else must be sufficient—that it is necessary to ourselves." Universal service, he held, was a desirable impossibility. The Polish people, he reiterated, were the most civilian in the world. To them a Polish soldier was a heroic abstraction, and a Polish army a secret book, closed with seven seals and only to be looked at on solemn occasions. The last two years, he said once more, had made the soldier popular, but not the army.

The interviewer ventured to suggest that a century of servitude would have produced like effects upon any other people. The suggestion roused Pilsudski to a diatribe which, spoken at the outset of his fiftieth year and, as it proved, on the eve of his rise to fame, is of surpassing interest. Indisputably, he admitted, nothing in history happens without a cause. "I do not reproach the Polish people. But I am a realist, taking things as they are, and not as I should like to see them. I strive, as I have always striven, to look at them without illusion. I profess whole-heartedly the principle of the world's greatest man, Napoleon: the art of breaking down obstacles is the art of not regarding them as such. We Poles, alas! excel in creating obstacles, and in suffering words to dominate reality. Throughout our history we lack actual achievement. In a narrow field we do well: outside it, we shrink back from every obstacle. Hence the argument that Poles cannot create.

"In talking with Germans," he continued, "I have always noted that with them we find a different civilization. Theirs comes from the State; ours, of necessity, from the people. Hence our misunderstandings. A few generations must pass by before a national Polish civilization is formed anew. This generation is inadequate to solve the complex social problems which confront it." "Must we, then, expect a gloomy future?" the journalist enquired. "I think not," replied Pilsudski, "for two reasons. First and foremost, history is working for us," and he burst into a merry laugh. "Yes," said the other, "we have gained our independence in the most seemingly incredible fashion." "Destiny," was Pilsudski's answer.

Every section of the Poles, he declared, longed for law and order based on their own exertions. This longing was the outcome of the ruin spread in all directions by armies millions strong. To base an independent Polish State upon this popular goodwill was difficult, but at any cost it must be done. Only the nation itself could cure its ailments, correct its deformities, and establish a healthy being. It must profit by discoveries which the outside world had made, but in which Poland had as yet no share. "Develop, or become the sport of fate"—such was Pilsudski's message to his countrymen.

"INDEPENDENT POLAND"

Pilsudski was undoubtedly right in thinking that the Polish cause would be advanced if many Poles were trained to arms. He was also strong enough to prevent the useless sacrifice of Polish forces, so long as he held the portfolio of War. The Germans, moreover, rightly saw in him the one outstanding Pole who could give them, or withhold from them, a considerable reinforcement. A genuine independent Poland, however, was to them a nauseating and fantastic dream. If they had realized the inflexibility and the incorruptibility of Pilsudski, his period of office would have been even shorter than it became. "The P.O.W.", he wrote to a friend in mid-March, "stands to arms, as formerly in August stood the Riflemen at my command. These new soldiers are happier than their predecessors, for they can obey the call of their own government."

In February, 1917, he had addressed more than 500 representatives from almost every district of Russian Poland who had come to the Warsaw assembly of the Auxiliary Military Committees. Now he spoke to an all-Polish congress. "Build, build, build a national army", was the burden of his addresses. There must be no dividing line between the army and the nation.

Meanwhile, the records of some ten meetings of the Temporary Council of State show how futile were its endeavours to move the German authorities, and how hard Pilsudski was labouring to build up the army.

At the second meeting of the Council as a whole (17 January, 1917), it received an assurance that the resources and the blood of the P.O.W., with some 11,000 members, were at its disposal. The Marshal (or Chairman), having read the letter, took occasion to dwell upon the work of Pilsudski, "on whom the eyes of our nation are turned today", and, to do him honour, the cheering members rose.

At the fifth session (1 February), speaking for the Military Commission, Pilsudski emphasized the unabated difficulty of their position. The status of the Legions with regard to the Polish State and to the Council, he said, had not been made clear, so that 2000 would-be recruits had merely given in their names and had been sent home. It appeared that an appeal to the Austrian Emperor might do more harm than good. "All is in darkness", he complained; "we do not even know who keeps it so, nor why." The position had not improved nine days later, when the Council devoted its ninth session wholly to army questions, and a majority favoured the extension of recruiting to Lithuania.

Early in March, Pilsudski reported that the Legions received no sugar, that their insufficient clothing had caused cases of fainting during manœuvres, and that when the people of Sandomierz wished to send them potatoes, they had been frustrated. He therefore drew up a plan for committees to assist supply, arguing that the nation, as well as the Germans, made difficulties for the Polish army, and that such bodies would furnish useful propaganda.

In mid-March, unhampered by the exigencies of debate, he defined the situation in a letter to a Cracow professor. When he marched from that city on 6 August, 1914, he now declared, he had underestimated the extent to which Polish strength depended on the action of other Powers. After two years of bitter experience, he would assuredly march a second time, but with more precautions. For neither of the Central Powers could change in a moment its frantic distrust of Poland. Their failure to esteem her civilization and her character seemed to him to cause them to treat her like an Asiatic colony, and to destroy with one hand anything that the other may, to her profit, build. Years of servitude, moreover, had made the Poles timid and self-depreciatory, indisposed to support any new thing of which someone may disapprove. So it had been with the idea of the Legions, and so it was then with the policy styled "Fulfilment of the Act of 5 November".

"For a man like myself," he went on, "grown up in combat, the position is peculiarly difficult. From the environment in which my character and mode of work were formed, I am wont to conclude clear and precise agreements, and to respect them without mental reservation, respecting at the same time all that is honourable and worthy. But I cannot imitate the natives of Ceylon, who groan in secret, but murmur their delight on the palace steps.

"As for the Legions, I deplore the burden placed on their young shoulders of fighting for the rights and honour of the nation, amid a passive and not self-respecting people. Still more do I deplore the fact that I cannot be with them to help to bear their heavy cross. Fate has made me turn politician, but every instinct draws me to my brethren under arms. Of course, when I speak of soldiers, I do not mean those heroes of the rear who are the curse of the Polish army in the World War. You ask about the P.O.W. From the birth of the Council of State it has stood to arms, like my Riflemen in August, 1914. It is happier than they, for it can answer the call of its own Polish government."

Next day, as chance would have it, Pilsudski elaborated this last text to representatives from all parts of the Polish kingdom at Warsaw, whither the Council had convoked them to give it strength. He strove to rouse the Poles by a comparison with the twin miracle of Napoleonic days, when first the French people, and then the German, rose from seeming ruin to find salvation in a people's army. But to follow their example, he contended, military service must be universal, an institution no less necessary than the school. Whether born in the palace or the hut, everyone must pay his debt to the fatherland. Only thus could the people and the army mingle into one, so that every family had its soldier, and every soldier his family in the fatherland.

Every soldier, moreover, must have his own government, which could give him lawful orders. At present, however, neither their Legions, nor any part of them, and therefore no recruiting, were in the jurisdiction of the Council. Hitherto, in army matters the Council lacked any power. He would not be a false prophet, and therefore they should receive from him no guidance as to the future. They could only form the will to create an army, and await the opportunity of action.

In this spirit of frank realism, Pilsudski went on struggling, to secure at least good treatment for the Legions, and an unblocked road for that army which he still hoped to form. He failed to free the Polish soldier from his unwonted diet of sea-fish, but secured attention to his lack of sugar, potatoes and fats. As to the question of *cadres*, he could only emphasize the fact that unless the Legionaries were used in that capacity, the creation of an army would suffer an enormous loss of time.

Reasoning and resolutions, however, could accomplish nothing, when the Germans were resolved that nothing should be accomplished. By 19 March, the Council had declared that if a Polish army as designed by it were not soon formed, its own *raison d'être* would vanish. A fortnight later, it prayed a speedy answer, and resolved to send a delegation on the subject of *cadres* to the governments of the Central Powers. A *communiqué* to the press drafted by Pilsudski, in which this and other resolutions were set out in historical sequence, stirred the German Commissioner

"INDEPENDENT POLAND"

in the Council to demand abundant time to scrutinize the document and perhaps to amend it before publication.

A week later, on 13 April, 1917, the currency came under discussion. Pilsudski declared that in Poland the Russian, German and Austrian currencies were dancing a wild country dance such as the world had never seen. One might buy something for 50 Russian farthings and incur a fine of 100,000 marks. The people, accustomed as they were to furtive conduct and concealment, would meet a new currency with passive resistance. In Warsaw the presence of the administration, backed by heavy fines, might secure a temporary success, but in the provinces there was in general no authority which would systematically fine men for trifles.

Immediately afterwards, Pilsudski made the all-important announcement that a Polish army had at last become known to the law. The Austro-Hungarian Emperor, he declared, had placed the Legions, hitherto a portion of his army, at the disposal of the Temporary Council. Their commandant, indeed, was Beseler, who was not a Pole. But Pilsudski himself had survived four commanders, of whom one was a Ruthene and two others could hardly speak in Polish. Under them the army had remained Polish in fact: it was now Polish in theory also. This was a great advance, though, as usual, he did not shrink from facing the uncomfortable aspects of the situation. Since the Act of 5 November, 1916, President Wilson had demanded a free and independent Poland (22 January, 1917) and, through Prince Lwow, the Russian Provisional Government had conceded Polish self-determination (29 March). The effect of these challenges to the three old empires had been to raise the expectations of the Poles to a height which staggered their present masters. As to recruiting, Polish officers were few and the war-weary populace longed only for peace. By nature the Poles trusted no one, and the Council had not changed this psychological defect. Free recruiting had brought only in the dregs. The P.O.W. was trustworthy, but it numbered only 15,000 men, organized, save in Warsaw and Lodz, in scattered groups of some ten or twenty members. Including these, recruiting in the best possible conditions could not produce an army more than 25,000 strong. Pilsudski gravely warned the Council against setting its name to a falsely optimistic proclamation, which would merely damage its prestige.

The session of 13 April, 1917, was the first and last in which the Council could congratulate itself on even the most unsubstantial progress. Within a fortnight it had begun to discuss its own abdication, and the discussions continued until mid-June. Their starting-point was a proposal to double their own membership, making it fifty strong, and to change the "Temporary" Council into a permanent organ of the State. At the same time a deputation was to move Berlin and Vienna to set up immediately a Polish government, with Poles as ministers, establishing a ministerial standing Council in addition to the enlarged Council of State. In these debates Pilsudski spoke often, forcibly and with effect. His voice was always raised for abdication, since the foundations of the Council had been undermined. The people, he argued, did not trust it, and without popular trust government could not remain effective.

At the same time the general framework of the war, upon which the fate of Poland depended, underwent violent change. The deposition of the Tsar, in March, 1917, meant that Liberals would rule in Russia, and that the Russian armies might develop a peace policy of their own.

"INDEPENDENT POLAND"

Before the end of March, the new government had welcomed an independent Poland, but one in military union with Russia. This set the allies of Russia free to follow suit, while the entry of the United States into the war promised a further liberal influence upon the terms of peace. Germany, it was clear, must seek a swift decision, and to this the rapid armament of a large and subservient Polish force might well conduce. If, on the other hand, the Poles proved disappointing and the Russians made a separate peace, the less of Polish armament and independence the better.

Three hectic months, April, May and June, 1917, sufficed to drive Pilsudski into revolt and resignation. The all-Polish congress in March had adopted clear and final resolutions. They demanded that the Legions should be transferred to the Polish government as *cadres* for the new army, which must depend upon it alone. Although for the time being enlistment must be voluntary, only universal service could give an army worthy of the population and able to defend Polish independence. The Germans desired a large number of Polish auxiliaries which would fight as they should direct. These auxiliaries, therefore, might have to cross swords with the Polish section of the Russian army, which was now to form a separate unit.

The Temporary Council of State proved itself more and more, in Pilsudski's words, "a dead institution . . . built upon a fiction . . . incapable of organizing society", and he felt that he and his friends could not with honour remain mere tools of Germany. In the twentieth meeting, on 2 July, he prefaced the reasons for his resignation with a characteristic request that his salary for June should not be paid, since at the beginning of that month he had formed the intention to resign.

MARSHAL PILSUDSKI

The oath to be exacted from the Poles, moreover, gave great offence, for although they swore to serve their Polish fatherland, they undertook to obey the German Emperor as Commander-in-Chief, with his brother of Austria-Hungary and all other military superiors. A week later, the Legionaries from Russian Poland followed their Commandant and refused to take the oath. The Legions, therefore, were immediately broken up. Austrian subjects to the number of some 3000 were sent to the Italian front; Russian, to concentration camps. Nearly 200 officers and more than 3000 men were thus interned.

Pilsudski himself met von Beseler for a final interview at the Belvedere Palace in Warsaw. Standing before the chair of the Brigadier, the Governor begged him to give Poland her strong army by joining with the Germans. "If I did so," was the reply, "you would gain one Pole, and I should lose a whole people." "Not so," rejoined von Beseler, "I would assure your army freedom of movement, the most modern armament and first-rate supply. And for yourself, whatever you wish—power, fame, honours." "Does your Excellence believe", replied Pilsudski, "that the hand which throttles Poland will throttle her the less if it has on every finger a ring engraved with an eagle?"

Chapter XV

PILSUDSKI A PRISONER (July, 1917–November, 1918)

ON 22 July, 1917, early in the morning, two motor-cars came to Pilsudski's lodgings. They brought Germans who carried him off, with Sosnkowski, his Chief of Staff. Five Prussian fortresses, Posen, Danzig, Spandau near Berlin, Wesel on the Rhine and Magdeburg on the Elbe, successively received him, a prisoner of rank but kept in an isolation stricter than that of any of his Russian gaols. For nearly a whole year, until Sosnkowski was suddenly restored to him, he lived with no companion, visitor or Polish news-sheet, and with only strictly censored correspondence. For more than fifteen months, it may be said, he was forced to live in a world of his own creation.

No man was better fitted for the task. Though torn from the full, varied and fraternal life of a soldier and politician, only to be plunged into solitude and German monotony, he accepted the challenge to his manhood, and proudly refused to be broken down. Among the creative work in which his active mind found solace, the philosophy of prison life and the history of his recent battles took a foremost place. In Magdeburg, he noted with surprise, and not without a certain gratitude, the German authorities were aiming rather at his soul, which they could not reach, than at his body. He, the Brigadier, found himself treated as a General, endowed with three rooms and full access to a small garden, served by orderlies, and allowed to read German newspapers.

By an ingenious stratagem, he even secured a supply of writing-paper sufficient to contain, in the most minute handwriting, his narrative of three phases of the 1914 campaign. The paper was furnished in order that the prisoner might complain to the authorities of his solitary confinement as contrary to Prussian law. As his German was defective, he explained, he would need a great deal of paper. His first section, on Ulina Mala, a brilliant sketch in some 25,000 words of the southward march to Cracow, was finished on 7 September, 1917—a fact which demonstrates its author's industry and vigour. These were the more remarkable that the manuscript was a mere exercise which only chance preserved for unexpected publication.

The complaint, indeed, was actually made, almost a year after the arrest. Meanwhile, Pilsudski's life had been greatly changed by the advent as a fellow-prisoner of Sosnkowski. From August onwards, endless debate and games of chess replaced the former self-scrutiny and composition. On the eve of this happy change, however, he had composed an interesting apologia which has since been given to the world. Designed to support the efforts of his friends to have him set free, it took the form of a letter, which with appendices covers some forty printed pages, to a member of the Council of Regency established soon after his incarceration. He seldom wrote without making some contribution to his own biography and to history. This letter of 25 July, 1918, embodies the results of a year's quiet reflection, and is perhaps unrivalled as illustrating the writer's forensic side. We need not suppose that he expected the Germans to be much affected by legal arguments, but to demonstrate the injustice of their proceedings to his friends might do no harm.

Pilsudski's first contention is that he is now a mere private civilian. The Council, to which he had the misfortune to belong, and the Legions, with which he may claim to have linked his name for ever, both have disappeared. His private affairs, which have suffered from his almost unpaid military service, urgently demand his attention. No reason for his arrest has been assigned. Newspapers have spoken of forged passports and of misconduct in the P.O.W. Yet he has undergone, for a whole year, solitary confinement which would not have been allowed in Russia. His proffered parole has been refused; his request to see a relative or friend, ignored; his correspondence, so impeded that in some months not a word has reached him. Such is the reward for two years' fighting on the German side.

The Germans, indeed, he continued, had a regulation empowering the higher command to inflict preventive imprisonment on enemy subjects. Could this apply to Poland, summoned by both Emperors to fight against the common foe? or to Pilsudski, on whom they had conferred high office? If he was in fact a Russian subject, he was not an enemy, for they had made peace with Russia. His war record was unassailable, from his beginning as one of a minority fighting against Russia to his end as an open and loyal critic of the method of forming an army. Surely some grave treason must be secretly laid to his charge, for he was not interned but rigorously imprisoned. For a year he had been unable to exchange a word with anyone. He was ready to face any tribunal, Polish, Austrian or German, civil, military or mixed, and, if guilty, to accept the sternest punishment.

"After my resignation," Pilsudski added in effect, "I was in Warsaw only to offer loyally to von Beseler my opinion on army questions, and to await the solution of the difficulties of the Legions arising on account of the oath. I did not conceal my opinion that volunteers were unlikely to swear allegiance except to a Polish government. My last duty, and that a hard one, was to endeavour to avert violence arising from the ruin of all the soldiers' hopes, and from the fact that the Galicians did not stand solid with the rest. To the last, I was not sure what issue to expect. I determined to petition von Beseler that I might share the Legions' lot and give them moral help to bear their burdens. My memorial was written, but my arrest prevented it from being handed in. A few days earlier, however, I communicated its general sense to the German Commissioner on the Council, and by his advice gave it to a German for translation."

Such was Pilsudski's defence against imputations of treason as an officer in the army. With no less vigour he repelled the insinuation that he had sinned in forming and directing the P.O.W. This, he maintained, was not a "secret" organization. It was constantly discussed by the German and Austrian Commissioners. The Warsaw Field Police had witnessed its manœuvres, and had then conveyed Pilsudski in their motor-car to the town. Both in the capital and in the provinces, such manœuvres required and received government permission. If the organization had not been legalized, the same was true of almost all organizations in Poland at that time. An army organization it was not. His function was rather to prepare its members for the army, leaving the Polish government to organize. Its two unlegalized serial publications avoided politics and dealt only with the technique of war. In any case, no charge on this account could be brought against himself, for with the Press, whether legalized or not, he had no dealings.

Far from issuing conspirative instructions to the P.O.W., Pilsudski continued, he wished it to become a legalized sporting institution. The German assertions that the P.O.W. was on the way to become a secret State, demanding absolute obedience from its members, seemed to him simply absurd. The charge, indeed, had brought a touch of comic relief into the tragedy of his life since the arrest. The taking of oaths he had opposed at every stage. Money and advice were all that the P.O.W. had received from him. Among his assistants, indeed, were numbered his friend Sosnkowski, ex-colonel in the Legions, and men belonging to the P.O.W. But each of these was confirmed in his office by the Marshal of the Council, and their antecedents were perfectly known by the German police. The police had given Sosnkowski a special invitation to Cracow, and the German and Austrian Commissioners accepted him as a substitute for Pilsudski. If these were the crimes which brought solitary confinement, all the Warsaw authorities should have been condemned. He had entered the Council confident that the system of recruiting would be changed. When this proved baseless, and for two years recruits did not flow in, it would have been a crime to refrain from turning to the P.O.W. His relations with that body, he concluded, could not give the key to the mystery of his imprisonment.

Pilsudski's arguments were as convincing as many an advocate's speech for the defence which has not averted a conviction. It may be that the boon of Sosnkowski's company in prison was consequent on his appeal to the Prussian law on the subject of solitary confinement. It is no less possible that this came from a premonition of defeat, and that the Germans sought to propitiate a leader who might soon be able to do them harm. During his captivity his fame had grown, and his captors punctiliously guarded many thousands of postal packets conveying to Magdeburg the homage of the Poles. We may well doubt that Pilsudski thought himself insignificant or that he in his heart expected the Germans to release him. "The safety of the State is the supreme law" was not a maxim that he could ignore.

Now, indeed, the harvest of the five-and-twenty years through which Pilsudski had poured out his strength for Poland was growing ripe. With complete devotion, even when his efforts appeared most futile, he had lived the doctrine that the imponderables have the first claim on life. All the vastness and giant strength of Russia, he felt, could not make the extinction of Poland right. Therefore, at twenty-four, he had determined to defy the tsardom. The P.P.S., the *Workman*, Bezdany, the Riflemen—these made small impression on the enemy, but they sowed a seed. On the field of battle, the Legions did little more than these towards winning the colossal war. But, in the blood and fire of four campaigns, the seed sown by Pilsudski grew a thousandfold and spread all over Poland. The Legionaries became apostles, and their gospel was "Poland and Pilsudski".

No human being can rouse such devotion as a fearless and resourceful soldier who loves his men and shares their dangers and privations. In this no soldier has ever surpassed "the Commandant". His men told, and still tell, of his unfailing courage. He was the first to attack, the last to retreat. He would choose an adventurous plan, and himself occupy the front-line trench—by his mere presence, as it seemed to them, dispelling danger and, as they felt, driving care and weariness away. Withal he was ever jocose and kindly, jesting with the men, sacrificing his share of an unwonted dainty to a sick child, caring for the wounded, pressing on the brow of a crippled subaltern a paternal kiss. Legionaries scorned distance and suffering if only they might see the Commandant, and thousands who were not Legionaries revered him as a prophet. The P.O.W. diffused the cult, and the martyrdom of Magdeburg increased its hold upon an imaginative race. The cry of "Poland and Pilsudski" became irresistible.

Pilsudski's seclusion, however, had been so complete that the revolution in his fortunes which November brought filled him with genuine surprise. A hint of what was possible came in the last days of October, when he was shown a German illustrated paper with a photograph of himself as the new Polish Minister of War. This reflected merely a vain effort by the Warsaw Regency to form a new government. Berlin, meanwhile, was moving towards attempting a bargain with Pilsudski, who was to be summoned from Magdeburg with that intent. On the evening of 7 November, however, the rapid collapse of Germany found expression in an order for his immediate transfer to the capital.

Next morning, Magdeburg was in the throes of revolution. German officers, if they ventured out, slunk through the streets in mufti: trains and newspapers failed: the mob might at any moment storm the citadel and set the prisoners free. In these conditions the local command, still linked with the capital by telephone, determined to smuggle Pilsudski and Sosnkowski out of Magdeburg, and to take them to Berlin by road. The scene on Friday, 8 November, a sunny morning, was perhaps the strangest even in Pilsudski's chequered life. He was, as usual, strolling in the garden with Sosnkowski, quite unaware of anything unusual in the city. Suddenly the two Poles were accosted by a figure in a huntsman's hat and cloak and military top-boots, in whom they recognized a German officer well known to them. He told them that they were free, and that in ten minutes he would take them to Berlin.

Ten minutes later, a crowd of guards and invalids in the citadel watched, with amazement, their departure—Pilsudski in Legionary uniform, Sosnkowski in civilian attire, each carrying a small bag. The two men silently followed their scarecrow pilot to the bridge over the Elbe, where a female typist whispered that all was well. For in the meantime the Commandant of the great fortress had passed unmolested through the crowd, and the car was waiting for them on the Berlin road. Soon the four soldiers were rushing towards the capital through a countryside as yet untouched by revolution.

Reaching Berlin at five, they found all quiet there, but Warsaw was reported inaccessible. Pilsudski and Sosnkowski were therefore escorted by their German hosts to a hotel. Next morning, 9 November, Berlin was electrified by the Emperor's abdication. Although the revolution still tarried, street demonstrations took place, and the well-known imperial motor-car was covered with red flags and paraded through the streets. Formal negotiations with Pilsudski became impossible, though in the afternoon a representative of the Foreign Office joined the party at a restaurant. To the Germans Pilsudski seemed grave and sad, fearing the influence of current events on Poland. In the evening he and Sosnkowski were able to leave by train for Warsaw. While to the exile the jog-trot of the train cried always "To Poland, to Poland", his German escort was asking at every station whether the government was still in power.

Chapter XVI

THE RESTORATION OF POLAND
(November, 1918)

PILSUDSKI arrived in Warsaw on 10 November, 1918, a misty Sunday morning. For many days the capital had been on the *qui vive*, in hourly expectation of his coming. The secret, however, had been well kept, and he was welcomed only by Commander Koc, of the P.O.W., and by Prince Lubomirski, one of the three members of the Regency established by the Central Powers. From the railway station he made his way to a simple boarding-house, and there began to envisage the task which destiny had thrust upon him. From morning until late at night he was in conference with Lubomirski and a long list of other Poles, as well as with the representatives of the German garrison of Warsaw.

There was, in fact, no effective government. Von Beseler, the Governor-General, had fled before the revolutionary wave, and the German soldiers had formed a council to guard their interests. Besides the crumbling Regency triumvirate and this German Soldiers' Council, a "Temporary People's Republic" three days old had been formed by the ever-eloquent Daszynski at Lublin, little more than a hundred miles S.S.E. of Warsaw. The ferment of Bolshevism was working in some sections of the population, and it was certain that the removal of the German incubus would impel the traditional Polish individualism towards new self-constituted authorities. "I discoursed with hundreds of people," said Pilsudski, "representing districts, organizations, societies and businesses. Each wanted his own government and threatened to obey no other."

The lack of a government, moreover, was accompanied by the lack of much that a community could not dispense with. Warsaw, indeed, was not in the grip of actual famine. For three years, the vast agricultural district near the capital had been safe and firmly ruled, and the harvest of 1918 had been gathered in with due regard to the needs of its German garrison. But the first necessity of government, general consent, was unattainable so long as the Polish National Committee in Paris continued to regard itself as Poland. The second, a well-disciplined army, had yet to be created. Revenue and rolling-stock, a diplomatic service and a constitution, peace, industry and trade—such were among the urgent needs of Poland.

Perhaps the most difficult of Polish problems was that of boundaries. Pilsudski, it was said, found a capital without a country. Between reviving the unpartitioned Poland of 1772 and creating a State out of the aggregate of Polish homesteads in 1918, lay a hundred possible solutions, none of which could be called entirely just.

Before the close of November, 1918, Pilsudski had achieved results which by themselves would go far to prove him a great man. The first, and the most essential, was the removal on good terms of the German garrison, a force superior to any that the Poles could set against it. On 11 November, Pilsudski addressed the Germans in a speech which, for its contents and for the conditions under which it was produced, merits verbal reproduction. The man who, transplanted from another sphere, struggling with an ever-growing mass of business, distracted by the news of the Armistice, and thrilled, in all likelihood, by the first sight of his eldest child, could utter so delicate and so telling an appeal was rare indeed.

"German soldiers!" he cried. "I speak to you as a State prisoner of your late government. That government drove you to the brink of the abyss, but you have taken the reins from its hands, and have established a soldiers' government of your own. You are spent by well-nigh five years of bloody warfare. Your new government, your Soldiers' Government, aims at bringing you happily to your homes, to your wives and children, to your fatherland. Remember that this can only be if you give absolute obedience to your new authority. Around you is a people whom your late government treated with unqualified brutality. On behalf of the Polish people, I tell you that they would not, and will not, avenge the sins of your government upon yourselves. Remember that blood enough has flowed; shed not another drop. I have heard that German soldiers are selling their carbines and machine-guns to the dregs of the people on the outskirts of the town. Remember that a soldier does not traffic in his arms. I ask you to bear yourselves with perfect calm, to provoke no more the Polish people, and to return as one man to your fatherland. Here is Captain Boerner, whom I appoint to keep me in touch with your Soldiers' Government. Go to him with all your requirements and complaints."

As he left the building, he said to the crowd of Poles: "In this building, the German Soldiers' Council is in session. It commands all the German detachments stationed in Warsaw. In the name of the Polish people, I have taken this Soldiers' Council under my protection. Do not presume to offer any of its members the least offence." Thus, at the outset of his *de facto* dictatorship, Pilsudski struck the keynote which resounded through his career. Quiet, straightforward, firm administration, based on the people's will, and aiming at peaceful co-operation—such was the formula of his home and foreign policy alike. As the next sixteen years were to demonstrate, it resulted in the establishment of reborn Poland and of new-born eastern Europe.

During November, 1918, and indeed during most of the twenty-three months that followed, every day confronted Pilsudski with some new and difficult demand. First came the question of his own power and of the future government of Poland. Two facts, and only two, were clear—that the German-made Regency could not continue, and that, in Poland, only Pilsudski found favour with both civilians and soldiers. The transference of power was proclaimed on 12 November, when he announced that the Regency had invited him to form a national government, to which it would resign its authority. In agreement with the Lublin Republicans, he therefore proposed to summon representatives of the several parties. At the same time he accepted the Headship of the army, and appealed to all soldiers to abandon cliques and to save the fatherland by uniting.

There was, however, another Polish government, which, though cut off from Poland, deserved and possessed great influence with the Allies and with the American Poles, while it actually possessed an army. Dmowski, Paderewski, Haller and Zamoyski were names which weighed far more than did Pilsudski in Paris, now the metropolis of reconstruction. While Pilsudski had been an Austrian brigadier, a War Minister of the puppet of the Central Powers, or a German prisoner, his National Democrat rivals had become Poland in the eyes of the victorious west. To them, the temporary dictator at Warsaw was a mere creation of the mob, and in that sense they influenced the Allies.

For Pilsudski, thus handicapped, it remained to expedite the return of the German forces to their own country, where a Socialist government had been instituted on 10 November. To this end, he issued a proclamation demanding that the Polish people, suppressing their natural longing for revenge, should in no way disturb the withdrawal of the army of occupation. The profits from his restraining influence were manifold. The Poles were freed within a week from a force whose presence was at once an insult, a burden and a danger. Assured that the Poles would not attack them, the Germans surrendered their arms, of which Pilsudski stood in need. His moral authority, moreover, was strengthened by the contrast with the National Democrats in Paris, who had invited the Allies to prolong the German occupation. He also succeeded in securing the withdrawal of the far more numerous German army of the east by a route which avoided the heart of Poland.

Meanwhile, he had come to grips with a problem which time alone, and not a short time, could fully solve—that of the political organization of the Poles. At a moment when Bolshevism threatened to capture great sections of the people, when the Ukrainian nationalists held half the city of Lwow, when the boundaries of Poland were still undetermined, when Poznan, Danzig and Polish Silesia were still in Germany, when a fiscal system, an economic system and an army had still to be created, Poland could not afford the luxury of party strife. Party strife, however, is seemingly the perennial fruit of seeds which, if not ineradicable, are at least deep-sown within her soil. For two days Pilsudski listened to group leaders. He liquidated the rival government of Lublin and made Daszynski the President of the

Cabinet of Ministers. This Cabinet, he told the people, was provisional. Within a few months he hoped to summon a Legislative Assembly. In the meantime no far-reaching social changes would be made.

Having thus done his utmost to provide a government, to reassure those who had something to lose, and to convince the have-nots that Bolshevism was not their only source of hope, he turned to present the new-born Poland to the world. No man could have heralded a puling infant State more bravely than he who had invaded Russia with a few score of Poles. Paris, however, save by wireless, was inaccessible, and diplomatic communication with every capital must be slow and uncertain. On 16 November, therefore, Pilsudski as Head of the army sent a wireless message to the Allies, to Germany and to all other States, notifying them of the existence of an independent Polish State comprising all the territories of united Poland. The victories of the Allies, he explained, had restored freedom to the Polish people. By their general will a democratic State, based on order and justice, was an accomplished fact. As Head of the Polish army, he expressed the hope that in future no foreign force would enter Poland without his consent. He also declared his conviction that the mighty democracies of the west would give brotherly support to the Commonwealth Reborn and Independent. At the same time he appealed to Marshal Foch to augment the forces of the fatherland by the transfer of "the Polish force which is now a portion of the French army".

The notification and the appeal were despatched at the end of the week which had begun with Pilsudski's arrival in Warsaw. Could the Allies believe that in one week a united Poland had emerged from chaos? What they knew of Pilsudski was that, while Russia was their ally, he had

Ignatius Daszynski (b. 1866).

Roman Dmowski (1864-1939).

led a small force of volunteers against her. What they might now suspect was that a leader of the Left, supported by the Warsaw mob, had been deluded by some trifling successes into believing himself important. Having induced the Germans to bestow their arms on fourth-form boys in the streets of Warsaw—so sneered the Poles in Paris—this man poses as the saviour of Poland, which the Bolshevists may now invade. He is already at war with the Ukraine. When the wireless message was despatched, indeed, the man who countersigned it as Minister of Foreign Affairs did not in fact hold that office, and the Polish army was still unorganized.

There was indeed a Polish army, numbering 430 officers and nearly 17,000 men, serving under Polish political control with a Head appointed by the Polish National Committee in Paris with the consent of the Allies. That, however, was the army of General Haller, for the support of which Pilsudski appealed to Foch, and its disposal lay in the hands of the Paris Committee. Dmowski, in fact, assured of the ear of the Allies, mocked Pilsudski's efforts to supplant him. Unfortunately for Pilsudski's prestige, he appealed to Foch at the same time to transmit to President Wilson a request for the services of the Polish detachments in the American army, of which none existed. On the political side, in the hope of conciliating the National Democrats, he arranged that a less aggressive Socialist, Moraczewski, should replace Daszynski as Premier.

The labours of Pilsudski's first week in Poland comprised also an earnest effort to save Lwow. That city forms a Polish island in a Ukrainian sea, and the forces of the Ukraine bade fair to conquer it. Within the town the Poles fought desperately, even women taking a part, but weeks passed before any help could come. Then Przemysl, almost seventy miles away, was recaptured by a Cracow force, and Pilsudski urged General Roja, an old Legionary, to hasten thither with five regiments and three heavy batteries for the relief of Lwow, spreading the report that this was only the vanguard of a larger force. Roja played his part well, and, by 22 November, the relieving force, some 1500 strong, had made the Poles masters of the city. Further they could not go, but they held Lwow intact against its Ukrainian besiegers, and their achievement helped to consolidate the new *régime*. Pilsudski's task now became before all else to win a race with his eastern enemies. Could he collect an army and support it by a stable administration before the Bolsheviks and the Ukrainians had overrun the borderlands and, it might be, had brought central Poland to revolution?

Posterity is fortunate in possessing a photographic glimpse of Pilsudski in action at this crisis. Among the ex-Legionaries who served him with selfless devotion, one then sought his aid, and has since become the Boswell of this and many another meeting.[1] Military doctor and civil administrator, his industry, solidity and driving power have kept him Premier for a longer term than any other Pole. In November, 1918, Skladkowski commanded the Polish force then forming in the difficult area of "the Basin"—the Silesian mining region some 200 miles southwest of Warsaw. Many of the arms surrendered by the armies of occupation had found their way into the hands of the Communists, who were drilling at many important points. Could the young, untrained, visionary Polish levies be ordered to shoot down these, their kinsmen? They had also to guard the frontier against the Germans, and their position was not easy.

[1] General Felicjan Slawoi-Skladkowski.

THE RESTORATION OF POLAND

Skladkowski, like many another, turned to Pilsudski, and was allowed to see him. He found Warsaw teeming with life, the streets full of men in civilian dress carrying arms, the palace guarded by members of the Academic Legion in civilian overcoats, and a long queue waiting to interview "the Commandant", as his comrades still called Pilsudski. By favour of the Adjutant, Skladkowski after only three hours' waiting stood before his pale, thin, weary hero, who cut short his compliments with a curt "Well?" as they shook hands. Before the tale of woe was fully told, Pilsudski said: "I want to resign in a parliamentary Poland. The elections must be peaceful, though I expect the Communists will boycott them. There may be strikes. So you must provide a six weeks' coal supply and keep order in the Basin." Questions of method were stifled with a second handshake and "That's all", and the visitor felt that all his problems had been solved. He had seen the Commandant.

CHAPTER XVII

PILSUDSKI AND THE NEW POLAND
(DECEMBER, 1918–FEBRUARY, 1919)

PILSUDSKI himself was resolved to trust the people. He never ceased to hope that a free democratic vote would enable him as Head of the army to serve a regenerated Poland. Such a Poland, he believed in 1918, would be a member of a federation embracing both Lithuania and the Ukraine. He had fixed the elections for the end of January, 1919, and had promulgated a most liberal franchise. All adult women as well as men were accorded votes, which were to be given by ballot and assured of due effect by a system of proportional representation. This meant that Jews, Ruthenes, Communists and extremists of many kinds could certainly find a place in the new assembly, while it could only be hoped that the inexperienced electors would choose a majority of moderate and disinterested men. But the danger from Bolshevism was great, and the widest franchise might well be the best antidote against it.

In forming an army, on the other hand, Pilsudski was unsurpassed. His handling of the Legions and of the Germans showed how well he understood the soldier. Of Moraczewski he said in jest that he had summoned that Sapper Captain, cried "Attention!" and ordered him to form a government. He had already proved, moreover, that he realized the danger from the traditional but transient boulevard enthusiasm of the heady Poles. His discouragement of those who clamoured to be led to Lwow caused him to be suspected of lukewarmness. To the boys in the highest class of the middle schools, who wished to leave and join the army, he replied that their patriotic duty was to stay on and qualify themselves for future office. But he sought, found and quickly transformed masses of more suitable recruits. Members of the P.O.W., Polish soldiers from the Austrian, German and Russian armies, the Russian "fourth division" under General Zeligowski and volunteers from all sides filled the ranks. Two months after Pilsudski's arrival at Warsaw, the army was more than 100,000 strong. That army, if united, might well secure the recognition which foreign Powers had not yet accorded to the Polish State.

But the instinct of Poles to combine with their friends in voluntary groups rather than to submit to a large national organization was visible in the army no less than in politics. Nothing attests Pilsudski's greatness more than the measure of success which his impassioned appeals for military unity produced. In the first critical ten weeks of his administration, his constant cry to the soldiers as well as to civilians was for a united army in a united State, that army helping the State to union. As one device to this end, regional political officers were appointed within the army. Pilsudski himself instructed them loyally to inform their superiors of the political situation in their district, to convince the civilians of the importance of the coming elections, and, between officers and men, to promote Legionary feeling.

To all he appealed for unity as men favoured above their forefathers in serving a free and independent Poland. Among the happiest days of his life he counted that of his first journey from Warsaw to Cracow with no frontier to cross. But every day brought fresh proofs of megalomania and of disunion, and innumerable factions turned to him. His watchword was, Wait until the elections decide: you will then know your power, and my commission will then expire. He firmly refused to allow his Chief of Staff to resign because the National Democrat Press declared that, as the brother of a Greek Metropolitan, he was unfit to deal with the Ukraine.

National sentiment, however, was far too weak and uncertain to heal political divisions out of hand. Besides the non-Polish minorities and the many independents, some eleven parties were already taking shape. Those of the Left inclined to support the government, though to his old associates Pilsudski always refused to proclaim himself a partisan. The Peasants (*Piasts*) found a leader in the cautious and inscrutable Witos, their so-called Pope, a former Austrian deputy, conspicuous for the top-boots and lack of neck-tie which advertised his rural character. Among the parties of the Right, the National Democrats were the chief, and these looked naturally to Dmowski and the National Committee in Paris, which in Polish matters kept the conscience of the Allies. This body regarded the Pilsudski *régime* as a weak, self-advertising rival, which had already gone far towards annihilating the credit which their own policy had gained for Poland. They prevented its representatives from approaching the Allies except through themselves, and they failed to establish a common government for Poland.

Pilsudski, however, set the national cause above party or personal considerations. He sent a deputation to the Committee, appealing to Dmowski to rise above cliques or groups, and to unite at the coming Peace Conference. When the great pianist Paderewski came from Paris, his presence plunged Poznan, or Posen, into a war between Poles and Germans. He connived at an attempt to seize Head and government in Warsaw, but Pilsudski suppressed the plot and went on with the negotiation. Characteristically, he desired no vengeance, and, in mid-January, the two bodies came to terms. Paderewski, with his high repute in America and Europe, became Head of a National Government, and a national Polish representation appeared at the Peace Conference. Before the end of February, the principal Allies had fully recognized the Polish State.

The formation of a considerable army and of a national government, the presentation of a single Poland to the Allies, and the peaceful conduct of democratic national elections—these great results were achieved in January, 1919. The co-operation of the United States in averting famine had also been secured, and every day without disaster strengthened the new Power. But it was a ruined country in which Pilsudski had to build, and a people so ill-informed that he had actually to explain to a deputation that Warsaw desired union with Posen (Poznan).

The Ukrainian war continued, the conflict with Bolshevism promised war at no distant date, Germans and Poles still fought in Poznan, and the Czechs attempted to occupy Teschen (Cieszyn) in Silesia, thus severing the land connection between Poland and the Allies. In the Baltic countries on the morrow of the elections (27 January, 1919), in replying to a French interviewer, Pilsudski declined to predict their consequences or to base any hopes on the mission to Lwow or any other gestures of the Allies. Deeds alone counted, he declared. Within Poland order reigned, but the foreign situation was bad. He himself could not deal with domestic policy. "To me", he said, "it falls to secure order, to command the army and to submit to the will freely expressed by the people."

Four days later, to an Italian, the soldier-statesman proved himself a veteran journalist by as close-packed and incisive a survey as he ever penned or spoke. Nine weeks earlier, he declared, Poland had been in chaos, with 4000 disorganized soldiers, the Ukrainians in Lwow, and Bolshevist agents essaying a Warsaw revolution. Now her army numbered almost 100,000, and could be larger, if the Allies would send munitions. All his own efforts centred on the Constituent Assembly and, even if this proved Conservative, as a soldier he would obey.

Bolshevism, as he often repeated, offered no internal danger, and the people would bear with fortitude unemployment, high prices and want. But war, though ended in Europe, was beginning to envelop Poland. "The Ukrainians threaten Lwow, the Bolshevists have taken Wilno and are at the gates of Brest and Grodno, saying as they advance that their goal is Warsaw and the whole of Poland. The Czechs have fallen on the province of Cieszyn (Teschen), which is purely Polish, and on the Polish districts of Spiz and Orawa. The Germans fight against us in Poznan. We are surrounded on all sides by foes and cut off from the world."

Poznan, he declared, was in a particularly painful situation, remaining in servitude when Russian and Austrian Poland were free, and forced to await the pleasure of the Peace Conference. There the rifles might go off of their own accord. It was impossible that Poland should refrain from the defence of Lwow. The blame must fall on the ex-Emperor Charles, who had cramped Polish Galicia and excited the Ruthenes to war. "Many", he said in effect, "hold that all Eastern Galicia should be joined to Poland, giving us a common frontier with Rumania and invaluable access to the Black Sea. I believe in the national movement of the Ukrainians and look forward to Polish-Ukrainian collaboration. By their treachery the Czechs have created in the coalfields a ferment dangerous for the general situation. They have the business men and technicians, and their conduct has made the workmen hate them more than the Germans. Danzig is absolutely indispensable for our trade and national life. We demand that it should be recognized without reservation as a Polish possession."

Ten days later, in solemnly opening parliament, he declared that they would not surrender a single foot of Polish soil.

CHAPTER XVIII

PILSUDSKI AND PARLIAMENT (1919)

ON 20 February, 1919, Pilsudski closed the first chapter of his career in reborn Poland by resigning the Headship into the hands of parliament. He was immediately and unanimously re-elected, and returned to the hall of meeting amid cries of enthusiasm from the deputies.

The Headship, "the great reward for the heavy labour of my whole life", was not rejected, but with all sincerity he doubted his own fitness for the post. He obeyed, he said, as a soldier those who could speak for the fatherland. His own design had been henceforth to devote himself to the army. He could only hope that parliament and he together might make free and independent Poland united. His election gave rise to an expression of strong hope from Poznan for union with Poland.

For several years yet, Poland must struggle for her territory. Her situation, like that of Europe, was full of complexity. At Versailles and in a dozen theatres of war the Polish frontier-line must be laboriously hammered out. Many principles, some of them conflicting, and many personal idiosyncrasies contributed towards the ultimate result. The Allies set out to remedy injustice, to safeguard self-determination and to construct a Europe in which democracy should be safe. These noble aims, however, were by no means easily applied to intertwined communities whose conditions were imperfectly known or apprehended. Some lands which had been unjustly torn from Poland at the Partitions were now inhabited by people who would resent being returned to her. To set up as many new States as there were nationalities, might be to facilitate aggression by Germany or by Russia at their expense. To create a new considerable Power would jeopardize the European balance. If Danzig, for example, became Polish, her German inhabitants would feel themselves enslaved; yet without recovering Danzig how could Poland secure access to the sea? Russia and Germany must in the long run be Great Powers. If they were separated only by eight weak republics, intrigue and peril would be endless. If, on the other hand, Poland regained her boundaries of 1772, could not her alliance make France the mistress of Europe?

As was inevitable, the prejudices of individual statesmen affected the verdict of the Conference. Clemenceau threw the weight of France on the side of Poland: Lloyd George opposed her claims. Some were swayed by fear that if full justice were done to the Poles, Germany would reject the treaty. Others predicted variously the dubious fate of Russia. Dmowski, battling at Versailles, made great territorial claims for Poland, particularly in the west; Pilsudski, whose army soon reached a total of 230,000 men, was even more concerned about the east.

All was complicated by the unique dimensions of the Polish Jewish problem in the regions concerned. While Danzig was alternately assigned and refused to Poland, while *plébiscites* more and more came into view, while one commission on Polish affairs was set up in the west and another sent to make investigations on the spot, Pilsudski strained every nerve to prepare against the menace of attack. It was impossible to foresee the future, he declared on 16 March. But he believed that, even if Russia got rid of the Bolshevists, she would be convulsed for many years. They, he was convinced, would try to attack Poland.

Imperialist, Russia would remain under any government, and Slavonic imperialism was a challenge to Poland which would always be met with defiance.

The government of Russia by the Bolshevists, we must remember, still appeared to many, Russians and Europeans alike, as a mere passing phase, and more than once the "Whites", or Counter-revolutionists, seemed to be carrying all before them. Five months after the Armistice had set Europe free to deal with the threat of Bolshevism to its existence, Pilsudski judged that the party was still strong, because it had at its disposal a large and ambitious ruling class, and obstinate, because that class knew that defeat meant death. Their course of action, he divined, would be shaped by material considerations. Having little food, they must turn to the rich Ukraine, while lack of horses must tie them to the railway. Success in the Ukraine would be followed by attack on Poland, but the attack would be limited as to route, and delivered through a region bare of supplies. In Poland, moreover, their doctrines would bring them few allies, for the country lacked workmen, and his contemplated agricultural reform would confront them with a mass of peasant proprietors. Pilsudski's need was now supplies, rather than men, and for these he turned to France, whence, at long last, and with some doubts as to its harmony with his ill-paid volunteers, he now expected Haller's army.

All through the winter of 1918–1919, Pilsudski had struggled with a weight of public care which left him time and strength for little save repose when not on duty. In such a life the epistles of his conspiratorial days could find no successors. When he wrote, as when he spoke in public, he was usually discreet and brief, though never false. To an old comrade he might unbosom himself on occasion, but such utterances have rarely been recorded. On 8 April, 1919, however, "Thy Joe", "with a hearty embrace", revealed his mood and policy to Wasilewski, his spokesman on the National Committee in Paris.

Few regions concerned the future of Europe more, and few were less well known, than that compendiously described as "the Baltic States". In 1914 a part of the Russian empire, in 1918 they seemed to be destined to serve Germany as one or more dependent kingdoms. Now they were striving to free themselves from Bolshevist armed propaganda and to secure recognition as independent republics. Estonia had a clear-cut racial basis for a State of little more than a million people; the Letts of Latvia, for twice as many. Some two million Lithuanians were neighbours to their Lettish cousins, but the question of their boundary was far from simple. Past history and mixed settlement impelled heady Lithuanian statesmen to make wide claims, especially at the expense of Poland. Wilno was to them Vilnius, their capital, though within the city indigenous Lithuanians were few.

Pilsudski knew Lithuania far too well to suppose that its problem was easy. In his eyes, Wilno was a Polish city, which could not be cut off from Poland. But Lithuania and Poland had united in 1569. Both were republics, and in religion the Latins had a great majority in each. Was not collaboration their true policy? Why should not Lithuania become the Scotland or the Brittany of Poland, thus safeguarding herself against Russian or German claims? In December, he had declared to a Lithuanian delegation that their imperialism, supported in her own interests by Germany, and therefore obnoxious to the Allies, must cease. Poland had no designs on ethnographic Lithuania, but historic Lithuania (the Grand Duchy of pre-partition days) comprised districts essentially Polish. Lithuania might be independent, but it seemed that her government would be officially associated with that of Poland.

With extraordinary daring, Pilsudski was now meditating the occupation of Wilno by force. His letter to Wasilewski was written in the interest of the Baltic federation at which he aimed. "You know", he said in effect, "that I will be neither an imperialist nor a federalist, while I cannot speak with some authority—with a revolver in my pocket. Since chatter about the brotherhood of nations, and American doctrines, seem to be carrying the day, I gladly take the federal side."

While Sir Esmé Howard was representing the Entente in Poland, Pilsudski had asked for his sympathy in Polish efforts to rid the eastern borderlands of Bolsheviks, but Sir Esmé insisted that the greatest obstacle would be the Lithuanians. Pilsudski judged that if, when the Poles pressed forward, Latvia would exercise pressure, Lithuania would be unable to resist. "I suppose", he continued, "that both America and England would guarantee such a pact, and that they would give us Libau and Riga as an easy compensation for doubtful Danzig." Besides pressing Latvia, Wasilewski should urge on his colleague Paderewski. "An ardent federalist, but weak," Pilsudski goes on, "and I greatly fear that vicious imperialist influences may lead him from the steep and thorny path which leads to the federalist paradise. Therefore guard his virtue. As for the Estonians, although it breaks the frame of the pretty picture that I tried to paint for Sir Esmé Howard, I do not reckon that entirely a drawback." That they should wish for federation with Poland was all to the good.

Chapter XIX

WILNO AND THE UKRAINE (1919)

AT this juncture, Pilsudski dared to defy the whole world by attempting to capture Wilno. Even among the Poles to whom his plan was breathed, the only politician who favoured it was Wojciechowski. It was a military project by a mere self-taught brigadier lately set free from a German prison. But, as he later recorded, he knew that his presence gave the soldiers heart, and that every light horseman felt him by his side. Then his troops went through the Bolshevists like butter, and on 19 April, 1919, victorious in the face of heavy odds, they forced their way into Wilno. Near the city, peasants suffered their vanguard to cross sown fields. Civilians joined them in the street-fighting, and the heroism of the railwaymen, who procured reinforcements in spite of the Bolshevist fire, finally turned the scale. Only the Jews, the ruling class during the Bolshevist *régime*, fired and threw hand-grenades from their windows, and were barely saved by Pilsudski from a massacre.

On Easter Monday, as the author and director of the campaign, Pilsudski received the symbolic key of the city at the feet of its miraculous Virgin. His bold stroke had achieved the "accomplished fact" for which he hoped. The Bolshevists made no counter-attack, nor could the Allies condemn the deliverance of Wilno from its tyrants. There, as in Poland, he was resolved to stand for self-determination, and he hoped that the local parliament would meet and take over the administration.

At this juncture, Pilsudski exercised all his statecraft in drafting his Proclamation of 22 April, 1919. After long meditation on the most telling title, he addressed it, To the Inhabitants of the Former Grand Duchy of Lithuania, thus giving a historic hint at federation once again with Poland. Poland, he declared, however, would content herself with having put an end to the long tyranny of Russians, Germans and Bolshevists in Wilno. Although in the countryside cannon still thundered, and blood still flowed, no military occupation would be established. A civil administration would provide for self-determination by way of secret, universal and direct voting without regard to sex. It would give the necessary help in victualling, in assisting industry and in securing law and order for all, without distinction of racial origin or confession.

The full scheme proved too liberal for Polish or for Lithuanian opinion, but a temporary civil administration for Lithuania centred in Wilno, and, in November, 1919, the university of Wilno was re-established. The Polish parliament, however, which had whole-heartedly desired the deliverance of Lithuanian Poland, repudiated Pilsudski's Proclamation a week after it was made, and all his efforts failed to bring the natives—Poles, White Russians and Lithuanians—into agreement. Pilsudski reflected sadly that the enslavement of Poland had arrested the development of her sons, so that one might meet men of the mid-eighteenth or nineteenth century, but rarely men of the twentieth. At least Bolshevism, following its collapse in Hungary, had been driven back sixty miles, and the main line of German communication with Russia had been cut.

Not the least important results of Pilsudski's brief campaign were the physical and spiritual recreation which it gave him, and his first-hand experience of Bolshevism.

WILNO AND THE UKRAINE

Two months of Communism, he wrote to Paderewski, had brought Wilno to complete ruin. The Bolshevists were not civilized people, but wild beasts, thirsting for blood and plunder. Houses requisitioned for their commissars had been turned into stinking sewers, and all their adornments shattered. In five days the invaders had issued more than a thousand decrees, with the practical effect that trade was carried on by barter, while the city starved, and the hatred of the people became terrible. Lenin, who sought to renovate society, had almost killed it.

Wilno, he said, had been made the capital of an independent Lithuanian Soviet republic comprising "governments" or counties of Kovno, Grodno, Wilno and Minsk. The budget of this republic for 1919 provided for an expenditure of 134 milliard roubles and gave no indication regarding income. At the same time, the refugees who spoke for non-Bolshevist Russia were demanding that Poland should accept the frontier of the Bug: a line running westward from Pinsk to Brest-Litovsk and cutting off Bialystok, Grodno and Wilno. The Jews were loudly denouncing the Poles as persecutors. Lloyd George invoked the racial principle against them. Germans and Lithuanians threatened them on one flank; Bolshevists and Ukrainians, on the other.

Pilsudski was hampered at Warsaw by Polish imperialism and peasant discontent; and at the front, by the *doctrinaire* behests of the Peace Conference. He could count on the sympathy of France, of Rumania, which held Bessarabia, and of Hungary, partitioned in favour of the Czechs, but all had their own battles to fight. True to his character, he looked inward for inspiration, and to swift independent action to turn its promptings into fact. Thus April, 1919, which taught him the difficulties of the situation and the loathsomeness and inefficiency of the Bolshevists, gives the key to the amazing campaigns which followed.

Pilsudski's lieutenants, Rydz-Smigly foremost among them, maintained their ascendancy over the Bolshevists in the north-west. It was not until June, 1919, however, that they could be regarded as secure against the Germans. Then, Danzig having been made a Free City, and *plébiscites* in other areas conceded, Germany signed the Treaty of Versailles, and gave Poland *de jure* recognition. Meanwhile, Pilsudski, refusing the armistice dictated by the assembled Powers, sent 50,000 men against the Ukrainians in mid-May.

Within six weeks, the Poles had proved that for the Ukraine the choice lay between Bolshevist domination and their own, and had been empowered by the Supreme Council to occupy the Galician lands formerly held by Austria. This left Pilsudski face to face with the Bolshevists, and at the head of an enthusiastic army. He could desire nothing better, especially as Haller's army had arrived from France, and on the home front progress was being made. Dmowski's National Committee was in dissolution. Parliament had at least begun the work of drawing up a constitution. Czechs and Poles were in conference on their conflicting claims to Teschen. Most important of all, parliament now provided that inoculation against Bolshevism on which Pilsudski counted to make Poland immune against its poison. This took the form of the so-called Parcellation of the large estates, by a drastic transfer to small holders, the principle of which was carried in July by a bare majority.

From 28 June, when Pilsudski himself came to make good the damage inflicted by Ukrainian counter-attack, until 17 July, when the eight months' struggle for Galicia ended triumphantly upon the river Zbrucz, he was perhaps entirely happy. On 10 August, the town of Minsk, about 110 miles south-east of Wilno, was wrested from the Bolshevists, who retreated along the railways. Pilsudski was soon at Minsk among the victors, smiling as each division "of course" declared that it had been the first to enter. "Never", wrote one of them, "shall I forget the expression on his face, such fire and joy as none of his later political triumphs ever called forth."

On the morrow, giving the toast of "The Polish Soldier", he revealed in part the secret on which he had built up the army. The fashionable Prussian system, based on a caste of officers, cut off by a Chinese wall from the civilians, and by an abyss from their men, he rejected as unsuited to modern times. It was the French Revolution that had furnished Napoleon with the material for his deathless achievements. The foundation of the Polish army must be the rank and file. He adopted the French military system, and declared that the two countries were man and wife.

During the remaining months of 1919, Pilsudski had frequent occasion to rejoice at Polish progress in the field. Suwalki, 120 miles south-west of Wilno, was won, and cooperation established with Latvia and with the anti-Russian force of the Ukraine. Early in October, he could say that, while the attempts of Germans in the Baltic lands to restore the monarchy were dangerous, Bolshevism was a Russian disease from which Poland had little to fear. At this time he was preparing to welcome the incorporation of the independent army of Poznan, some 60,000 strong, and a stranded force was making its way homeward from Siberia.

CHAPTER XX

THE RUSSO-POLISH WAR (1920)

ON New Year's Day, 1920, with all due ceremony, Pilsudski received the diplomatic corps at Warsaw, and soon afterwards declared to his fellow-Borderlanders that Poland had learned by her own bitter experience how they should be treated. "I am Head of the Nation, not of a city or a party," he cried at Lublin, "a soldier, and the soldier's mistress is war." He toasted the victorious Latvian army at Dwinsk, on their common front against the Bolshevists. Early in February, when the enemy had offered peace, he asked a correspondent of *The Times* if in politics it was possible to be sincere. The Bolshevists, he argued, must have an alternative in store, for use in case their proposals were rejected. But their strength, he said, was spent, and their people had every reason to press for peace. In his opinion a Polish defeat was impossible. Poland could not lose the war.

To a Frenchman he declared that the Bolshevists lacked stomach for the fight. They were wont to defend themselves for a few hours and flee at nightfall. Their numbers, though great, would not intimidate the Poles, who knew too well the fruits of their revolution. In some provinces, population had fallen by more than one in eight. So many children had died that a whole generation had been sacrificed to the doctrines of Lenin and Trotsky. Laying stress on every word, he repeated that Poland would never begin negotiations under threats from the Red Army. He was sure of his soldiers and confident of victory.

Signs were not wanting, however, that, since Pilsudski's earlier triumphs, the balance might well have turned. The Poles, indeed, would be stronger in 1920 than in the previous campaign. Numbers, equipment and experience had all improved. But as a new State, compounded from dissimilar fractions of jarring empires, with a people divided, inexperienced and poor, Poland lacked the solidity and discipline which should exist behind the army. A hard winter had inevitably evoked a cry for peace. Paderewski, the open-handed conciliatory idealist, had left the country— a parliamentary failure. The dispute with Czechoslovakia dragged on. The Germans felt—and the feeling would long continue—that their country had been partitioned in favour of a worthless nation. With the Germans "Polish economy" had long been a synonym for chaos.

In the west, indeed, Germany was helpless, but the Western Powers neither understood nor cared sufficiently for the situation in the east. There, others besides Pilsudski might attempt to create accomplished facts, and German adventurers could form and equip their Legions. Pilsudski understood both war and politics too well to ignore the danger of a Russo-German combination. The Allies, moreover, by issuing edicts and withholding supplies, could hamper the Polish movements. They had lately outraged Polish feeling by according to the conquerors of eastern Galicia a mere mandate to administer the province for a term of five-and-twenty years, thus encouraging Ukrainian separatism. At any moment they might wreck Pilsudski's plan.

On the Polish side, there were therefore by no means negligible grounds for avoiding fresh adventure. The Bolshevists, meanwhile, were fast improving their position. On the moral side they made a great advance by frankly accepting the principle of self-determination. Men who had followed Russian history, among them many Russians, could not believe the successors of the great Peter sincere in thus abandoning the historic mission and the conquests which had made Russia a European Power.

The move, however, seems in retrospect to have been supremely wise. Two years after the November Revolution, the Bolshevists must at all costs win over Russia. The country was lamentably poor, and "White" generals gravely threatened to restore the old order. To admit that Finns and Estonians, Letts, Lithuanians and Poles had a moral right to rule themselves was at once to repudiate tsarism, to propitiate the new governments, and to claim for the Russians the right to rule themselves as they pleased. Once secure of Russia, they might make their creed triumphant in the Border States, the rest of Europe and the world. They were primarily international revolutionists, not Russian patriots, and classes, rather than States or nations, were their chief concern. In Lenin's eyes, Germany was of far more account than Russia.

To us, who know what was at stake, and what the summer of 1920 brought to Poland, Pilsudski's decision to reject the Bolshevist peace-offer becomes one of the foremost factors in an estimate of his powers. Did it spring from the intuition of genius, or from far-seeing calculation, or from mere illusion and pride? A just verdict, it may be at once confessed, cannot be reached with ease. To the civilian, Pilsudski's boastful words in February cannot fail to suggest a coming fall. Charles XII, Frederick the Great and Napoleon had underestimated Russia, always with dire results.

It must, however, be remembered that soldiers, like boxers, may boast to heighten the morale of their own side, and to depress the enemy. War had changed since the eighteenth century, and in brains, machinery and transport, Poland might well be superior to ruined and decimated Russia. In the Great War, Russian supply had been notoriously weak, and the officer class was that which the Bolshevists had done their utmost to destroy. There was every reason to believe that, for some years at least, they would not be able to attack. If, on the other hand, they or the "Whites" were given time to consolidate their power, the problem against which Pilsudski had dashed his head for forty years would be revived. The Poles would once again become a rebel people against an almost invulnerable State five or six times as populous as Poland.

There was, therefore, strong temptation to present the Russia of the future, whether Red or White, with accomplished facts which would spell security for Poland. In Pilsudski's opinion, an ethnographic Poland should be flanked by allies in the shape of other emancipated peoples. Lithuania, White Russia and the Ukraine, with her support, might well be able to maintain their independence. But his first thought must be for the campaign of 1920, from which, and from which alone, he could expect these great results. If the morale of his young army suffered, all might be lost, and nothing impairs morale so much as talk of peace. An enemy offers peace when he is weak. He is wont to suggest it when the idea will weaken his opponents more than himself, as when their troops will hear of it and his will not, or when their discipline is inferior to his own.

In this case, the Bolshevists asked for an armistice and aimed at gaining time. The Poles refused the armistice and stated peace-terms unacceptable to Russia. Pilsudski, indeed, was an ardent campaigner and an ingrained anti-Russian. But the most dispassionate general in his place must have disliked a negotiation which would rob him of victory over men whose creed forbade them to regard a "capitalist" State as having any right to live. It could not be doubted that they would seize the earliest opportunity to retrieve what Poland had wrested from them. Since the Germans were outraged by "the Polish Corridor", a crushing anti-Polish coalition might well arise. Pilsudski, however, was more than a general serving Poland. He was above all a State-founder, whose thought is always for the future of his creation. In his eyes, the army was the mainstay of Poland; and victory, the inspiration of the army. To him, the campaign of 1920 was necessary for the immediate consolidation of Poland, no less than for future safety. It was waged by the first man in history to receive the title "Marshal of Poland", in which at this juncture the army expressed its gratitude.

At the same moment, early in April, 1920, Pilsudski made an important profession of faith to a deputation of the German inhabitants of his country. Warning them that as Head of a constitutional State his power might not be as pervasive as they supposed, he declared himself an opponent of all hatred and revenge. His lifelong principle, he said, was that every people had a right to the protection of its speech and culture by the State to which it belonged. Democratic Poland wished, and was bound, to guard the cultural rights of all its citizens.

Towards the end of April, the diplomatic fencing with the Bolshevists was cut short by a sudden onslaught in the Ukraine. Pilsudski had agreed with Petlura, a fugitive Ukrainian general, that Poland should keep the southeastern lands within her present frontier in return for aid in freeing the remainder of the Ukraine from the Bolshevists. The Poles, whose boundaries 240 years earlier had included

Pilsudski in the Russian campaign with General Rydz-Smigly (b. 1886), his successor as Marshal.

Kiev, pledged themselves to evacuate the new Ukraine at the end of the war. Pilsudski himself began the new offensive on 25 April, and next day Jitomir, some eighty miles west of Kiev, was in his hands. He at once proclaimed that his army would remain only until a truly Ukrainian government should gain control. Within a fortnight his small force had reached the Dnieper, and, on 8 May, it occupied Kiev.

Expert English journalists reported him as saying that the Russians showed valour only when in an armoured train. With a loss of less than a hundred killed, he had taken 30,000 prisoners, whom he proposed to release, as he loved experiments. He could march as far as he pleased, but he would only fortify his bridge-heads across the river. Poland was ready to reopen negotiations for peace, but her demands would be the same as those which the Bolshevists had found unacceptable in April. Imperialism, he declared, was foreign to the Polish character, and those who laid it to her charge did not know Poland.

In the sunshine of a triumph such as historic Poland had seldom known, the reserve and even antagonism of parliament melted away. "On its sharp bayonets", declared their Speaker, "our army bears freedom to long-downtrodden peoples, and peace to people of goodwill. In thee, chief General, unheeding party differences, we see the symbol of our beloved army, an army mightier than in the days of our greatest glory." When these words were spoken, however, the Bolshevist counter-stroke was already making itself felt. In the north, three weeks of alternate attempts at envelopment by the two sides left the position little changed. But at that moment, in the south, Budienny was dispelling Pilsudski's illusion that the lack of horses and of enterprise that he had seen extended to the whole of Russia. At mid-summer, his Cossack cavalry, some 40,000 strong, covered on occasion seventy-five miles in a single day and night. They ate on horseback, and slept in farm-carts which still moved on. Before mid-June, the Poles were in retreat from Kiev, and early in July the whole Ukraine was lost.

The causes of this sudden change of fortune are not obscure. In seizing Kiev, "the city of a thousand golden domes", the Poles had outraged the feelings of every Russian, whether "Red" or "White". To many, it was as though Canterbury had been captured by the French. Europe, moreover, knew and cared little for Pilsudski's Proclamation, but much for what seemed a wanton aggression, far from the Polish frontier, upon an enemy who had offered peace. The presence of Polish invaders in the eastern Ukraine roused Ukrainian feeling, while the Russians knew as well as did Pilsudski that, without the rich Ukraine, their economic future would be hopeless.

Moreover, when the Poles attacked, as the Bolshevist Commander-in-Chief concisely stated, the position of his side was "relatively favourable". Thanks to the aversion of the peasants for the old *régime*, the "Whites" had almost disappeared from Russia. "Kolchak", he wrote, "was liquidated in the east; Denikin was liquidated in the Caucasus. Of Wrangel's men only a nest survived in the Crimea. In the north and west (not counting the Poles) all was over. Peace with Latvia was signed. . . . In the spring of 1920 we could throw almost all our strength upon our western front, and begin the heavy struggle with the Polish 'Whites'."

The Poles were now disposed in a long cordon, and lacked mobile reserves. With some 200,000 men, the Bolshevists outnumbered them by five to three, and were equipped with the excellent arms and munitions which the Allies had sent to the Russian "Whites". In the south, Budienny led a Cossack force which could move swiftly without depending on the railway. Perhaps more formidable still was the sympathy outside their own dominions on which the Bolshevists could reckon. In 1920, as for years to come, millions accounted them friends of the working-class. In the Ukraine, in Czechoslovakia and in the west, thousands, perhaps millions, of "workers", therefore, wished them well against the Polish tyrants, and perhaps against their own governments. "To Wilno, Minsk and Warsaw!" cried their Commander Tutachevski. "March over the corpse of Poland to kindle the world-wide fire of revolution." It is said that Lenin's hope of bolshevizing Germany influenced both the fact and the plan of the campaign. It is certain that foreign sympathizers prevented arms from reaching the Poles, and swayed more than one government to press them to give way. Arms sent by Hungary through Rumania were all that arrived in time, and Britain telegraphed advice so fatal that her local representatives refused to pass it on in its entirety.[1]

In face of this peril, the Polish government did its utmost to rally the nation to a united effort, and with success. At the beginning of July, parliament gave full powers to a special council with Pilsudski at its head. The army was strongly, or at least numerously, reinforced, and both men and women by tens of thousands volunteered. Pilsudski knew only too well the difference between a trained and an untrained soldier, and firmly opposed the movement towards composing a whole army of volunteers. Volunteer battalions, however, he welcomed, and furnished them with

[1] "Pertinax": *Journal of the R.I.I.A.*, March, 1930.

a share of the funds which were placed in his hands as a national testimonial to himself.

While these measures were taking effect, and while Poland was beseeching the Allies to intervene, the Bolshevist forces advanced on converging lines towards Warsaw. Budienny's march on Lwow, indeed, was checked before it reached the city, but the northern invaders covered on the average nearly ten miles a day. Successive rivers, the Vilja, the Niemen, the Narew, failed to stay their progress, and on 1 August they captured Brest-Litovsk, some 130 miles east of Warsaw. Thus success cut the line of the Bug, behind which Lwow also lay, and frustrated Pilsudski's plan of assembling behind that river a force with which to attack the Russian rear. A keen student of the history of war, he was meditating the operation with which Napoleon in 1813 had almost frustrated a more formidable converging movement upon Paris. On the morrow of the fall of Brest he returned to Warsaw (2 August). His work in the next fortnight was to form a landmark in the history of civilization.

Chapter XXI

THE DECISIVE PHASE (August–October, 1920)

WHEN August began, the Poles were in a singularly friendless state. Hungary alone could supply munitions, and of these some were obstructed by the Czechoslovak workers. Germany by her neutrality cut off material provided by the Allies, and the Danzig Germans refused to unload their ships. While Poland cast herself at the feet of the Western Powers, these urged concessions and sent only missions. Labour in many lands longed for a Bolshevist success.

The national peril, however, united all parties in support of their Head of State. Witos became Premier; Daszynski, Vice-Premier; even Dmowski supported Pilsudski, though wishful to depose him from the Chief Command. This the Marshal was prepared to share with Weygand, the adviser of Foch, but when the Frenchman declined, his plan was also rejected. Overruling the Polish generals also, Pilsudski, after a long agony, decreed, on 6 August, that his northern armies should retreat to the Vistula and so regroup that he might lead from the south a flank attack upon the Russians in front of Warsaw. This, in the main, the General Staff accepted. Their decree fell into Tutachevski's hands, but its boldness made it seem incredible and he ignored it.

If all the Red troops had been Bolshevists, indeed, Pilsudski could hardly have hoped for victory. Many, however, were peaceful peasants dragged from their homes, or Whites forced into their conquerors' ranks. While the officers were good, the forces were driven from the rear by Commissars who were not unmindful of their personal safety, and in the main the countryside detested the invaders. Budienny, moreover, was out of harmony with the rest, and there was no Pilsudski to dominate and to inspire the Russians. It was notable that, throughout the campaign, victory was swiftly determined by morale, the force which felt itself inferior usually retiring. The total Polish loss did not exceed 50,000.

Pilsudski's plan was based on the belief that his own presence and the obvious danger would lend wings to the Polish soldier. It involved, of course, the strategic use of fortresses and rivers. From Pulawy, some eighty miles above the capital, to Modlin, some twenty miles below, the middle Vistula flows roughly north-west towards the Baltic. This hundred-mile stretch of the wide and rapid river is guarded by two great fortresses, each at the mouth of an important tributary. At Modlin, the green waters of a triple flood flow in, for the Narew, coming from the north-east, has lately received the Bug, curving inwards from the far south-east, and the slighter Wkra, running straight from the north-west. The Wkra, indeed, seems to prolong the line of the middle Vistula, which, near Modlin, bends due west towards Plock, before sweeping on to Danzig and the sea.

Against an invader from the west, therefore, Warsaw had both an outer and an inner line of defence. The outer was the line of the Bug, stretching for more than three hundred miles from Modlin, past the great fortress of Brest-Litovsk, to the region of Lwow. The inner was the broad Vistula, on which the abundant works and guns of Warsaw were flanked by the two strong places of Demblin and Modlin, with Plock beyond, and also with such protection as the Narew and the Wkra could afford.

THE DECISIVE PHASE

On 12 August, 1920, the middle Vistula was menaced by five Russian armies, which were advancing towards it on a front roughly parallel to its own bed, and more than twice as long. The two hundred and fifty miles between the southern frontier of East Prussia and a point some fifty miles south-east of Chelm were covered by the 4th, 15th, 3rd, 16th and 12th armies, with the "Mozyr group" interpolated between the last two. The Bug, the Narew and the Wkra had all been safely crossed. In the north, the Polish left wing was outflanked, and Plock, perhaps, in peril. Pilsudski himself was at Pulawy with his 4th army, awaiting the Legionary First, while the weak Polish 3rd army on his right guarded his flank and rear against aggression by the Russian 12th. Before him he had the Mozyr group, a body of which the strength, though probably considerable, was uncertain.

His own forces, though equipped with miscellaneous weapons and ill-clad, some even barefoot, he found better in morale than he had feared. Wishing to inspire and marshal his men, and to give the strongest enemy forces time to engage closely in a futile and costly assault on the capital, he determined not to move before 17 August. Then, if all went well, he might roll up the flank of the force at death-grips with the vast garrison of Warsaw, thus cutting in two the line of invading armies, and launching a destructive pursuit towards Brest and Grodno.

Next day, however (13 August), the conditions of the struggle changed. Tutachevski's object was not, as Pilsudski had supposed, to conquer Warsaw from the east. On 8 August, he had directed his three northernmost armies to make for Plock, cut off the Poles from Danzig, and pave the way for an attack on Warsaw from the west. This strategy conduced to a swift appearance of the Bolshevist arms in Germany, where they hoped to kindle a world revolution. These armies, the 4th, 15th and 3rd, therefore swung towards the west and south, and, on 13 August, the small town of Radzymin fell.

The capture of a town only some fifteen miles from Warsaw was widely accepted as heralding the collapse of Poland. Russian patrols appeared within six miles of Praga, Warsaw's suburb across the Vistula. The Papal Nuncio, later Pius XI, the Italian minister, the representatives of the United States and Denmark—these stayed on in Warsaw, but the remainder of the diplomatic corps withdrew. It was rumoured that Dmowski at Poznan was preparing a Right *coup d'état*, and Berlin Red newssheets announced the fall of Warsaw. "Long live independent red Poland," was Trotsky's triumphant cry.

The Polish General Staff, indeed, morally supported by Weygand and his subordinates, did not give way to panic. Sikorski, counter-attacking, drove the invaders first across the Wkra and then across the Narew, and three days sufficed to re-conquer Radzymin. Meanwhile, however, Pilsudski granted the earnest request of the General Staff, and began his northward march at dawn on 16 August. The Legionary spirit which the Marshal had breathed into his men, with the conviction that for Poland it was now or never, gave a morale with which the Bolshevists could not compete. By the next evening, 17 August, three of their armies and the Mozyr group were in retreat. While the 4th army continued to advance towards the west, its neighbour, the 15th, was retreating north-eastwards, and part of the next army, the 3rd, at right angles to that line. East of Warsaw, several divisions stood firm, while Pilsudski drove his routed opponents across their rear. A disaster such as he had dared to hope for thus threatened the invaders.

THE DECISIVE PHASE

Tutachevski's plan, indeed, was ruined, but the Poles were too weak to press home their advantage. On 18 August, Pilsudski at Warsaw was compelled to divert his attention to the Russian 4th army, which was about to cross the Vistula and capture Plock. While his forces redeemed Plock and drove these invaders into East Prussia, other Poles and Ukrainians were foiling a belated effort by Budienny to redress the balance from the far-off south. These distractions saved the Russian 15th and 3rd armies from ruin. Within ten days of Pilsudski's onslaught they had formed a new line beyond the Niemen and contemplated a new attack. It was estimated, however, that Tutachevski's offensive had cost him some 150,000 men, while the Polish captures of material had been great. Perhaps more valuable still was their gain in confidence and in prestige.

On the tenth day of victory (26 August, 1920), Pilsudski discussed his position and prospects with a representative of the Warsaw newspaper which was wont to accompany his morning tea. The Allies were pressing for that limitation of Poland to her ethnographical frontiers with which, seven weeks earlier, she would gladly have purchased an immediate truce. To yield now, however, would be to abandon Wilno, to belittle the Polish State, and to leave Warsaw insecure. Direct negotiations with the Bolshevists were in progress, and three sittings had already been held at Minsk. Wherein lay wisdom for the Poles?

Pilsudski expressed his strong conviction that the peril from the Bolshevists would recur. For the moment, indeed, they had lost about two-fifths of their army, and only 125,000-150,000 demoralized men would return to Russia. For the Poles to fortify their ethnographical frontier would be absurd. The transport of the necessary barbed wire alone would claim all their rolling-stock. They must demand a tenable frontier, and shatter the enemy if he refused. In two months, winter would be upon them. Pressed as to the recovery of Wilno, the Marshal said: "That is a political question. The government, as expressing the people's will, should decide it." After a pause he added, as if talking to himself: "The northern defences ought to be made safe. The Lomza country (one hundred miles north-east of Warsaw) is ruined—harvest, cattle, horses especially carried off. Unsafe to winter there. Hunger. The peasants will devour the Bolshevists, take bloody vengeance. But——" He then turned to the interviewer and insisted that in some places the Jews had fought against the Bolshevists. Some had been imprisoned along with the local bishop, others executed. Yet in other places near by—"a strange thing, like many things in Poland"—multitudes of Jews had turned traitor.

The Bolshevist invasion had caused the Teschen question to be settled on bad terms for Poland, and it helped the East Prussian *plébiscites* in Allenstein and Marienwerder to go against her. Pilsudski's victory, however, won her the sympathy of the Allies and, when the Bolshevists refused to make concessions, the Polish offensive was not condemned. After Budienny had been repulsed from Zamosc, some seventy miles north-west of Lwow, the Poles, in September, made a victorious advance, and drove the enemy beyond the confines of Galicia. In the north, the Lithuanians gave up Suwalki, and a series of great struggles on the Niemen routed the Bolshevist armies. Instead of the fulfilment of the Russian plan—a new onslaught on a front stretching eastwards from Grodno with its flanks guarded by the Lithuanians and the marshes—Pilsudski's manœuvre had gone far to restore the Polish position south of Wilno. This he used immediately to effect a drive towards Minsk known as the battle of the river Szczara. Within a fortnight, four Bolshevist armies were shattered, and 50,000 prisoners taken. Meanwhile, at Riga the negotiations begun at Minsk went on.

In mid-September, a month after the victory of the Vistula, and a week before the onslaught on the Niemen, Pilsudski had once again placed his views before the French public. Of Lithuania, he would say but little. Her antagonism he ascribed to German influence, and by deed and word he expressed his own longing for brotherhood. He likewise refrained from discussing exhaustively the Ukrainian question. The country, he said, was too rich. Impoverished Russia turned to that well-filled granary and taught the Ukrainians Bolshevism so that she might exploit it. "Besides the Russians", he continued, "there are others who gaze at the Ukraine from afar, turning their eyes to every quarter of the globe where riches are to be found." As to Poland, after seven years of war, which in parts had almost ruined her, she needed that peace which alone could enable her to develop her natural resources. Collaboration with all her neighbours was her desire, but its fulfilment depended upon them.

Czechoslovakia, he said, composed of diverse elements in a continual ferment, made Poland apprehensive. Germany, which coveted much that other possessed, was staggering in a struggle to find her feet. His most earnest desire was that Poland and Russia might forget the endless quarrels of their ancestors and agree to differ. But the present Russian government was insecure and dangerous to its neighbours. Of Wrangel, whom France had lately recognized, he declined to speak. The Bolshevists, in his opinion, had created a threat to Poland which a treaty of peace could not remove. They had made the people poor and therefore dangerous, while, to maintain a power not based on the people's will, they would distract them by aggression.

Pilsudski's victories on the Niemen and on the Szczara could not change these essentials, but they could teach the Bolshevists the futility of fighting on. In mid-October, an armistice was signed, and, a month later, a peace conference began at Riga. Meanwhile, another long-vexed question, that of Wilno, called for all Pilsudski's resource. The city must not be lost to Poland, but Poland, despite her victories, must not alienate the Allies. Unable to hold it longer, the Bolshevists had bestowed Wilno on the Lithuanians, who made it their capital, and began to drive out its Polish people. When the Allies arranged the Suwalki pact, Wilno remained on the Lithuanian side of the line drawn between their army and that of the Poles.

On 9 October, 1920, however, Zeligowski and his division from Lithuania and White Russia drove out the Lithuanian occupants and were welcomed as saviours by the people. For form's sake, the General posed as a filibuster, and declared his independence of the Polish higher command. The natural consequence was an official enquiry, addressed to Pilsudski by the French and British representatives at Warsaw. The Marshal countered by invoking the principle of self-determination. If the Allies wished to hand over Wilno to Lithuania without consulting its people, he declared, he would be forced to lay down his office and do his duty as a Wilno man. For the time being, Zeligowski entrusted the government of "Central Lithuania" to a Temporary Government of its inhabitants. The question was destined to remain unsettled for more than two years, and Pilsudski did not live to see the Polish-Lithuanian concord that he desired and regarded as inevitable. For nearly eighteen years the neighbouring peoples were severed by a closed frontier, until, in 1938, Poland threatened to use force and the grotesque estrangement ended.

Chapter XXII

PILSUDSKI AND POLAND (1920–1921)

WITHIN three months, Pilsudski had rescued Poland from the verge of ruin and had restored her proper boundaries. Against Weygand's advice, he had clung to Lwow; against the Allies' precepts, he had in substance recovered Wilno. Much, indeed, must yet be done, and swiftly, if his work was to be rounded off. On almost every frontier, Poland was faced by problems still unsolved. Her sole outlet to the sea was Danzig, with its hostile German population subjected, in a manner complex and not yet defined, to her control. Between Germany and eastern Prussia now lay Polish Pomerania, over which the resentful Germans must be conveyed. Southern Silesia, with its coal and fertile soil, was inhabited by millions whose Polish or German allegiance had yet to be determined. Still further south, the frontier between Poland and Czechoslovakia must long give rise to friction.

Four running sores, besides the White Russian, Lithuanian and Ukrainian, were thus vexing Poland while she negotiated peace with Russia. Yet none of these, perhaps not all of them together, gave Pilsudski such concern and personal distress as did the running sore in Poland. For his country's sake, up to a point, he could endure the envy, hatred, malice and all uncharitableness which fell to his own lot. "The world over," he growled, "Chief Generals are held in honour. When their name is linked with victory, the honour is twofold. When their victory ends the war, it is threefold. Not so in Poland."

In Poland, even the sorest peril had not induced Dmowski

to join in a united government. He had left menaced Warsaw for Poznan, where, Pilsudski's partisans assert, a *coup d'état* was prepared and demonstrations against the Marshal organized. In a Warsaw palace, they say, at a given signal a band of aristocratic women knelt before Weygand and kissed the "victor's" hand. At the same time, at a political meeting, a church dignitary branded Pilsudski as a mean traitor and poltroon, while the rumour ran that he was in communication with the Bolshevists by means of a secret wire. Hitherto the patriot in Pilsudski had mastered the egotist, though he was sad that such foul weeds as these could flourish in Polish soil.

In Magdeburg, he said, he had tried to calculate every possibility that the end of the war could bring about. If Germany lost, he expected Poland to be surrounded by States in chaos, seeking new forms of public life. All the future depended on which of them could first achieve order based on freedom. When fate made him ruler of Poland, he aimed at surpassing all her neighbours in this endeavour, but he found appalling chaos and party strife. His hope lay in summoning a constituent assembly at the earliest moment. This was the condition on which he empowered first Moraczewski and then Paderewski to form a government. "And still," he declared in January, 1921, "when two years of life in Poland have belied not a few of my lonely dreams in Magdeburg, I remember with pleasure that the first step—the summons of the Constituent to work out a constitution—accorded fully with my prison calculations, anticipating all our neighbours and disappointing all our enemies. I freely confess that I was proud when, early in February, 1919, having broken down a thousand obstacles, I could hand over my power to the first parliament of reborn Poland."

PILSUDSKI AND POLAND

A month later, on 19 February, 1921, Poland became the pledged ally of France, then by far the most formidable Power in Europe. The alliance was the outcome of an official visit which Pilsudski paid to Paris, the city in which his brother Bronislas had died, aged by Siberia, but to the last a gracious scholar and a patriot.[1] The Marshal struck the keynote of the visit in a few sentences uttered to an interviewer in the train. "Our will", he declared in effect, "is all for peace, and peace is possible, if we will it strongly. Yesterday (in Germany) I saw no devastation. Today, I see the devastated areas which France has sacrificed for us all. France and Poland have always been linked by the two most potent bonds—interest and love. I am no phrase-maker, but one thing I can say to France—I bring her all the love of Poland."

He was soon to prove her readiness to exchange with France promises of mutual consultation on all questions of foreign policy which concerned both States. If either suffered unprovoked attack, both were to take concerted measures for defence. They specifically undertook to consult each other before concluding new agreements with regard to central and eastern Europe. Having thus shown the West the spokesman of new Poland and proclaimed her friendship with France, Pilsudski returned home. On his way, he took occasion to present a Polish decoration for valour to the city of Verdun, the symbol of indomitable resistance to German aggression.

Early in March, 1921, a convention for joint defence was concluded with another natural friend of Poland—Rumania. That France and Rumania thus courted Poland, proved that Pilsudski had made her something more than a mushroom State. But at Riga he now reaped a far richer harvest than

[1] Cf. Stan. Szpotanski: *La Pologne Nouvelle* (Paris, 1920).

even at Paris and Bucarest. On 18 March, 1921, the Riga treaty made secure, so far as a compact with the Bolshevists could do so, the frontier of Poland on the east. After hard bargaining, Lithuania was in substance abandoned by the Bolshevists, while they divided White Russia and the Ukraine with the Poles. Poland thus recovered a substantial part, though far from all, of the Borderlands which she had lost to Russia in 1772. Its population was now nearly five and a half million, of which almost one-half were Poles. Mutual recognition and mutual abstinence from hostile propaganda or tariff warfare were agreed on, and the Bolshevists undertook to return the chattels and works of art of which they and their predecessors had plundered Poland.

It now remained, first, to secure from the Allies the unfettered ascription of "Central Lithuania" and Eastern Galicia to Poland, and, what was more difficult and more important, to win over her Lithuanian neighbours and her Ukrainian and White Russian subjects. For this last, Pilsudski's principles were beyond all doubt the best, and none so well as he could compel their application. Poland, however, lacked trained and upright officials, while in the Borderlands she had to govern masses of alien peasants, poor, backward and remote, united by language and religion rather with their brethren to the eastward than with the west.

On the eve of the treaty of Riga, parliament at last voted the new Polish constitution. True to the tradition of ancient Poland, it carefully secured the liberties of the people against monarchical excess. The king of pre-partition days was now represented by the President; the people, which had in earlier practice meant the nobles, by the Seym or Lower House. A Senate was indeed created, but in comparison with the Seym it possessed a negligible share in the sovereignty.

Fearing Pilsudski as first President, the parliament decreed that in war the President should not exercise the chief command. It would elect him for a seven years' term, with power to nominate ministers and judges and to act as chief of the executive. The Seym, however, could compel any or all of the ministers to resign. The basis of the constitution was broad democracy, with full regard for human rights, including that of individual and collective property. National minorities were amply secured, and wide local and corporative autonomy was contemplated. The Roman Church was recognized as that of the majority, and the State looked forward to a concordat with the Pope. Revision of the constitution was to take place at least every quarter of a century.

The constitution of 1921, whenever it should be put in force, would go far towards making democracy dominant in Poland, but it could not ensure either the wisdom or the continuity in policy of the Seym. Though loosely drawn, it clearly provided no adequate place for the one man who might be reckoned indispensable. Although Pilsudski always desired to limit his own share in the government to the inseparable departments of Foreign Affairs and War, the position of Poland in these early years made his dissociation from other fields impossible. The army, for example, depended on the budget; the budget, upon agriculture, industry and trade; while all these were closely linked with education.

In 1921, the year in which agriculture, the staple of five-sixths among the Poles, seemed to be well on the way to recovery, the half-built economic structure was gravely shaken by a currency collapse. In post-war years, indeed, prices in many lands underwent wild fluctuations, such as the nineteenth century had never known. The British pound and the francs of Belgium and France lost for a time between two-thirds and nine-tenths of their respective powers of purchase. The value of the Austrian crown and of the Russian rouble fell to almost nothing. The German mark in 1923 was called down to one million-millionth of the value which the government had printed on its notes. As to the causes, no agreement has yet been reached. The amount of gold held by the State with which to redeem a given amount of paper, the relation between its income and its expenditure, its reputation for prudence and honesty or the reverse—all these must affect its currency and credit, thus helping or hindering the public revenue and the livelihood of the people.

A government which cannot draw from the taxes sufficient currency to pay its way is often tempted to print more paper money than its subjects need for their transactions. The natural result is that prices tend to rise. As wages are not raised with equal speed, for a short time industrialists make great apparent profits and workmen can buy less. Soon officials and workmen, with good cause, demand more currency as wages, and foreigners mark down the swollen currency to a lower ratio against their own. Government in reply may borrow, if it can, or print yet more paper money, or reduce the salaries, pensions and grants paid by itself, or raise the taxes, or make a capital levy. All these expedients are painful; and some, disastrous.

The Polish mark, which early in 1920 stood at about one-thirtieth of its normal gold-price, fell during the year to about one-hundredth. Something, it was evident, must be done, but the general poverty and the manifold need for reconstruction made it difficult to determine what to do.

One class, the Jews, was conspicuous in that of the total wealth of Poland it held a share some four times as great as its numbers seemed to warrant. A capital levy was voted, but by no means fully carried out. A too drastic reduction of the army was averted by the personal influence of Pilsudski and by the obvious needs of the situation. Poland, still insecure, required an insurance policy and a police force: the army furnished both.

An increase in wealth and credit, however, came from the measure of success which Poland gained in the question of Upper Silesia. In that industrial district, capital and enterprise were mainly German; labour and agriculture, mainly Polish. Before the war, Polish racial consciousness in the region had made itself felt, and in Korfanty the Silesian Poles possessed a parliamentary spokesman and a leader. Two years had passed since the Peace Conference had resolved on a Silesian *plébiscite*. This, on strictly racial lines, was expected to show a Polish majority of nearly two to one. The Germans argued that to divide the district would ruin both Silesian industry and Germany. The eager Silesian Poles, in 1919 and 1920, rose in arms. At last, in March, 1921, the vote was taken, and the well-organized Germans prevailed. Even without voters brought specially from Germany, they polled in a proportion of some $5:4$. With out-voters, they were almost $3:2$. At the prospect of continued German domination, the miners struck, and Korfanty headed a formidable rising. Poland stood aloof; Germany, now disarmed, could not quell the revolt; but, in July, the Allied Commissioners brought it to an end, and Poland at last had peace. The final adjudication was left to the League of Nations.

In August, 1921, Pilsudski's first wife, long childless and separated from her husband, passed to her rest among the family sepulchres at Wilno. There a great glowing stone pays tribute to her warm heart and untiring championship of Polish liberty and independence. The event influenced the course of history, for with his second wife, Alexandra Szczerbinska, and their two daughters, the Marshal entered on a serene domestic life which notably economized his strength. He had already passed the life-span of the Great Peter and of Napoleon, and, amid the exacting labour of his proper offices, he had always been confronted by a dubious or hostile parliament.

In the first half of 1921, the Polish currency had lost three-fourths of its value, while the new constitution had not yet been put in force. September saw the installation of a ministry of experts from outside parliament, since the Premier Witos now laid down the burden from which Pilsudski had refused to release him at the end of May. Personal changes, however, could not cure the essential disharmony between a congeries of groups of Deputies and a Chief of State, each of whom was resolute to have his own way. Friction with parliament absorbed Pilsudski's time and sharpened his temper.

His brusque administrative method is well illustrated by a subordinate who, by his own confession, often provoked him. The question at issue was the status of the army sanitary service. In Russian times, much rough surgery and medicine had been entrusted to the unqualified, and the profession lost prestige. To impress Pilsudski, its champion had drafted a long history of the question, from ancient Egypt, through the barber-surgeons of the Middle Ages, down to modern times. He had already defended the field hospitals against the Marshal's charge of lagging far behind in the last campaign. Their horses, he said, were bad, telephones were lacking, and the troops moved away too fast. "No doubt," broke in Pilsudski, smiling, "you would like to have good horses, and news by telephone a few days before we move, and we must wait for the hospitals and not go too fast. Take note that, in the next war, I shall move still faster. You must keep up with me, and without telephones."

He then gave leave to raise the question of status, "but," he said, "be brief." "In the Egyptian army," began the doctor. "Be brief, please," said the Marshal, thumping the arm of his chair. "I will, Marshal," replied the other, and scrambled through the barber-surgeons to the early nineteenth century. There Pilsudski stopped him with the words, "The army doctor must be an officer, for he works in contact with the men on the battlefield and close behind it. Without an officer's rights he cannot do his work. Thank you, gentlemen"—and the deputation, chastened but happy, left the Belvedere.

In Foreign Affairs, of course, the executive had a freer hand than in domestic, and here Pilsudski continued to make progress. Cordial relations with Danzig were hardly to be hoped for, but Poland by avoiding German routes could mightily enlarge the city's trade, and, in October, an elaborate treaty recorded their agreement. Early in November, an admirable convention with Czechoslovakia for mutual recognition and defence was signed, only to be wrecked on a small difference before ratification.

Later in the month, the question of Wilno, or "Central Lithuania," became Pilsudski's foremost care, and bore witness to the lack of unanimity in Poland. Wilno, still under the interim *régime* of Zeligowski, embodied the thorny problems of the Polish-Lithuanian boundary and of Polish-Lithuanian federation. On paper at least, the Bolshevists had abjured further interference, but it remained for the Lithuanians, the Allies, the inhabitants of "Central Lithuania", the Pilsudski party and their opponents, if possible, to reach agreement. The Lithuanians firmly demanded Wilno, and with no less firmness declined to jeopardize their independence by entering into a form of union with a tenfold stronger nation. They thereby frustrated the well-meant efforts of the Allies to work out a solution on Swiss lines.

The inhabitants were ready at any time to show a great majority for union with Poland. The Poles wished for a "popular" vote, but whereas Pilsudski would have a vote by all the disputed regions, the Right opposed the federalism to which that form of self-determination might conduce. Feeling ran high, and the Marshal expounded his views before a meeting of the many party leaders. As a son of the Wilno region, he declared that the historic question, "Was it part of Poland, Russia, Lithuania or White Russia?" had been obscured by the age-long aggression of the Russians, so that few now knew the answer. In history hitherto, differences on such matters had been settled by the sword. The sword had spoken in the case of Wilno, but Pilsudski held that Poland should act upon a higher plane. In Poland's evil days, Wilno had shown great moral strength. Hence, after hearing all sides, the government proposed self-determination by the Wilno region and the district south of it, in no way prejudging the question of annexation or federation.

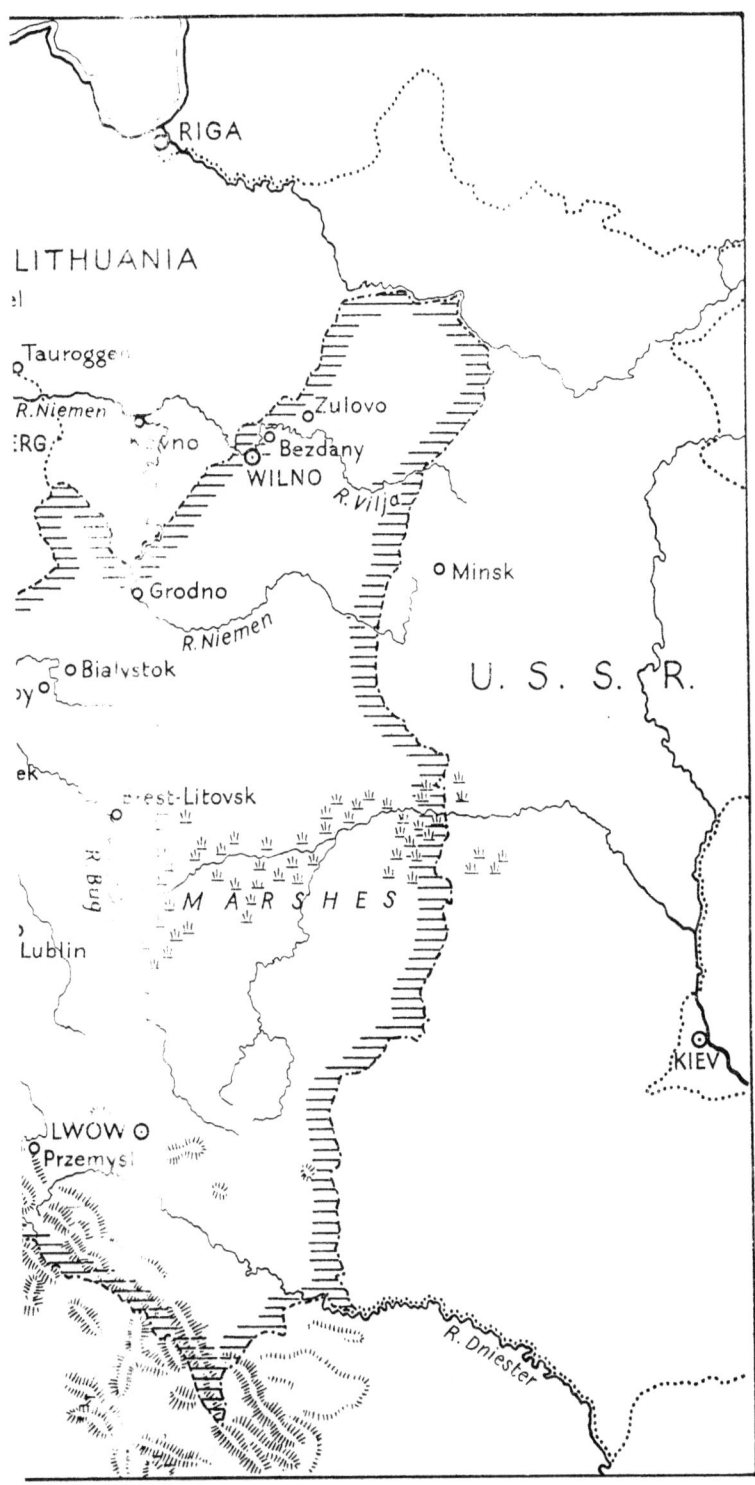

Chapter XXIII

POLAND IN 1922

ON 16 November, 1921, Pilsudski, by a majority of thirteen, had gained the approval of the Constituent for his policy with regard to Wilno. This, however, was but an episode in a humiliating and embittering contest, which did much to sour Pilsudski's later life. His relations with the Seym, or parliament, indeed, epitomize his most bitter disappointment and his greatest failure. No national emergency, it seemed, could move the Poles to lay aside their divisions. Even when the Bolshevists were marching on Warsaw, his political opponents denounced him as a traitor in Russian pay, and, when he went to Paris, they sent a secret counter-mission. The wastage of his energy through friction, and the damage to his reputation by the ebullitions thus provoked, were alike incalculable. From 1919 to 1935, disagreement between Pilsudski and the Seym formed one great thread in Polish history.

The Constituent, at its second meeting, in mid-February, 1919, was convulsed by the narrow defeat of Witos in the election of its Marshal. "Down with the traitor!" cried the Left. "The gentlefolk will lead us by the nose." All were unanimous, however, in returning to Pilsudski the Headship of the State which he resigned into their hands, and in voting five resolutions known as the "Little Constitution". Thereafter, except when some great victory had just been won, harmony was at an end, chiefly, so the Pilsudskists maintain, through the ambitious and disloyal policy of the National Democrats under Dmowski. This led to such phenomena as charges of corruption against Paderewski, ministerial crises and frequent changes of government, and two years of wrangling over the words of a new constitution.

When the din was greatest, the reporters would gather round the Speaker's chair and record the sentences of suspension which he pronounced. "I exclude the priest Okon from five sessions for continued disorder," he cried on 5 November, 1920. The priest Okon then stood before him and roared with all his lungs, "Down with the Senate." "Deputy R—, who is kicking the bench, I exclude for five sessions"—and so on, until he was compelled to suspend the session. On resuming, the Right were in a minority of five. The Speaker then deducted the votes of five suspended members and carried the resolution of the Right by his own vote. Sessions of indescribable disorder followed, and the constitution of March, 1921, was born after thirteen hours of whistles, groans and shouting. The final scene, none the less, was marked by an impulsive thanksgiving in the Cathedral and by cheers of the Left, for Pilsudski, and of the Right, for the Speaker and the constitution.

The depth of the party cleavages in Poland was shown by Session 262 of the Seym, on 29 November, 1921, after the emancipation of Wilno—a proceeding which caused an illiterate deputy to cry aloud that Pilsudski was a traitor. A member of the Left now indicted deputy Zamorski for declaring, in a pamphlet published in Chicago, that the Head of the State was in secret league with Germans and Bolshevists, while the army was in the hands of Socialist officers, who expected it to depose the government and Seym. Pilsudski was further charged with connivance at his own confinement in Magdeburg, and with designing to cede Lwow and Wilno. Such charges, it was urged, menaced the success of the Polish loan among their fellow-countrymen in the United States. The Seym should cause a court of honour to investigate Zamorski's work. In Pittsburg, a collection had been made to effect the overthrow of Pilsudski.

Heat, insults and the widening of the debate on Pilsudski *versus* Dmowski lines naturally followed. The Minister of Justice revealed that the Head of the State did not wish the courts to concern themselves with his honour. Emotion rose so high that one would-be speaker could not articulate. In the end, Zamorski was condemned and the National Democrats walked out. Such were the preliminaries of the full incorporation of Wilno.

Early in January, 1922, "Central Lithuania" responded to a visit from Pilsudski by a free and democratic vote, of which the Lithuanian government and the Wilno Jews expressed their disapproval. "To Poland!" was the watchword of the electors, and next month the new assembly voted unconditional reunion by 101 to 0, three deputies abstaining. Lithuania protested, the Allies urged caution, the government desired to show the utmost moderation. March, however, brought the natural response from Poland —the incorporation of the Wilno district and the addition of its representatives to parliament. In due course it became one of the sixteen shires of modern Poland, and international endorsement of the incorporation followed. Early in 1923, only recalcitrant Lithuania cherished a Wilno question. In 1938 the anniversary of her loss was still marked by a minute's silence. From 1922 onwards, however, Pilsudski's city could rejoice that its historic mission of upholding Polish culture in the north-east had been resumed.

March, 1922, may rank as a beginning of spring sunshine

for reborn Poland. Three years of national effort, evoked and directed by Pilsudski, had given her an honourable place among the States struggling for reconstruction. The Russian question, the Ukrainian question, the Silesian question, the Danzig question, the questions of Wilno and Teschen—all seemed to have been solved or to promise peaceful solution. The Constituent had duly met. The capital levy was bringing in considerable sums. Poland was gaining in status, both as a Baltic and as a European Power. In March, the representatives of Finland, Latvia and Estonia came to Warsaw to concert joint economic action at the forthcoming Genoa Conference. Soon, it might be hoped, Lithuania would find Memel a problem so absorbing as to still her clamour for Wilno. Then Poland might head a Baltic league to which her four partners would contribute numbers equalling one-third of her population. Her own victorious army numbered a quarter of a million, and every year must increase her cultural and economic unity.

Over this fair prospect, however, there hovered gloomy clouds. Despite all retrenchment and heroic taxation, Poland, a poor country, poor in capital, in technique and, on some sides, in human material, found a balanced budget almost unattainable. Poznan had learned much from the Germans, but the Austrians had kept Galicia backward, and many years must pass before the traces of the Russian occupation vanished. To this day, in Russian Poland, the Vistula pursues its course almost unregulated, the clerk juggles with his abacus, doctors, like cabs, are divided into two classes, and men smile at their own unpunctuality and lack of enterprise. In 1922, the exhaustion produced by war increased the torpor of a generation oppressed by Russia.

POLAND IN 1922

Again, the German threat to Poland might be veiled but could hardly be obliterated or renounced. Danzig, Pomerania, Poznan, and now Silesia were wounds that, until the German changed his nature, would never cease to throb. In words ascribed to a Japanese ambassador, "one cannot collaborate with the Germans. They are much too rigid ... a people who must rule or be ruled". In 1922, internationalism seemed to hold the upper hand among them, but it was hard to suppose that Bismarck had lived and taught in vain. If Prussia should once more seize the helm, Poland would be in peril, not only as the State which had robbed the Germans of their Partition gains, but as the State which stood between them and their half-grasped booty of the war. To revive the German Baltic kingdom or the German Ukrainian republic, Poland must become a vassal.

The Russian menace likewise survived the victorious treaty. While Russian imperialists could not forgive the Polish appropriation of Russian districts, the Bolshevists were confident of class revenge. Next year their defeated commander was to declare that strategy, not policy, had lost the war, and that if the Russians had wrested that *bourgeois* army of the aristocracy from the hands of the Polish *bourgeoisie*, a working-class revolution would have followed. This would have flowed over all western Europe, as any new challenge to the Red army would swiftly show.

On every Polish frontier, moreover, both within her confines and without, lurked questions of national minorities which at any moment might burst into flame. Even in the summer of 1938, hardly a week passed without some "incident" affecting Poles resident in Germany, Danzig, Lithuania and Czechoslovakia, or subjects of those States in Poland. The Ukrainian question and the Jewish question must breed trouble on a still larger scale. In 1922, the progress towards good neighbourhood with the Czechs was stopped by a conflict over a small mountain village—a conflict which eventually came before the League of Nations. Poverty, a grievous education, exhaustion, perils on all sides—these handicapped a State whose new-found democracy had not yet learned to express itself in workable political institutions. In this Poland was far from singular. Most of the new States of Europe, indeed, and not a few of the old, produced a heterogeneous mass of parties which ensured instability in the administration. The nations, preferring order and strength in arms to politics, commonly accepted dictatorships, except in north-west Europe. The Poland of 1922 was not ripe for such a counsel of despair, and Pilsudski, the only possible dictator, would never countenance it. The summer months, therefore, were spent in grappling with a crisis which illuminates that stage of politics in Poland, and affords some insight into the enduring characteristics of the Poles.

Chapter XXIV

THE POLISH CRISIS (1922)

THE political crisis of June and July, 1922, was heightened by the threatening aspect of the foreign situation. Lithuania had ostentatiously declined the hand of friendship which Pilsudski held out to her in April, when he ceremonially incorporated Wilno. In May, Germany abandoned Polish Silesia under protest, with a display of draperies which recalled the long-drawn mourning in Paris for the loss of Strasbourg. Poland, however, deemed these trifles in comparison with the news in which the Genoa Conference recognized its own death-warrant—that the Germans and the Bolshevists had signed a treaty at Rapallo. For the moment, indeed, this made the Poles more necessary to the Allies, and they stood side by side for the defence of Europe. But memories of the Partitions by Germany and Russia could not but revive, and Pilsudski's policy of peace and a strong army seemed more than ever needful.

With added weight, therefore, the Marshal turned to his next task in internal politics—the replacement of the Constituent by a parliament normally elected. In the transition period, he held, the government should be as far as possible non-party. With this view the parties did not agree. Early in June, he criticized the ministers, particularly for showing weakness towards Russia. They therefore determined to resign. The parliament claimed, in effect, that so long as a ministry possessed its confidence it was inviolable. Such was the doctrine laid down by a meeting of the chiefs of the several parties and formally communicated to Pilsudski by the Marshal, or Speaker, of the Seym. Next day, therefore (8 June), Pilsudski attended a similar meeting in the parliament house, and complied with its request that he would explain the origin of the ministerial crisis.

From a legalistic point of view, indeed, his own conduct seemed to need no apology. As Head of the State, it was assuredly his duty, not merely his right, to summon the ministers to discuss policy. If they did not refuse to attend, it was no less his duty frankly to express his views. If, after hearing these, they chose to offer resignation, he could reply, as he had done to Witos, that the interest of the State forbade him to let them go. But if, in his judgment, the State would best be served by their resignation, he not only might, but must, accept it. The parliament, of course, might differ in their estimate of what policy required, but they could hardly frame a valid criticism of the form of Pilsudski's action.

In his cogent narrative, however, he expounded only the substance. The elections, he said, would soon be held, the passions of the untrained electorate ran high, and, in the gloomy international situation, disorder would be dangerous to the State. At such a moment, Poland must have a strong administration. The Premier, as all knew well, had resigned when the Wilno difficulties were acute, and had remained in office as a necessary evil. The ministry had asked Pilsudski to give them greater power, but he, alas! had nothing to bestow. When, therefore, they made the assurance of his confidence a condition of remaining, a Head who believed them incurably weak could only let them go.

After the meeting, Pilsudski conferred with the Premier and other ministers. He then sent a letter to the Speaker, showing that the resignation was the fruit of an adjourned discussion, and that he had at first judged some questions of organization too severely. This letter, like the verbal explanation, left the substance unaffected. The Head of the State refused to endanger Poland by supporting ministers whom he believed inadequate.

Warsaw being Warsaw, wild rumours of Pilsudski's chauvinism were soon in circulation. He meant to mobilize, men said, and he could not tolerate a Premier who stood for peace. To this he answered through the Press with a pungent summary of his position which both Poles and their enemies could read. "Poland", ran this brief document, "has no aggressive purpose. As policy and as strategy, that would be absurd. Even if war could clear the threatening atmosphere, to wage it when the moral structure of the nation is weak would be the height of folly. If the Bolshevists intended a desperate measure, the initiative in making a show of disturbing the peace should be left to them."

Nothing, however, was less likely than that either Pilsudski or his Right opponents would give way. The country, after all, must have a government, and what would happen if the Head of the State refused the only government that parliament desired? In drafting the so-called "Little Constitution", three months after the Armistice, it had unanimously resolved "that the Head of the State commission the government on the basis of an agreement with the parliament." What did these words imply?

At Pilsudski's desire, the heads of parties again met him for discussion on 12 June. He himself had no clear opinion as to the true construction of the earlier resolution. According to the unauthorized report of a hostile journal, he began by emphasizing the ambiguous nature of the gathering, while the Speaker maintained that the parliament would be in honour bound to support its spokesmen's decisions. Professing himself a sincere democrat and hater of lack of law, Pilsudski then demonstrated the confusion in the existing constitution. Its terms could be interpreted, he said, as placing the initiative in forming a ministry both in the parliament and in himself. Was there to be a Derby race between them? If so, he was a non-starter. When his fine-drawn argument came to an end, the Speaker pointed out that while the constitution was no masterpiece, constitutional usage, in Poland as in other countries, eked out its written terms. The meeting itself should rank as the highest among committees, and might properly consider questions of nomination and communicate with the Head of the State.

Four days later, after a committee had laboured to interpret the constitution, parliament voted, by 188 to 179, that the initiative in appointing ministers lay with the Head, but that if he refused to nominate, or if parliament declined his nominee, a majority in a special body should appoint. The special body took the form of a miniature parliament, and to it Pilsudski resigned his right of designation. On 18 June, the body named a leading industrialist. Pilsudski acknowledged their letter and did nothing more. He was still, at fifty-five, the wag who had sent the Siberian *dossier* to Vladivostok, but the struggle exhausted him far more than the 1920 campaign.

Check and countercheck went on. The body and the Speaker shrank from issuing actual commissions to the Premier and ministers. Within a week, the industrialist withdrew, and the body unanimously asked Pilsudski to nominate. Pending a decision of the constitutional question, he gave office to the Vice-President of Warsaw. Nine days later, the Right, by a majority of six, voted no confidence in his nominee. On the same day, 7 July, Pilsudski accepted his resignation, and enquired if the body desired to try again. The body wisely replied that if the Head did not wish to take the initiative, they would nominate, and Pilsudski at last set to work to effect an agreed solution. He stipulated, however, that the ministry should represent a victory for no party, and for this the parties were not yet ripe. On 13 July, therefore, Pilsudski resigned the initiative. Next day, by a small majority, the body nominated Korfanty, a name as welcome to the Germans as Zeligowski to the Lithuanians. Pilsudski immediately made it clear that a Korfanty ministry would compel his own resignation.

The tension now became extreme, and Pilsudski could scarcely bring himself to address a military gathering. But he made no false move, and gave the excited deputies time to choose between himself and a policy of adventure. Korfanty, none the less, produced a list of names, only to be referred to his supporters. These proposed a vote of no confidence in the Head of the State, but, on 26 July, it was rejected in parliament by a majority of twenty. Pilsudski thereupon named Professor Nowak, and, on the last day of July, the Nowak ministry took office.

When, therefore, during August, it fell to the Head of the State to present himself for the first time in Upper Silesia, he could meet the German minority on friendly terms. His duty, he declared, was to bear himself towards them not only as Germans but as Polish citizens, and at the same time to watch over the international obligations of Poland. He urged them to use their influence beyond the frontier to make life easy for the Polish minority there.

On the same day (28 August, 1922), he joined in celebrating by a banquet the beginning of common life between

Poland and Silesia. Although in Silesia unemployment was rife, the occasion justified the optimism which he professed. The cleavage between the Polish brethren which the old boundary kept open had endured, he said, for nearly six centuries, and he had often crossed the frontier in disguise. In 1918, Poland, a devastated country, was fighting without arms and looking to foreigners to feed her, while trains of shattered carriages drawn by worn-out engines passed drunkenly over ruined rails. Now all was changed. Victorious, self-nourished Poland had demobilized nearly a million soldiers, and within her frontier unemployment was practically unknown. By her side, Silesia must face the future with full self-confidence.

The general election had at last been fixed for November. While the Nowak government prepared to organize the administration of Eastern Galicia on a basis of justice and tolerance, Pilsudski paid a state visit to Rumania, Poland's natural ally. As a matter of course, he was accompanied by his Foreign Minister, Narutowicz, and by representatives of the army. The meeting with King Ferdinand gave the Marshal opportunity to pay neat compliments to Rumania, united, as Poland was revived, by the triumph of right and justice. Pilsudski proclaimed the ideal of one people, with two national standards, stretching from the Black Sea to the Baltic. "Our countries", he declared, "both thirst for peace based on justice, peace in which freedom may be ensured by right." The tangible fruit of the visit was the development of the defensive convention of March, 1921, into an alliance fortified by economic agreements.

This Rumanian success, an improvement in relations with the Bolshevists, and the prospect of Ukrainian collaboration strengthened Pilsudski's hands in dealing with his next formidable task, the management of the newly-elected parliament. In November, 1922, two-thirds of the thirteen million electors cast their votes. In the Seym, the Left secured some 190 seats; the Right, 163; the centre, only 6; and the National Minorities, more than 80. These last, Jews, Ruthenes, White Russians and Germans, obviously held the balance between Right and Left, and Pilsudski's scrupulous fairness and large tolerance might well meet with due reward at their hands.

In the Senate, of which the membership was 111, the National Minorities, with 26 seats, also held the balance between the Right, with 49, and the Left, with 36. It was observed that in the new parliament the standard of education was higher than in the old. On 28 November, Pilsudski addressed both Houses. He could congratulate the Seym on the contrast between Poland at that time and four years before, when they were not masters of great portions of the country. He urged them in discussing foreign affairs to avoid the turbulence of their predecessors, and observed that hitherto the political life of the Republic had not given evidence of Polish capacity for that collaboration between the different organs of State which the constitution prescribed. Finance was their most urgent care, for Poland was suffering from the same disease as other European nations.

In the last three years, indeed, the budget deficit had multiplied nearly eightfold, as expressed in Polish marks. At the same time the cost of living had risen thrice as fast. Notes with a face-value some 1500 times as great as at the close of 1919 were now in circulation, while the past year had witnessed a further fall of more than four-fifths in the value of the Polish mark. Poland, an agricultural country, was favoured by a bounteous harvest, while, with Silesia Polish, her industrial future seemed secure, and she engaged in friendly conference with almost all her neighbours. Yet parliament failed to check her currency depreciation. That class of question lay outside Pilsudski's sphere. He gave freely, lived sparsely, and strove to spare his country unnecessary outlay and taxation, but left economic science to those to whom it appealed. His ancestors, from time immemorial, had regarded such matters as proper for the Jews, deeming their own duty fulfilled if they obeyed the call to farm, administer and fight. Their great descendant was no less indifferent to gain than to the grandiose schemes of manifold development which were largely responsible for the embarrassments of 1922. "I", he said, "do not love money."

In opening the Senate, Pilsudski charged the new senators above all else to practise moderation. In Poland, he declared, their body enjoyed a great tradition, not only in the works of historians, but in the people's hearts. The present constitution, however, like those of other democratic countries, gave them a more modest rôle—that of applying judgment, deliberation and moderation to the proposals of other bodies. Moderation must be their watchword, to avert internal struggles, and the bitter, though often aimless, party strife in which reborn Poland abounded. Such was the admirable prelude to one of the most chequered and painful chapters in Pilsudski's life and in the modern history of Poland.

Chapter XXV

THE POLISH PRESIDENCY (December, 1922)

ON 1 December, a follower of Witos was elected Marshal, or Speaker, of the Seym, by a majority of more than two to one. This showed what a "deal" between the Peasants and the National Democrats could accomplish. But it was clear that in parliament as a whole the Left had the upper hand, and that Pilsudski, if he stood, would be chosen President on 9 December. On the 4th, however, he explained to the Nowak government and to his supporters the reasons which prevented him from standing. Both in scale and texture the speech was worthy of the crisis, and it is valuable both as a criticism of the constitution and as an example of Pilsudski's mode and power of thought.

The inevitable review of the past Presidency was enlivened, he said, by a discovery which he had made on the previous day—that in February, 1919, the Seym had declared itself commander of the army in time of war. The so-called constitution of March, 1921, had limited and directed the President far more minutely. "Every action", he complained, "must be countersigned by a minister, though the ministers were responsible to him, not he to them."

It may perhaps be regarded as characteristic of the Marshal, at least during his later years, that he perceived slights where none were intended. Such counter-signature formed not only a safeguard against some human aberration —mistake, illness, momentary impulse, undue influence— and against a signature procured by forgery or fraud; it also invested the minister with so great a share in the responsibility for the contents of the document that, if these proved distasteful, he, rather than the President, would suffer. Pilsudski's instinct was to resent and to deride any general rule that did not fit his personal measure, which was that of a clear-sighted, careful, disinterested, patriotic autocrat.

Only if endowed with an almost feminine sympathy, he argued, could a President probe the minds of his ministers so as to avoid conflicts between his power and theirs. Perhaps by an oversight, however, the constitution had armed him better against the Seym and Senate, for they could only bring him to trial before a State Tribunal. Pilsudski went on to complain of the burdens imposed upon the President by the duty of acting as the ceremonial representative of the nation. Life had punished him for smiling when in early days he read that kings made this complaint. Even in working with his colleagues indoors, a President must cease to behave normally. With a monthly civil list of little more than £100, moreover, an official dinner had sometimes left him bankrupt.

Turning to the army, he asked, What were the duties of a President towards it? In peace, apart from ceremonial, he was supreme judge—a burdensome, if sometimes moving, task. In war, even this function was not clear. He must appoint a commander on the proposal of his ministers, but that was all. He would not, however, stand there in uniform and discuss the army. It was hard to be an official, but an officer bore a still heavier burden of duty. He himself, chosen Head of the State against his will, had used his power freely during the two war years, but in peace he chafed at the long delay in forming parliament. Then for the first time he realized the absurdity of the constitution framed in February, 1919, and ejaculated "Not for me!" His last two years had been a journey through sand and marsh, though cheered by the loyalty and kindness of some of those to whom he was then speaking.

Whom should they choose as President? He himself, in representing his country, had enjoyed advantages—"a marvellous life-history, the aureole which destiny had set about him, a proud, calm head, arousing the far-reaching interest of all". His successor should be spared what had weighed upon himself—the fact that thousands upon thousands of those who had spoken with him believed his power to be far greater than it was. He must expect bouquets and also stink-bombs. "As a soldier," said Pilsudski, "I stand shells easily, and they make almost no impression on me. When hunted, I walk at ease, for I have a light tread, though sometimes a heavy hand. I am not caught. After crossing the marsh, I survey my slightly muddied feet and go on. Enough of this!"

With heartfelt gratitude for their invitation to stand for the Presidency, he declared that his character was not such as would conform to its requirements. He advised them to choose a man whose tread was heavy but his hand light, who would keep out of swamps and make the compromises which democracy demanded. He should not be an outstanding party man, liable as such to a conflict between national and party obligation. On 9 December, 1922, Seym and Senate united into the National Assembly to elect a President of the Republic. Five candidates were nominated, and the result was not easily to be predicted. The candidate of the Right, however, received 222 first preferences against 319 distributed among the rest, whose supporters were more hostile to the Right than to each other. As successive ballots removed those who failed to reach the necessary quota, Narutowicz, the Minister of Foreign Affairs, attracted the bulk of the Left and National Minorities, and, at the fifth ballot, gained the day. With Pilsudski at the head of the army and an avowed supporter of his policy in the Belvedere, Poland might well avoid a sudden change of course. Feeling, however, ran high, and the hostile behaviour of the Right was answered in Warsaw by a twelve hours' protest strike.

On 14 December, the new President went to the Belvedere, where Pilsudski, with the Premier and other high officials, waited to install him. Pilsudski welcomed his successor in the short grey tunic of a Legionary, in which he had made his entry four years earlier, and in which he wished to depart. With his calumniators in mind, he invited Narutowicz to inspect the accounts of the funds subscribed for his personal disposition, and an inventory of the Treasury possessions. He then invited him to breakfast and proposed his health. "As the only Polish officer on active service who has never stood at attention before any man," he cried, "I now stand at attention before Poland, incarnate in your person."

Later in the day he left the Belvedere. Not for the first time or the last, Pilsudski had to face that searching test of character—the duty of self-suppression for the sake of a successor and of the cause. This duty he fulfilled by vanishing into the workroom of his remaining charge, the army. Narutowicz, conscious of his own inferiority to his predecessor, and so ill that he passed the nights in an armchair, placed any room in the Belvedere at his disposal, but he declined such a show of condominium. Narutowicz was left in sole possession, and to him the Premier handed in his resignation. Before the gap could be filled and the new order fairly started, the new President, on 16 December,

*Stanislas Wojciechowski.
The Second President.*

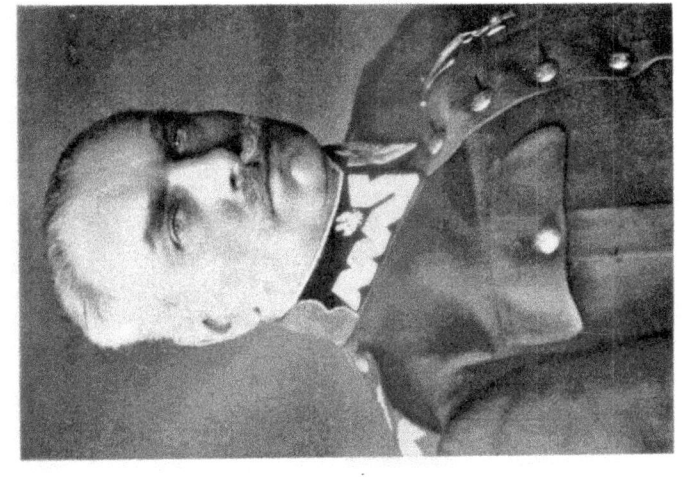

*General Skladkowski.
Premier (1936-   ).*

was shot dead. The assassin declared that he had wished to kill Pilsudski, and in his absence killed his docile instrument, for Poland's sake. This crime did more than any other stroke of fate to make the Marshal an embittered man.

The vacancies which it caused were quickly filled. Within four days, by a somewhat increased majority, the National Assembly chose, as President, Pilsudski's old friend Wojciechowski. A Socialist when they toiled together at the *Workman*, he was now a follower of Witos. Sikorski, Chief of the General Staff, became Premier, and, under his firm hand, Warsaw regained her calm. Pilsudski, for the time being, acted as Sikorski's successor. The gravest consequence of the assassination, however, was probably its effect upon Pilsudski's mind. The shot had been aimed at him, and the guilt, he felt, attached to his opponents. The Right had bitterly resented their defeat. Their German counterparts had murdered many statesmen. On his way to installation, Narutowicz had been assaulted in the streets.

The Right, moreover, had long enjoyed and might soon regain a majority in the Seym, Pilsudski's rival for the exercise of power. Financial stringency, coinciding with improved prospects of lasting peace, would almost inevitably lead to the reduction of that army by which he hoped to consolidate and to regenerate Poland. After the fatal 16 December, he abandoned the longed-for holiday, to toil as the chief administrator of the army and the chief guide of the government, but he had no reserves of patience, and the notion that the Right were murderers fermented in his brain.

On the last day of the old year, 1922, a Polish journalist found Pilsudski at his work on the General Staff, and drew from him an important indication of his state of mind. The assassin had just revealed his expectation that the Marshal would be his victim. "Had he fired at me," declared the Marshal, "in accordance with my luck, he would certainly have missed, but in all that have been aimed at me, his would have been the only Polish ball." "It is painful above all else that another, and he a friend, should perish in my stead. But I am also aghast at the moral aberration which can transfer responsibility so lightly from one person to another. If my responsibility is such that someone feels himself entitled to shoot at me, I feel it incompatible with the spirit of our race that, without a blush, he should shoot down someone else. That is the spirit of the east."

While Head of the State, he declared, he had often observed the fatal influence of that spirit upon Russian Poland. He had striven to arm the nation against its destruction of individuality. Among normal Europeans, the election of a President would impel people to find out the truth about him. "With us, on the other hand, above all things, men seek for lies. And they believe in the lies and build their political structures upon them. I know the Narutowicz family of old, long-settled gentry from the Kovno district, like my own." The President's ancestors must have turned in their graves to hear him called a Jew, with all the political implications of such a lie.

Pressed later to develop his doctrine, Pilsudski emphasized Polish susceptibility to even fanciful suggestions, against which public life gave no protection. His own personality, prominent and enigmatic as it was, must, he knew, occasion much enquiry. But the discoveries made about him were such as proved his thesis. For instance, when he provoked the crisis of the previous June, a deputy asked him in all good faith whether he had given orders to mobilize. Those who said this must have taken him for a madman, if they were themselves not mad. Yet the public was much disturbed.

Before the battle of Warsaw, many believed that Pilsudski had run away, and that he had made off with vast sums, presumably given him by the Bolshevists. In 1919, when he had sacrificed wise strategy to politics, and hastened overmuch to rescue "his beloved Wilno", he found Warsaw declaring that he did this to become Grand Duke of Lithuania. In 1921, after Zeligowski's stroke, deputies had hurled insults at Pilsudski, calling him a hired traitor. When at Lwow, in 1918, the blood of starving heroes was being lavished for the fatherland, those who disposed of Haller's army [the National Democrats] believed lies and withheld their help. Every Pole in public life could multiply such instances by thousands. Thus lies, he said, brought Poland into situations from which it was difficult to escape.

CHAPTER XXVI

PILSUDSKI'S RETIREMENT (1923)

THE early months of 1923 witnessed developments which could only inflame Pilsudski's contempt for the parliamentarians whom universal suffrage and proportional representation sent to Warsaw. Both within and without, Poland encountered difficulties, which the government did its utmost to solve, and at the same time she gained notable successes. The currency lost half its value in a month, but all known medicines—new units of exchange, taxes both general and special, domestic and foreign loans—were courageously applied, and peace buttressed by alliances and extolled. To secure an independent outlet to the sea, since Danzig was politically uncertain and commercially inadequate, a new port was begun on the western shore of the gulf which bears her name. Gdynia, begun with French gold, embodied Poland's ambitions towards self-sufficiency, commerce, industry and sea-power. Its birth coincided with the final sanction by Europe of the Polish eastern and northern frontiers. At a time when military service was out of fashion in the west, the army won high praise from western experts. Yet the Seym moved steadily towards the Right, and Pilsudski's enemies seemed to be attracting the cautious Witos.

During the earlier part of May, 1923, the Marshal, who only then received the Grand Cross for his work in 1920, was preoccupied by the visit of Marshal Foch, whom he decorated with the highest military Order.

About this time he endeavoured to dispel, so far as a

brief article could serve, the deep ignorance of the Polish people on questions of strategy and defence. High costs, he wrote, had abolished the mass armies of pre-war Europe. A new force must defend a new strategic being, Poland, compounded from three fragments of old empires. Like pre-war Germany, she had two fronts, but she lacked the mobility which the Germans gained from their network of communications, their administration, their magazines, reinforcements and the like. Her railways had been designed not to connect with each other, and not to correspond to the density of population. Her people thought of war as a man might think of arithmetic if he did not know the difference between zero and a million.

In politics, thanks to their long enslavement, they were equally inexpert. They must learn to resist rumour and such panic as the enemy achieved by false reports in 1920. Morale among the people went far towards winning a war. Universal military service should improve both their morale and their grasp of warfare. Uniformity of law and administration throughout Poland was her greatest need. During the war the worst transport blocks had been formed at the old frontier stations. Three years' work had brought immense improvement in technique and education. But an incalculable task remained, especially in the field of popular morale.

This brief sermon may be regarded as the testament of Pilsudski to his people. The deal between the Right and Witos was completed, and, on 26 May, the government was defeated by more than two to one. Two days later, Witos became Premier, and, on 30 May, Pilsudski indignantly resigned from the General Staff, "for reasons unconnected with that body". At midsummer, the Rumanian royal pair were due in Warsaw, and for a brief space the former Head of the State shrank into a President of the Army Council to do the honours. As such he gave an interview to a Rumanian journal, revealing himself as studying the Russo-Japanese War on the eve of a long rest-cure. Europe, he said, was faced by only three complications—the French occupation of the Ruhr since January, the settlement between the Allies and Turkey, which was approaching a favourable conclusion, and the disturbance of the balance of the north by Russia. But all nations were striving to avert war, and he did not expect it to come in 1923. Russia was differently organized from all other States, and could not have normal relations with her neighbours. She always caused alarm, but, undermined as she was by the Revolution, he did not think her dangerous. Poland, her boundaries settled, had now a firm basis for national and popular development.

The Rumanians departed; the murderers of Narutowicz, as the Marshal held, remained in power. They soon taught Poland the consequences of the Peasants' bargain with the Right. These seemed to be, in brief, the proscription of their opponents in the Civil Service, the persecution of the hostile Press, and the reduction, in their own favour, of the land-tax. The reduction, moreover, was sweeping only in the assessments of the greater landowners, whose natural allegiance was to the Right. Soon, it was evident, the Pilsudskists in the army might expect to be attacked. As the only General who dared to brave Pilsudski, Szeptycki became War Minister. Resenting Pilsudski's criticisms of his plan for making the army more dependent upon the politicians, he sent his seconds to the Marshal, and only the efforts of the cautious Witos and the authority of the high-minded Wojciechowski prevented the scandal of a duel.

On 28 June, however, by a small vote and a majority of

less than two to one, the Seym had pronounced Pilsudski's service meritorious. He accepted a pension of some £600 yearly, but, though without patrimony or savings, he assigned the whole to the university of Wilno. On 2 July he left the army, unable as an honourable soldier to defend such men as Witos. Next day, at a banquet, given in his honour by upwards of two hundred friends, he declared that after bearing calumny for five years in silence at last he was free to speak. As a lover of history, and one whose name would be found on countless pages, he might gratify his natural egoism by a few words on his share in past events.

The "few words" became perhaps the most famous utterance of his life. He first etched unforgettably the vision of the prisoner of Magdeburg, suddenly and mysteriously finding himself dictator over Poland. "Why he and not another?" the future historian will ask. Whence came this strange phenomenon that suddenly appeared in Poland?" Standing before them in his Legionary uniform, he declared that the sole moral force that gave millions of Poles into his hands was the fact that he was the Commander of the First Brigade. "Justly or unjustly, new Poland took as her first symbol the figure of a man clad in a tattered grey uniform soiled in the Magdeburg prison." Poland made him dictator neither by election nor by a *coup d'état*, but by a moral achievement. In so doing, she broke with her own bad past. "Poland, so Poles themselves have said, stands by disorder. Poland is anarchy." Every future historian must regard her moral achievement, not Pilsudski's faults or merits, as the outstanding fact.

After a few months of dictatorship, he went on, in February, 1919, he had opened the first Seym and handed to them his power. He stood before them the same man in the same uniform, wearing the sword which his officers of the First Brigade had given him. For himself, he desired service in the army, but the Seym unanimously chose him Head of the Polish State and of the Army, whose only previous Head had been the immortal Kosciuszko. The regenerate democratic Poland, by a moral achievement, had broken with the old. Most of the deputies who did this were strangers whom he had never seen.

But then his fabulous fortune suffered change. Everywhere—on the battlefield, in peaceful labour at the Belvedere, in the caresses of his children—he was haunted by a shadow. A stunted monster with crooked legs, spitting forth its filthy soul over all that should be sacred, friends, relations, intimates, following his every movement with ape-like grimaces, distorting his every utterance—this monstrous inseparable, assuming divers forms, now Polish now foreign, shrieking foul insults with twisted lips, in weal or woe, in victory or in defeat, this dwarf was ever with him.

This, declared Pilsudski, was no mere metaphor, as a few amazing facts would prove. He, the representative of the nation, had been charged with theft, and a commission appointed to recover the crown jewels. What other free people would suppose its representative to be a malefactor? In time of war, he, the Head of the Army, had been deemed a traitor. Such was the poisoned soul of the filthy monster who had assaulted every aspect of his life. When he thought of that incessant soiling, it seemed that his very clothes must stink.

Why, the first speaker had asked, did he resign? A soldier must guard his tongue, belonging as he did to what the French called "the great dumb". Now, for the first time, he was free to speak. It was true that he had covered the Polish arms with glory, and had triumphed over the foe before whom others trembled. It was true that his talents, his temperament and his experience made army work easy and pleasant to him. Yet he had left it all, because his soldier's conscience forbade him to draw his sword for men whose agents had first hurled missiles at the new President in the streets and afterwards fulfilled the crime.

He had often gazed at the bowed head of Poniatowski's statue—that Army Head who had perished in a marsh. In other countries, victorious generals were honoured; in Poland, marshes were their reward. He meant no more than that Poland was beginning slowly to return to her old bad ways, and that his audience must do their utmost to replace her on the right road. He was no prosecutor, counsel or judge, but only a seeker after truth. For himself he asked only remembrance and a long, long rest, that he might become as merry as his comrades of the First Brigade.

CHAPTER XXVII

PILSUDSKI AT SULEJOWEK (AUGUST, 1923)

PILSUDSKI'S "long, long rest" was destined to extend over nearly three years (July, 1923–May, 1926). His farewell to his friends bore the stamp of exasperation, not of exhaustion, and a quiet domestic life among the pines some thirteen miles from Warsaw might soon provide him with a full reserve of strength. There, at Sulejowek, he need never see his enemies, and his determination to support his family solely by his own labour kept him close to his desk. Each month $300 from the American Poles passed through his hands to charitable uses, while he himself prepared lectures and wrote history and articles on public affairs. In a land where men still lament that there is only one bookshop to 40,000 people, against one to 700 in France, even a Pilsudski could not command great royalties, and his housekeeping was proverbially sparse.

In his modest villa, as in the Belvedere, he kept a strict routine,[1] rising at ten for early tea and two newspapers, a first batch of work, breakfast proper at noon, work until dinner at three, rest and a walk, tea at five, and work until towards midnight, followed by newspapers, periodicals and a dreamless sleep. Meetings of the Legions and visits to Wilno formed his chief holidays, and army comrades were his usual guests. He was too eminent not to be a force in Poland, but, unless duty demanded it, he had no wish to interfere. For a time, at least, the army had no great reason to complain, and foreign affairs were handled with no

[1] M. J. Wielopolska, *Józef Pilsudski w zyciu codziennym.*

AT SULEJOWEK

grave departure from his principles. Poland advanced on the path of consolidation, and Europe felt more and more that she promised to be a useful and weighty State. Her weakness lay in finance, where Pilsudski could afford little help.

During this, the Sulejowek period, the chief monuments to his activity are his writings. In these, many clues to the workings of his mind are to be found, and history received no small enrichment.

In July, 1923, he produced a vigorous brochure, *Memories of Gabriel Narutowicz*. His thoughts went back to the early days when he had envied the murdered President those military studies in Switzerland which were denied to Poles at home. Their personal acquaintance, however, dated only from the establishment of Polish freedom, which brought home the engineer Narutowicz as a candidate for the Ministry of Public Works. Those were the days of gigantic plans, unfinished works and ludicrous and costly failures, while bureaux quarrelled among themselves and the Cabinet spent three-fourths of its time in conciliation. Narutowicz, unlike others, quietly proposed the abolition of his own ministry, served at the Genoa Conference and produced a striking report. Only then did Pilsudski perceive the knowledge of Europe and the possibilities of this cheerful, tolerant recluse, who had yearned to serve his country even in the lowest place. In the constitutional crisis of 1922, he desired to mediate, thinking Pilsudski's criticisms too ruthless, and defending even faults if they were Polish. He then became his close collaborator.

In his passion for work, he kept no time free for rest, while he laboured to find the grain of good in every man. Free from the usual assumption of omniscience, he strove to deprive Warsaw of its reputation as the most gossiping capital in Europe. Foreigners, he said, believed that Poles always told lies. He did not entirely agree with Pilsudski that the ill repute of Poland came from the existence outside the government of an irresponsible Ministry of Foreign Affairs recklessly seeking victory for itself, not for the State —Pilsudski's formula for Dmowski and his friends.

Narutowicz, he repeated, was strong where most Poles are weak—in knowledge of Europe. To Pilsudski, as Head of the State, he defended even his enemies, and refused to believe that they were working against him. As a minister, his hermit life cost him many friends. Toiling beyond his strength, the returning emigrant, happy to work for his country, declined into the uneasy, bitter, ineffective Pole. He claimed that Pilsudski should stand for President, and sacrifice his freedom in order to maintain foreign policy unchanged. When he stood firm, Narutowicz willingly worked for Wojciechowski. Although shocked by the passions which the Presidential election unloosed, he did not expect the "pushes" and murders which then abounded in Germany to find their counterpart in Poland. Pilsudski had warnings that such were in train against himself. He took preventive measures against a *coup d'état*, and, as usual, ignored the Terror. For Narutowicz, he merely reinforced the guard.

In the few days between the election and the end, the ingrained optimism of Narutowicz must struggle against experience. Foul unsigned letters, threats by telephone in Jewish accents, sinister forms lurking near the Belvedere at twilight—these daily concomitants of a Polish President's life were his. "Stern sentences, because this is not Europe," became a policy with which he must agree.

If at Sulejowek Pilsudski had written only this fragmentary biography, he would have made an invaluable contribution

AT SULEJOWEK

to our knowledge both of the murdered President and of himself. Vivid, direct, sustained, the sketch establishes its author as undeniably a man of literary power. In July, 1923, moreover, it proves him anything but weary. Terse, pungent and picturesque, scathing towards the National Democrats, tender towards his friend, he radiates personality and force. Consciously and unconsciously he paints himself, both as he was and as he believed himself to be.

A man who will declare frankly what he loves and hates goes far towards revealing what he is, and to this the memory of Narutowicz impelled him. Who can doubt that the author loved his friend? or that, when a hard-pressed toiler in his fifties feels such a strong and sudden love, there must be some unusual, personal appeal. In this case, comradeship in the P.P.S. or in the Legions was wanting, and the humour, the culture, even the delicate honour of Narutowicz could hardly have stirred such depths within Pilsudski. The secret may well lie in a rare and triple combination—selfless devotion to Poland, transparent loyalty to its Head, and—the last charm to a battered hero—a *naïveté* unspotted by the world. Although the "canny Lithuanian" takes a certain pride in boasting with Henri of Navarre, "Many have betrayed me, but by few have I been deceived", he reverenced and loved the grown-up child.

Hard on the heels of this biography came a contribution, more than half as long again, on the history and art of war.

In the first week of August, Pilsudski attended at Lwow the second congress of the Legions. The fruits of his visit were a brochure on their military value, a speech against calumny, and a lecture on the defence of Lwow in the earliest days of reborn Poland. All bear the stamp of pugnacity and vigour, indicating that, although the Marshal might scorn to enter politics, he was no extinct volcano.

Sulejowek, indeed, might well prove a self-sought Magdeburg, a seclusion in which the fame of the absentee would grow until Poland, in her need, again cast herself at his feet. But he let no occasion pass of meeting his former comrades. This he did, as his declining years were to prove, because he loved them with all his heart, as they loved him. But his personal eminence and his continued contact with the army made "the lion of Sulejowek" a force which every Polish ministry must respect and even dread.

At Lwow, his history and analysis of the Legions and their spirit was followed by spirited invective against the lies which bring ruin to a people that builds upon them. Warsaw, he said, was the metropolis of falsehood, and to combat slander ranked among the hardest of social duties. When a volunteer had been killed in defending Warsaw, his widow with two orphans turned to the government, which would do nothing for her, and then to himself, who could not. Volunteers went back to their employers, and the employers told them to go to those who had summoned them to war. A Legionary died of heart failure, and there was nothing for it but to beg on behalf of his dependants. With these facts in mind, Pilsudski could take no salary. To frustrate calumny, they must raise the people's soul above the level at which calumny ceased to be effective.

On 12 August, 1923, Pilsudski arrived in Wilno for a fortnight. Two days later, he gave a local editor an interview on the subject of the newly elected Seym. He criticized the new *scrutin de liste* system for having failed to bring new blood to parliament. Only a fresh contingent from the national minorities had been elected. Beyond this, four years of freedom had built up nothing. He denied that the country was indignant at the presence of illiterates among

AT SULEJOWEK

the electors as conducive to demagogy. Poland, he held, like the rest of Europe, was disillusioned with parliamentary institutions.

Dispassionate self-command marked his bearing at this his first home-coming after his emancipation. At first sight, indeed, the interview appears perfunctory, the curt despatch of business in the August heat by a hard-pressed lecturer. The dictum on parliamentarism, however, may well mark a turning-point in Pilsudski's thought. It was uttered within five years of the triumph of those who fought to make the world safe for democracy, and at a time when Germany, Italy and Spain still had normal parliaments. It was uttered, moreover, by a lifelong believer in the people's will, and by the architect of the Polish democratic franchise. For a time he had hoped that experience would teach the Seym wisdom. Now he felt that the nation needed a moral reformation, and that the power of parliament for mischief must be checked.

Seven lectures completed the more than bounteous harvest of these two summer months. At Lwow, he said, the defenders had fought against great odds, at a crisis which stripped naked the human soul. When he reached Warsaw in November, 1918, Lwow had been ten days in arms. He spoke with thousands, but of Lwow no word passed their lips. In Russian Poland, little was heard of Austrian, but the most diverse rumours reached him. An airman reported a few young Legionaries as holding out, while the superior forces of the Ruthenes brought their seniors to negotiate for a *condominium*. Pilsudski could only send word that he must have time before he could send them aid. The Germans in Poland were then laying down their arms; and the people, stealing them. The arms went to equip private armies, which sprang up like mushrooms after rain. Almost every party had its own recipe for saving Poland, and its own army, which it sometimes threatened to use against Pilsudski. He, therefore, could only direct Cracow to send help to Lwow, if possible. But Cracow had many problems of its own, while soldiers returning from the several fronts were abandoning their arms and going home. To his joy, however, Legionaries from Przemysl rushed towards Lwow of their own accord. The city was reported as saved, but then as menaced anew.

Pilsudski could not call up conscripts, for he had no means of equipping them, while their value would have been reduced by political passion and thoughts of Poland as a merely temporary State. He therefore called up the P.O.W., thus sending new battalions to Lwow. For clothing in the grim winter and for supplies of men, the Lwow front became to him an ever-empty sack, but, however irregularly, it was maintained. Foreign observers told him that if they had ever doubted the Polish right to Lwow, they would have been convinced by the sight of the Polish soldiers enduring a hellish life which no others would have put up with for a fortnight. The immediate strain upon Pilsudski was almost shattering. Once, he confessed, he had threatened to shoot his adjutant if he breathed the name of Lwow. The cause was the trumpets of Jericho which the National Democrats were for ever sounding in his ears, while four-fifths of his strength was locked up at Lwow. They denounced him as a traitor and robbed needy Poland of Haller's well-found army. For four years the poison generated by the rival government upon the Seine had worked in Polish public life. Which had the greater moral worth—honest work or the trumpets of Jericho?

AT SULEJOWEK

Five lectures, of which only a hearer's notes survive, were delivered to the Wilno branch of the Society for Military Knowledge. They deal with Command during War—its nature, its significance, the psychic elements which compose it, and its several kinds. In Poland, said Pilsudski, where so many characters are weak, there is a tendency towards collective decisions, which always weaken command. The task of man's soul is to create. Conceptions are sudden creation, a kind of inspiration; Command, the supreme conception. A general must have some conception ready for every emergency, and he must guide the army as a good dancer guides his partner. Napoleon compared the creation of a military plan to the first travail of a woman, afraid and sure of nothing, but loving the child in her womb. All this Pilsudski illustrated from his plan of seizing Wilno in April, 1919.

Every commander, moreover, he declared, has to struggle with politicians. He is part of the political structure of the country, and his deeds influence its politics. Witness the career of Nivelle, suddenly promoted from colonel, whose success at Verdun, though a million soldiers fell, caused Lloyd George to wish him to direct the British army also. If they wished to command, they must seek the soul of truth, gazing straight into the eyes of the Goddess. The weak cannot bear this, and grovel before her in the dust. Even the strong totter, but they never fall, and in her eyes they read the determination of their will.

Such was the behest of one who declared that above all else he loved the truth. Two further lectures followed, their theme "the Wilno question." They comprise such interesting facts as that in the winter of 1919-1920 the Powers had attempted to unite Pilsudski and Denikin against the Bolshevists. Denikin, however, had demanded that the lands beyond the Bug should be governed in his name, and with the old insignia of Russia. That condition Pilsudski had declined, knowing that his soldiers would not be willing to defend their ancient foe.

Again, in 1920, when defeat in war had brought, at Spa, defeat in politics, Wilno and Brest-Litovsk had been adjudged to others. As Head of the State, Pilsudski could not himself defy her obligations. It was therefore necessary to create a new accomplished fact, and he devised and commanded the action of Zeligowski. Before its harvest could be reaped, however, the Bolshevists must be defeated, and also the enemies at home. Against the latter, the fact of possession was reinforced by the voice of the inhabitants of Wilno. But no other deed roused Europe to such vigorous opposition, and the Polish government took fright. Its representatives abroad were stirred up to send home warning despatches, and national scandal-mongers raised all manner of calumniating cries. "The League of Nations," he said, "obstructed our work, but we were aided by the follies of the Lithuanians." Pilsudski calculated on the effect of time, and maintained possession by girdling Wilno with troops. Then, at the request of the frightened government, he gladly took the question into his own hands, and Wilno remained to Poland.

All this, he stated, was done in spite of the national scandal-mongers who declared that he sought the throne of Lithuania for his daughter, who, they said, was the fruit of an intrigue with Madame Perl. Just before his visit he had received a cutting from a Poznan paper inscribed, "Know that on your conscience you have innumerable stains." A Wilno pamphlet declared that he had demanded the repurchase of his family estates, waving aside the objection that their acreage exceeded that now allowed by law. "Who pays the author", he asked, "to write such filth? Where, save in Poland, would anyone pay three farthings for it?" A farmer's wife asserted that when Pilsudski was quartered upon them, in 1915, he stole her husband's boots. A well-known deputy published the statement that the Legions began to plunder before they smelled powder, and that their leader was a bandit. When Pilsudski called for volunteers to defend Warsaw against the Bolshevists, the head of his Civil Chancellery responded, only to find himself suspected of being Pilsudski's agent in secret communications with the enemy. This nearly brought him to suicide. As soon as Narutowicz became Pilsudski's successor, men said that he was a Jew, and thanked God for his death. Now the *Warsaw Gazette* was hinting that Pilsudski was conspiring in Wilno.

Blackmail might have something to do with sudden libels and their withdrawal. With himself, who had been through prison and battles, blackmail had no success. Such was his purity and honour, he declared, that, in 1917, the first Polish congress in St. Petersburg had made him their honorary President, though he belonged to the rival party.

Then, after a month's absence, he returned to Sulejowek, and, on 4 September, wrote a highly characteristic letter to New York. The American "Pilsudski Committee" had, in effect, offered him financial independence. Deploring his resignation, they sent $200, and desired to make a remittance every month until he returned to lead the people to a great and glorious future. The money was for his personal use and not for charity. He replied that he was a man of work, proud that by his own work he could accomplish so much in the world and in Poland. Hence arose a constant ambition which forbade him to accept their most kind and moving proposal in its entirety. But he asked to be allowed to use such funds for extraordinary expenses, such as journeys and unpaid publications, leaving the support of his family to the fruits of his own labour.

Soon afterwards, at Warsaw, he received an ovation from the delegates of the school-teachers of Poland, whom he addressed as comrades in the regeneration of their country. In the autumn of 1923, however, disturbed as it was by currency inflation and by strikes, his only additional publication was a brief tribute to his fellow-revolutionary, Malinowski. An engineer, one of the band of brothers in the P.P.S., he had been arrested with Pilsudski in 1900, and sentenced to eight years in eastern Siberia, but on the way thither he escaped. He resumed the work of conspiracy, but found the Russian Revolution too bloodthirsty for his delicately scrupulous character. In the new Poland, Pilsudski wistfully remarked, he was one of the few citizens who could live quietly and who showed themselves morally prepared for freedom. Tender yet discriminating, this vignette honours the painter and his subject alike.

Chapter XXVIII

PILSUDSKI IN 1924

IN mid-December, 1923, the Witos government fell, as not radical enough in agricultural reform. Ladislas Grabski, who succeeded, gave the War Office to Sosnkowski, long Pilsudski's subordinate and friend. Pilsudski, however, refused to rejoin the army except on terms of independence in time of peace and of supremacy in time of war, which the National Democrats would not find to their taste. These he explained to several political meetings, and, on 9 January, 1924, he made a clear and vigorous statement to an editor. Warned by the prescription of several officers, he said, he was determined that the army should not be the football of parties or of commanders chosen by the Cabinet.

Later in January he produced another brochure, turning this time to the final unsuccessful struggle of the Poles in 1863. That rising against Russia, in vain dependence upon Austria, France and Britain, had coloured all Pilsudski's life and all the history of Poland for sixty years. Still, he declared, it waited for a historian. His own lecture, based upon much research, was prompted by his lifelong puzzle—how could deeds be at once noble and stupid? In it, he destroyed the legend that in 1863 the Polish nation was at peace within itself. A brochure on Chief Commanders followed.

In February, 1924, Pilsudski described how, after quitting Magdeburg, he gained a reputation for wisdom merely by holding his tongue. Everyone else proclaimed some impracticable plan for saving the country: he put forward none, and was credited with deep insight. "There lies the difference", he said, "between a man of decision, like myself, and a waverer." Next, he framed a merciless indictment of a new plan for the highest command. Sikorski, the War Minister who had replaced Pilsudski's friend, Sosnkowski, attempted to gain countenance by unofficially soliciting the Marshal's remarks upon his plan. Worse still, the plan and the request came through an intermediary. This did not escape Pilsudski's notice, and he replied with a surmise that the minister lived in an atmosphere in which discourtesy to him was accounted good form.

The plan, which was to play a leading part in Polish history, he characterized as a bad imitation of the French system, without regard to the radical difference between France and Poland. In France, the minister was a mutable civilian, who could, in some small measure, explain the army to the Cabinet, and the real minister was the Chief of the General Staff. In Poland, the minister was a mutable officer, but the Inspector-General exercised the chief authority, as he should do in an army which existed to defend the nation and not for a jumble of intrigues and tea-cup storms between passing ministers and cabinets. With military directness, but unprintably, he analysed the working of the plan, excused himself from returning the original on which he had scrawled his comments, and, after the formal assurance of his high esteem, added that he had kept a copy of his letter.

Soon afterwards, he sent his stipend to the university of Wilno, rejoicing that it possessed a faculty of art, and hoping that the tide of national economy would not submerge the young scholars.

At this time Grabski, with dictatorial powers, was struggling for a balanced budget. An English mission, headed by Mr. Hilton Young, was called in to advise. Currency inflation, it declared, had drained the country of its capital. The peasants, distrusting the currency, would soon supply no one except themselves. Inflation must stop, or economic paralysis would set in. Economic reform and the Sikorski plan were long to disturb the Poles.

The next round in the contest between Pilsudski and his military foes was fought in the law-courts. The higher command prosecuted a lieutenant for declaring that in October, 1923, he had received instructions to hire agents to spy upon the Marshal. On 21 March, therefore, Pilsudski gave evidence before a military court at Warsaw. In reply to the presiding colonel and to the Prisoner's Friend, he deposed that at Sulejowek he himself and all the neighbours observed the spies, at a time when there was a general expectation of some *coup d'état*. At such a time, he thought, the odds were four to one that the government would have him watched. He had often been watched for long periods, in Russia, Austria, Galicia and Warsaw. When he lived in the Belvedere, his watchers were probably directed by the group which killed Narutowicz, whether supplemented or not by the government he could not say.

In October, 1923, his telephone conversations were tapped by order. His personal relations were not of the best with the then War Minister, who, in 1917, as the servant of the occupying Powers, had ordered him to be watched. On the eve of the arrest, moreover, he had been seen to approach the Governor's residence. In October, 1923, the expectation of a *coup d'état* was attested by the summons of picked troops to Warsaw, and the War Minister passed a night at Headquarters. Pilsudski declared that he was not disturbed by being watched, and that he had taken little heed of the details reported to him.

Apart from the renewed insinuation that the Right had brought about the murder of his successor, Pilsudski's evidence must have weighed heavily with any court. That the government should seek to deny the fact suggested how much they feared him. From this, its fourth day, indeed, the trial stood adjourned, and, some eight months later, the charge against the lieutenant was withdrawn. In the meantime, on the day of Saint Bartholomew, the government had published a historical summary of the greater question—that of again employing Pilsudski. This indicated, in reply to a letter from the Legions, that he would soon be nominated for the post of Inspector-General. 19 March, the day of his patron saint, was becoming a high-day throughout the army, and signs were not wanting that, in many regiments, he was still reverenced as the Chief.

Care for the army, indeed, was at this time the main purpose of his life. To raise its morale, and to save it from the politicians, might well be the greatest service that he could give to Poland.

In 1924, apart from the Ministry of War, there was little in politics to rouse his indignation. The Grabski government was of the non-party complexion that he favoured. Economic questions reigned supreme, terrifying into silence many windbags and *doctrinaires*. Poland had cut loose from the discredited mark, to inaugurate with high hopes the gold-franc zloty, whose very name spelt gold and suggested safety. Until the bad harvest heralded renewed depression, the rational cure—taxes, economies and loans—seemed to be working wonders. Gdynia, embodying confidence in Poland's future, was now begun in earnest. At the same time foreign relations continued to improve. The Poles had many ill-wishers, and the Bolshevists, encouraged by receiving recognition from the western Powers, stirred up their Polish clients. The government, however, did not flinch, and outspoken remonstrances at Moscow, as usual, produced a good effect. Collaboration with the Baltic States, excepting Lithuania, proceeded, while relations with Czechoslovakia and Danzig notably improved. Firmly allied with France, Poland could hope that the admission of Germany to the League of Nations would procure a permanent seat upon the Council for herself. Within her frontiers, at least in theory, national minorities enjoyed full civic rights, and their language, their faith and their culture were exempt from interference. All this followed the precedent established while Pilsudski was Head of the State.

During this year and the next, therefore, Pilsudski, though the cynosure of the army and the bugbear of the government, had leisure for authorship, and for some time he used it well. Within three months, April, May and June, 1924, he dictated the most outstanding of his works, *The Year 1920*. Begun as a reply to the published lectures of his Russian opponent, Tutachevski, it grew under his hand into a volume of more than 60,000 words, invaluable alike as history, as autobiography and as a dissertation on the art of war. At the end of June, he threw off a suggestive lecture to the Warsaw Social and Political Club on "Democracy and the Army". Justice and honour, he contended, could reconcile two institutions, of which one was based upon freedom and the other upon command. In life, the reconciliation was best exemplified in Switzerland, where the citizen might spend half the day as a private soldier and half as a free civilian. He had seen a university professor, garbed as a colonel, marching with elastic tread to share in the marvellous feats of endurance of the Swiss. Symbols did much to help. Democracy erred in clothing judges in a modest black toga. "Wavering between love for strength and power and for the languishing force of freedom," he concluded, "I leave the problem like a diamond in your hands."

A week later, under the title "Czeremoszno", a village eighteen miles south of Kovel, Pilsudski sent to the new Institute for Research into the Recent History of Poland a reminiscence of a march between those places in September, 1915. The vigorous, jovial treatment of a military prank proves the author, then holiday-making on the bank of the Niemen, to have thoroughly enjoyed the task. On 10 August, he journeyed to Lublin for the third annual congress of the Legions, which were celebrating their tenth birthday. There he contended that the Legionaries had been compelled to struggle against the opinion of the great majority of Poles for their ideal of a Polish army under a commander of their own. Although they had proved that they could fight the enemy, they were too feebly supported by their own people to overcome the resistance of their masters.

Those masters themselves alienated the people by their misconduct. He remembered the fury with which they named the pan-Slav General Keller, who in his cups commanded wenches to be brought him from the district occupied by his *chasseurs*. Still greater was the rage against the Russians, who burned the villages and crops on their evacuation, and drove the people like sheep into a far-off foreign land. It was then that the Poles began to leave off speaking of the Russian army as "our lads". In Kielce (1914), he had remonstrated to a high officer on Hindenburg's staff against such conduct as asking women in the street for direction to the brothel, burning furniture as firewood or breaking all the lamps on leaving. Kalisz had been bombarded without due cause. Pilsudski begged his audience of men and women not to disguise the truth. A great man had once told him that "liar" and "Pole" were often used as synonyms. It was humiliating to pretend that the days of servitude had been better than those which the Legions had ushered in.

On the same day, the Legionaries addressed to the President, the Premier and the War Minister a request to employ the Marshal. The reply, made through a newspaper, was that the government had offered to make him practically Minister for War, that he had declined, that they had then discussed reorganization within the limits of the constitution, that they had placed a scheme before the Seym in March, that pressure of business, especially of budget questions, had caused delay, but that they expected an early and dispassionate treatment of the question in the autumn, and that the War Minister would then advocate the Marshal's appointment as Inspector-General.

Next day, 25 August, 1924, Pilsudski wrote a brief, temperate and crushing letter to the newspaper in question. The only government proposition of which he was aware, he said, had been brought by a minister to Sulejowek and declined. The present War Minister had sent for criticism a scheme which Pilsudski had pronounced unworkable. What might have been submitted to the Seym, or might then be preparing, he did not know. On *a priori* grounds, however, he would expect it to be in opposition to his views.

Early in September, he responded, with zest and with his own peculiar charm, to the request of a Warsaw firm that he would record two speeches on the gramophone. In the first of these, he extols the importance of an element not divine but human—the work of man. Of this, all history, all culture is the product. "But instead of being proud of mastering this, which he can master, man would be proud of mastering an element not his own but God's. In particular, he will not reverence the greatest power of his own element, collective work, although that is the greatest marvel of creation. To my mind, the basic postulate of intercourse is always contract and its loyal maintenance."

In the second, he speaks to his best-loved audience, the children. He is standing, he says, before a marvellous trumpet, which will take his voice and send it out into the world without its owner. It will belong, not to him, but perhaps to the trumpet or to some limited company. Children will listen to it, maybe his own, who will suppose that hiding behind the trumpet is Papa. It is curious to think that, when Mr. Pilsudski is no more, his voice will be sold for three farthings, like sweets or gingerbread. The records, they say, are everlasting, so he would like them to tell one beautiful truth, the truth about laughter. The essence of happiness is a laugh. And the more sincere and childlike it is, the more there is in it of heaven on earth. As a good soldier, he used to know how to laugh merrily when danger threatened. And he would be glad if through the machine he could make his laugh, rather than his words, eternal.

In October, 1924, at Wilno, where he had once been punished for speaking Polish, he realized one of his life's dreams—to pay tribute to the men of '63. The succeeding generation, he said, called the rebels "romantic", and made "romantic" mean the same as "stupid". In three sober lectures before the university he strove to rectify this injustice. He showed how in December, 1851, a new Napoleon, like his uncle in November, 1799, had assumed the burden left by a French Revolution, in this case that which had convulsed Europe in 1848. The consequence,

PILSUDSKI IN 1924

in 1859, had been the emancipation of the Italian people. In this emancipation the Poles might well discern a forerunner of their own. As the history of 1864-1871 was soon to prove, the unification of the third divided race, the German, was then at hand. The Poles had fought actively for others' freedom: others should fight for theirs. Russia at the same time had entered on a period of reform, and Alexander II seemed to stand for liberation. The Poles, moreover, exaggerated the importance of the Russian revolutionary movement, with disastrous results upon the conduct of their own. But historians have erred in regarding Poland in 1863 as derelict or half dead. The Poles in 1863, unlike their fathers in 1830, proceeded rather by conspiracy than by war. But the strength of the conspiracy, and therefore its chances of success, were, in his opinion, a hundred million times greater in 1863 than in 1830. In 1830, all hope lay in the army, and the army and the nation were far apart. In 1863, the day when nations decide wars had already dawned. The Polish nation had gained greatness and power sufficient to struggle for a whole year against the greatest empire in the world. Ought shame to be the portion of the conquered?

From this vigorous and suggestive criticism of historical writings, Pilsudski turned to a constructive survey of more recent events, "the first days of the (new) Polish Republic". At Cracow, in mid-November, he devoted two lectures to the history of November, 1918. When, he asked, could the new State be said to have achieved its birth? Cracow, for example, had overthrown its Austrian government at the end of October, but that did not mean that a new government had been set up. His commission of liquidation, the all-party twenty-three, was obviously a mere temporary device, designed eventually to liquidate itself, and having a narrow territorial sphere of influence. The German Revolution caused wild names—Soldiers' Councils and Workmen's Councils—to be imported from Russia. In Poznan, however, on 11 November, the Poles formed a People's Council, which did not claim sole sovereignty. When the approach of the Polish Legions was reported, this Council stood by the Germans. Analysis of other semi-governments, such as that of Lublin and the Council of Regency, shows that they could not be permanent. The National Committee in Paris, which, in 1917, received recognition from the Allies, claimed only to share in determining the lot of Poland, and was willing to postpone her claims. In the Armistice she is not mentioned. When Pilsudski arrived in Warsaw, it was to a sort of necessary concubinate with the Germans, in which he was the stronger party. It was not until 28 November, he contends, that his decree, countersigned by the President of the Ministers, speaking of the government of the Polish Republic, and ordering elections, really created the new State. Next day he took up residence at the Belvedere.

In November, 1918, he told the men of Cracow, what he had found in Poland was the ghetto. This he defined as a group of people, compelled, indeed, to co-operate in some things with those around them, but making for themselves an inner law and secret institutions, which have a stronger hold over them than any influence from outside. Every ghetto, he said, makes definitions which others cannot understand, and has a jargon of its own. In Poland, this ghetto spirit of cliques, mutually incomprehensible and hostile, flourishes as perhaps never before. He himself had always been opposed to it, and had striven to transcend its bounds. In whatever group he had lived, therefore, he had always been something of a heretic, with a reputation for combating words, relics and shibboleths without meaning. From schooldays onwards, such had been his fate. He often gained by turning from mere words to realities. In the World War, he passed through the joyous, fearless, vigorous ghetto of the Legions, and therefore returned to Poland with a ghetto of his own.

The strength of every ghetto was increased by the resistance which the successive shocks to Poland called forth. Since her fate depended, not upon herself, but upon what happened in Vienna or Berlin or on the battlefields, her history proceeded as by leopard's bounds, and the hours struck in rapid sequence. The ghetto acted as a brake. His own career, from solitary confinement to dictatorship, had been, of all, the most spasmodic. He found in Poland men who would co-operate in Lublin, but in Poznan withdrew each to his own ghetto. Men denounced each other as pro-Russian, pro-Austrian or pro-German, when those parties were of necessity extinct. Ignoring realities, they quarrelled about trifles, most often about words. Our children, he concluded, will sing of reborn Poland full of joy and laughter, while we, alas! will encounter her with splenetic sourness and dyspeptic growls.

In thus addressing the Polish Athens, Pilsudski admirably revealed his method, and himself, whimsical and brilliant by turns, but always contributing something both new and true. He ended his fifty-seventh year in full vigour, of all Poles the most admired and the most feared, whose countenance the government must for its own sake strive to secure. On 11 December, by Grabski's invitation, he discussed with a small committee the question of the reorganization of the higher command. After this, he gave an interview in which his position was made clear. The new plan, he argued, was marked by distrust of the Inspector-General, who might or might not receive the chief command when war actually broke out. In any case, he had no influence on the selection of his closest collaborator, and, in several spheres, other officials might share his powers.

After listening to his detailed and devastating criticism, the interviewer asked him whence came a plan which made the Inspector-General a mannequin, and the War Minister and Chief of the General Staff persons deciding matters for the conduct of which they would blush to take responsibility. "Perhaps the personal factor comes in," replied the Marshal in effect, "as it did in drafting the constitution. I am spoken of as a candidate for the post of Inspector-General, and they may wish to tie my hands, as in old times those of stupid monarchs, so that no harm can be done to the State, the army, the government or the Seym. If so, it would be a hundred times better to leave me out than to spoil the scheme and the life of the army. Or make the War Minister Commander-in-Chief in case of war. That would at least be logical, and we should neither dress up a future Commander-in-Chief as for a pantomime, nor the War Minister and Chief of Staff in borrowed plumes, making them blush and the army take offence." This was trenchant journalism, and perhaps the most unkind cut of all was the fantasy of Pilsudski's enemy, the Minister for War, commanding an army of 250,000 men. But was it politic or patriotic thus to deride and infuriate the government? A layman may surmise, however, that a plan which would give Pilsudski a completely free hand in time of war, while guarding against the abuse of such power by his substitute or successor, would not be easily drawn up. The Marshal's own ghetto met him face to face and remonstrated against his too drastic style.

PILSUDSKI IN 1924

Happily for Poland, peace was at this time undisturbed, and her progress in its arts remarkable. A Pole gained the Nobel prize for literature; another, Professor Moscicki, created a vast scientific production of chemicals. Pilsudski himself published *The Year 1920*, which was translated into many Continental tongues. This he sent to a few intimates, with tender and graceful letters. To Slawek, he reveals his mood on Christmas Eve, soon after the meeting of remonstrance. Using the old conspirative nickname, he writes:

"DEAR GUSTAVUS! Yesterday I saw your indignant eyes fixed on me, and thought how often in our lives we have looked at each other like that. We two old but unwearied horses traverse many trackless regions alone, but time and again meet on life's highway, exchange glad greetings, and harness up to pull the same carriage. In the old days we pulled light carts, now it is heavy-laden carriages, often bogged—famous old, unwearied horses that we are! Curious, is it not?

"For Christmas, dear friend, accept this book and the heartfelt greetings of all my family."

Since an unimpeachable Polish historian is constrained to say that on occasion Pilsudski could be a perfect brute, it should be observed that, as this note shows, he could take hard knocks without rancour, impenitent though he might remain. But the biographical emphasis falls on the word "unwearied". Corroborated at the time by the style and by the writer's obvious activity, it was in the next fourteen years to be amply justified. Pilsudski still possessed the energy for a decade of unceasing labour, and Slawek became Marshal of the Seym in 1938.

Chapter XXIX

THE PILSUDSKI QUESTION (1925)

IN the last days of 1924, Pilsudski contributed a few pages to the *Memories of the Legions*, which he had sponsored. In these, he reverted to 1915 and described the devastation of Poland by the Russians in their retreat. On Ozarow church they had poured petroleum thrice, either from military stupidity or senseless Muscovite barbarism. He felt as though struck in the face, and his cheeks burned for the shameful impotence of Poland.

At Warsaw, in January, 1925, he delivered two lectures on leadership, which stressed the human factor as ultimately supreme in war. In the Tannenberg campaign, it was the appointment of Hindenburg and Ludendorff, men capable of taking bold decisions instantly, and of racing the time-god in their execution, that turned retreat into overwhelming victory. On the Marne, von Kluck did the same, but the German Headquarters blundered almost beyond belief. Where is justice in the world, when Hindenburg is ranked as great and von Kluck as little? Von Kluck, commander of 400,000 well-found men, received orders to refrain from crossing the Marne—which he had, in fact, crossed three days before. Was he, then, to retreat before a foe whom he could see in retreat before his own force? He decided to remain one day. Time took its revenge, and the battle of the Marne was lost.

Soon afterwards, Pilsudski, proud to be a family man, spoke with exquisite tenderness to a newly-formed association of soldiers' widows. As Head of the Army he had issued the orders which forfeited their husbands' lives, but as Head of the State he had given them equal rights with men. Orphans of all ranks shared a common fate. Even in time of peace, life was not easy for a soldier's family, and they must not be too hard on their officers.

Other biographical and military lectures followed, and that on "Prison Psychology" may well take the first place among his minor works. When the summer came, two years at Sulejowek had certainly added not a little to Polish literature.

Still, however, he remained unemployed. His unemployment could be ended only by agreement between the will of the government and his own. Unless grave danger threatened, it could be safely said that the government would not give him that authority without which he would not return. Witos said openly that his career was over, and students declared that he belonged to history. Under Grabski's non-party ministry, therefore, Pilsudski's fate, as so often in the past his country's, depended mainly upon the action of foreign Powers.

During 1925, the Polish horizon was cloudy, but threatened no immediate storm. Both the great dangerous neighbours alternately blew hot and cold. Germany now joined the League of Nations, now made her fabled soldier President, now declared on Poland a tariff war intended to coerce or break her. The Bolshevists, who mocked at the League of Nations and evaded their debts to "capitalist" Powers and persons, attempted revolution in Estonia, and spoke fair words in Warsaw. The Baltic States continued their cooperation, and Czechoslovakia showed something resembling friendship. A friendly understanding with the Jews was mutually expressed in words. Above all, provided that she made no blunder, time must work for Poland.

MARSHAL PILSUDSKI

The tradition of her independence grew daily stronger, within her frontiers and without. Education in the widest sense progressed: the army accumulated trained reserves: statesmen ceased to raise their eyebrows at her name: she gained a recognized share in the equilibrium of Europe.

Only the finances seemed to defy the efforts of the government. Pilsudski, therefore, remained a great national figure occupied in retirement with authorship, with theories of military reform, and with a kind of honorary presidency of many regiments. The standpoint of the War Minister, General Sikorski, also remained unchanged. As a politician, he must endeavour to please the public; as a man, he wished Pilsudski far away. Since, in judging Sikorski's army plans, the public made the Marshal's approval the condition of its own, the minister strove to satisfy it by a show of acquiescence. His professed desire for Pilsudski's return, however, was at obvious variance with the scheme which he insisted upon preparing. To expose the cheat, Pilsudski on 12 August published his letter of the preceding February.

"The amazing system of discourtesy and lying", he wrote, "to which I am so often subjected, I confess not seldom makes me wonder if there is a pestering fly from the piggery droning around my head. Only a few days ago, I learned from the newspapers that I am going to take part in this year's manœuvres. It was announced without any authorization from me—obviously for someone's momentary advantage." Here, he concluded, was another example of the reckless mendacity and indiscretion with which foreigners were wont to charge the Poles.

This seemed a palpable hit, but the *riposte* was difficult to parry. At the close of his speech to the Legions, the angry Marshal had wildly denounced the official Polish records. These he advised the future historian to distrust. When he was preparing to write *The Year 1920*, he declared, he failed to find in the Staff archives many documents that he needed, and found false ones in their stead. The upshot, on 22 August, 1925, was a communication to the Press, in which the Chief of the General Staff, Stanislas Haller, announced that he had invited the Marshal to name the suspected or missing documents. A Commission should then investigate the charges.

Pilsudski at once replied publicly by stating that the surrender of Wilno in July, 1920, had been falsely attributed by Haller, then his own Chief of Staff, to orders given by Pilsudski to himself. His own direct order to the Commander at Wilno to defend the city at all costs was missing. Secondly, it had been impossible to discover in the archives his despatch of 20 August, blaming Joseph Haller, of which two copies should have been there. Again, what was the history of the falsification of his despatch to General Smigly, which caused him to retire from Kiev in a wrong direction?

Early in October, the Commission, in which a general presided over two historical professors and two colonels, began to investigate these charges. Pilsudski, meanwhile, was at bitter feud with two military critics who had belittled his victorious campaign. It was, therefore, in a mood of indignation against ministers, historians and Polish society that he faced the Commission on 18 October. The occasion was memorable, for one of the professors [1] afterwards published some of his notes, giving a unique view of the Marshal as seen by a political opponent whose veracity is beyond question.

"We must distinguish between the Chief Commander and the Chief Command", Pilsudski insisted. The former

[1] Dr. Wl. Konopczyński.

had often to fight against the latter. The army had been hastily assembled during the war: the generals were strangers who distrusted each other and often quarrelled, while all except himself feared the Allies. He could not trust the Seym and government, and believed that many of their attacks on him were paid for by the Entente.

There were few within the Chief Command or in politics whom he could trust, and therefore he planned his campaign with few assistants. Only the former Austrian officers were accustomed to the "book-keeping" of war, and most of those were morally decadent. In the Chief Command, as probably in the Seym, corruption reigned. He had forced Paderewski to appoint Wojciechowski his lieutenant when abroad, and Pilsudski and Wojciechowski had fought the evil side by side. After the victory at Wilno in 1919, the Chief Command took over economic matters, but he did not trust its opinion when waging war. He had flung all things aside, taken the command and conquered.

These valuable *obiter dicta* seem to have little bearing on the work of the Commission, whose unanimous report was signed on 5 November. The soldiers and the historians agreed that there had been no falsification of the order to the Ukrainian front, that General Stanislas Haller had been in no way to blame for the surrender of Wilno, and that the missing despatch had been transferred to the archives after the publication of Pilsudski's book. On the night of 20 August, 1920, the Marshal had discussed by telephone the change by the Chief Command of the line of pursuit. The Commission ascribed to polemics, especially between writers of military reminiscences, and to calumnies directed against the Marshal, the atmosphere in which these charges had arisen. In the confusion of the campaign, the raw material of archives had been imperfectly preserved, and where Rumania had twenty officers at work upon war records, Poland had only two. The chiefs of the Historical Bureau had been conscientious, and its present chief, one of the writers who had roused Pilsudski's ire, had done genuine service.

The President of the Commission added a declaration of considerably greater length than the report. As a soldier with complete confidence in the Marshal, he saw in his protest not merely a question of detail, but a protest against whole years of systematic damage to his authority. This had been detrimental to the soldierly spirit of the army. When the danger was greatest, however, his presence had electrified the men and they felt sure of victory. That was the deepest historical truth, though it could not be deduced from documents. The attempt by political groups, and also by some soldiers, to strip the Marshal of the glory which he had earned, aimed at the army a deadly blow.

While the Commission was considering its report, Pilsudski had again wielded his pen on behalf of his old associates in the work of revolution. The P.O.W. had asked him for a preface to a publication called *Turning-point*,[1] devoted to the events of 7-11 November, 1918. Many Poles, he declared, had no yesterday, even beyond a week. A month was too long for the ephemeral soul of the average man, who could only say, "I don't remember." Hence they sought justice, since the P.O.W. had a glorious past, by attempting to deny it any future.

While Poland was thus rent by controversy, the Powers of Europe, assembled at Locarno, had concluded agreements which were held to be guarantees of peace. France and Germany accepted the existing frontier between them, and Britain undertook that if either should violate it, she

[1] *Przełom.*

would restrain the aggressor with her whole force. On the eastern side, Germany, still a disarmed State, undertook to seek no alteration by way of war, and France gave her guarantee to Poland. Combined with the new courtesy of the Bolshevists and of Britain, this seemed to mark a further advance of Poland in prestige, and in 1925 she enjoyed a bounteous harvest. The disastrous and progressive fall of the zloty, however, ruined the credit of the Grabski ministry, and on 13 November it resigned.

Next day, Pilsudski, attended by a voluntary retinue, presented himself before President Wojciechowski at the Belvedere, and handed him a declaration drawn up to protect the moral interests of the army. Twice over, he in effect declared, War Ministers had been appointed for merely party reasons, and the soldiers, who were not electors, should not be made the sport of politics. On the morrow, several generals and about a thousand officers made their way to Sulejowek to celebrate the journey from Magdeburg for "his marriage to Poland" seven years before. In reply to their loyal congratulations and expressions of hope, he quoted the words that one of them, the President of the late Commission, had used in his appendix to the unanimous report. "Honour is the army's god: without it the force of the army crumbles." To safeguard the army's honour, Pilsudski said, he had stood before the President of the Republic on 14 November.

Both Pilsudski's remonstrance and this demonstration could not, and did not, fail to influence the political crisis. Four days later, on 20 November, a coalition ministry was formed, of which Sikorski was not a member. Foreign Affairs fell to an extra-parliamentary minister, and soon Zeligowski became Minister for War. The burning question of politics, the recall of Pilsudski to public life, however,

THE PILSUDSKI QUESTION

remained unsolved and apparently far from solution. His vigour, at fifty-eight, was unimpaired, and it no longer found a sufficient outlet in authorship. During 1925, little more than a lecture on Psychology and a few articles had fallen from his pen, and he had no considerable work in contemplation. His message to Poland had been clearly stated. It remained to transmute that message into life, and for that task who could serve so well as he himself?

On the lower plane of politics, a great part of the army ardently desired to be ruled by him, a weighty fraction of several parties agreed with them, and it might well be supposed that the great lukewarm mass would not disapprove of his return. On the other hand, the man who in time of peril could sweep all else aside, take the command and conquer, might well be an awkward yoke-fellow in time of peace. Sincere democrat as he was, no principle could make him tamely acquiesce when his colleagues did what seemed to him disservice to the State. Pilsudski in office might signify military rule, exercised in great part by soldiers less wise than he. There were generals who talked of "the Pilsudski myth", and high-placed officers who trembled for their careers. Party politicians could not but dislike a man who ostentatiously stood above parties. The National Democrats remained the strongest single group, and although Dmowski, declaring that he was never a politician by vocation, had retired, his party remained, by sentiment, by principle and by tradition, Pilsudski's inexorable foes.

CHAPTER XXX

PILSUDSKI AND THE GOVERNMENT (1926)

EARLY in January, 1926, one of the Marshal's friends among the ministers formally raised in the Council the question of his return. This was considered by a committee, and, on 12 January, the public learned through the Press that the Speaker would be requested to expedite the work of the Seym on the organization of the highest authorities in the army. Pilsudski immediately replied with yet another repudiation of the proposed arrangement. He described the influx of enquirers, particularly of soldiers, who turned to him rather than to the "political committee" which was discussing his return. The project itself still seemed to him "unworthy work, injurious to the army and the State", designed to prevent his own return to the army even when Poland was threatened with destruction, as its author, Sikorski, might very well desire. That, without consulting him, they again proposed what he had already rejected, and even covered it with his name, was characteristic of Poland, where it was an article of faith that not only a bad constitution but worse political usages must be maintained.

This outspoken, but not unfounded, indictment was repeated and sharpened in an interview two days later. Pilsudski then took occasion to speak of "the very low standard of decency" of Sikorski, thanks to whom a project which he had denounced was introduced unchanged on pretext of securing his return. The Chief Command, he explained, was a neutral institution, invented by himself to safeguard finance in the late war. It could not possibly direct an army. The General Staff, of course, was indispensable to every army. Even a company must have its little staff, for war required both command and bookkeeping. As hereditary monarchs must nominally command, although they might be almost idiots, or devotees of art, science or flirtation, a Moltke might direct the army as Chief of the General Staff. His organization had been copied everywhere, worst by Austria, which, unfortunately, set the Polish standards. When Napoleon was both monarch and commander, his own staff was the General Staff. Sikorski's plan gave so much power to the Chief of the Staff that only an idiot or an ass could accept the post of Commander.

Pilsudski expressed gratitude to the President for his courteous and loyal treatment of himself, when the question of nominating Sikorski's successor had arisen. He would only say that he had suggested that an officer of distinction (not a political intriguer) should be chosen, and that the bad traditions inherited from Austria should be broken. As to that agreement with himself which was so often claimed, the custom was to ask anyone who knew him, even an enemy, what Pilsudski thought of any matter, and to proclaim the result as his opinion.

Within the next six weeks (15 January–23 February, 1926) the Marshal six times responded to Press requests for his opinions on the crisis. But for a lecture on the relations between the army and society in 1863, these formed the whole of his literary output. The hiatus, indeed, was in part accounted for by the effects of a chill, but it also indicates the prolonged excitement which the crisis could not but cause.

On 20 January, the interviewer voiced the deep concern of the army and of the public at the Marshal's previous decision. Pilsudski explained that, as Poland obviously could not attack, the future war would be defensive. This meant that at first the enemy could choose his ground, and the General-in-Chief must make his counter-decisions quickly. How could his movements be swift, when the plan reserved the dislocation and concentration of the army for the approval of the War Council? Again, experience had taught him in 1920 the strength of a commander who is in sympathy with his troops, and, alas! the possibilities of crippling him by agitation at the front. This latter the project would increase. Further, he had no mind to be the sport of jarring parties. Sikorski had denounced those who honoured the anniversary of Pilsudski's return to Poland, and had punished their spokesman. It was plain that the atmosphere should be cleared. After fourteen months in parliament, the project had only been made more absurd. It was highly unlikely that it could be so transformed as to allow of his return.

Pilsudski's recall, of course, depended ultimately upon the Seym; the Seym, upon public opinion; public opinion, largely upon trade and prices. These last, despite the abundant harvest, were unsatisfactory. Inflation had not wholly ceased, and Poland still felt the effects of war-time ruin and post-war extravagance. Her people distrusted her currency, and it was necessary to allow some of the taxes to be paid in kind. The growth of population, moreover, exceeded what the land would bear. To reduce the number of rural unemployed, the great estates continued to be broken up, but world-wide experience has shown that small holdings cannot produce standard crops as economically as large-scale farming. Public opinion tended to doubt the competence of the Seym, and society was nervous and uncertain.

Such was the background of the political events of February, 1926. Zeligowski was at the War Office, but, apart from some external intervention, there seemed to be no hope of recalling Pilsudski to service. On 6 February, the Marshal sent the President an ultimatum. "Renounce the project or forgo my aid" was virtually its content, and, two days later, they discussed it at the Belvedere. The result, as the Marshal immediately informed the Press, was failure. Zeligowski, he said, had been made ill by the crisis, and went about with his resignation in his pocket. Another ministerial friend had been driven by the foul atmosphere to actual resignation. The way seemed open for a new Sikorski era, but it would be difficult to find a high-placed officer to follow in the steps of Zeligowski.

On 10 February, the day on which this interview was published, the Council of Ministers met, and Zeligowski moved that the project be withdrawn from the Seym. The Premier desired the ministers to consult the parties which they represented, and to report a week later. Zeligowski thereupon informed him that, if the project were not withdrawn, he would resign. Next day, Pilsudski gave another interview. They would have a second historical Commission, he sneered, to prove that his victories had been won by the Chief Command, and that all the deficits arising from corruption in war and peace were caused by him. Pressed once again to disclose his advice to the President at a second meeting in November, 1925, he said that it included a warning that, in their mutual strife, parties would be careless of the morale of the army,[1] and that it was

[1] Pilsudski, at Sulejowek, had most sternly declined to tolerate agitation in the army on his behalf.

time for the Polish Staff to break with the worst Austrian traditions. These would be continued if Sikorski and his predecessor came back.

Within a week, the Press was asking the Marshal for further light on the *rôle* of the army in the State. He replied with a reference to his lecture of 24 January. The Poles, he said, had long lost their military tradition, so that, of the six hundred members of the Senate and Seym, not more than twenty had seen service. How, then, could parliament rationally direct the soldier's life, or convince the soldier that his life should depend upon its caprices? The project marked the triumph of all the trickery and hole-and-corner confabulation of all the conventicles in the Seym, sometimes not even of parties but of individual deputies, in which some deputy's distant cousin counted far more than a soldier's blood. Why should military careers or men's lives depend on the chatter of politicians over black coffee, or something stronger, in the buffet of the Seym—A and B one day combining against C; B and C the next day against A, and so on, as Poland in recent months had seen? Since the interviewer kept on asking for his prognosis, he would point once more to the danger of a new Sikorski era.

Two days later, Pilsudski was again under examination, this time on the plea that the public was suspicious of militarism. Every war, declared the Marshal, must have an object, and Poland was too weak to deem any object worthy the hazard of a war. He remembered too much cowardice and treachery during the last war to wish to have another. The common charge of militarism brought against Poland was absurd. Nowhere could international projects find a readier hearing. Yet, although they were in the epoch of Locarno and disarmament, he fully expected to be charged with reducing by his bad reputation the chances of his country for a permanent seat on the Council of the League.

Militarism, he argued, was a historical conception bound up with the pre-war Europe, and it was unlikely that history would repeat itself. One great cause of the war had passed away—the existence of three great Powers whose partition of Poland displayed their feudal and medieval structure. This had changed, and the general weariness of war made renewed militarism unthinkable. Poland was not the only country with an army, and her central, weak and unguaranteed position made it most necessary for her safety. One deputy, indeed, was demanding army reduction, to provide capital for the development of building. Pressed for his opinion on the probability that the army project would be withdrawn, the Marshal answered that he neither knew nor sought to know. As the government was a coalition, it might well act like a woman—say "Yes" and "No" by turns, and put off the decision.

This interview was published on 19 February. On that day, the Council of Ministers rejected Zeligowski's demand that the project should be withdrawn. The President had called for a statement of their intentions, and they resolved to await the outcome of the correspondence between themselves and him. The news of these proceedings brought another interviewer to ascertain Pilsudski's verdict on them. He received it in one word of Lwow *patois*[1] implying muddled dawdling. The Marshal declared that he disliked the thing so much that he found the pronunciation difficult. Their action was what he had expected, and he could soon, in all likelihood, be surrounded with spies, as when Sikorski and his predecessor were in power. The ministers who had now opposed his return to office represented the parties

[1] zakałapućkać.

which had supported Witos in 1923. Witos had not long survived, and the same men now feared for their muddled dawdling, if Pilsudski regained his place. He had deliberately concentrated on the withdrawal of the Sikorski project as the pearl of the whole anti-Pilsudski system, which would in practice, as he had told the President, be found intolerable.

The Marshal had next to stand fire from those whom he had offended by his strictures on the heritage of the late Austrian army. The Commander in Cracow and eleven other former members of the Austrian General Staff demanded that the War Minister should defend them. Failing this, they would sue Pilsudski for notorious calumny. Zeligowski sent on their letter to the Marshal, whose reply to him was published on 21 March. It stated that if, as Polish citizens, the officers resorted to a civil court, the question lay outside the competence of the Minister for War. A Polish minister could hardly be obliged to defend the tradition of the Austrian General Staff, which all the world condemned. Nor could Pilsudski be called before a court of honour for having criticized his former subordinates to the President of the Republic in the presence of the Premier, during a national emergency. If anyone could complain, it was the President, who had asked in vain that he would refrain from publication. His warning had been directed against Sikorski and his predecessor.

Complete self-confidence no less than complete devotion to his country was probably the secret of Pilsudski's power. The defects of his qualities plainly appeared in his apparent unconsciousness that what could properly be stated to the President might be a wrong to private persons, if published to the world. In this case the eleven, when publicly assured by Zeligowski that the warning had not been a general one, withdrew their complaints, while the leader, who had circulated his letter throughout the army, received no further satisfaction.

On the day when Warsaw perused the reply to Zeligowski, a cheering crowd assembled to hear the Marshal lecture on "The Commander-in-Chief in Theory and in Practice". If any had anticipated sarcasm or invective they were deceived. The lecture was a contribution to politics, partly because Pilsudski explained what the Commander must be and do, but chiefly because he gave proof that in himself Poland possessed a rare man, lucid, vigorous, restrained, experienced and, above all, human.

"If in every theory," he maintained, "there must be some exaggerations of the truth, in the theory of the Commander-in-Chief they are, alas! very numerous. I begin, of course, with the Polish. One of the most common is the consideration of the task of two beings who may quarrel during war—the Premier and the Commander-in-Chief. The exaggeration of Polish statesmen always tends to give the Premier the right of command in war, and that to such absurd lengths that we may say that it would be better to have no Commander-in-Chief, but to let the Premier take his place. From the well-founded theory that the former must always work with his government comes the exaggeration that the Premier, who is usually ignorant of war, is entitled to direct him in his military work. If Poland goes on thus, the Premier's ignorance may make it necessary to give him a technical adviser, perhaps the distant cousin of a subaltern, or, it may be, a retired general. Then, in accordance with Polish practice, if the Commander-in-Chief criticizes a subordinate, he will be judged by a court of honour presided over by the

Premier. From the sound principle that government and Commander must co-operate, since a lost battle sweeps them both from place, comes the exaggerated conclusion that the Premier advises the Commander in everything. I say from experience that, with such a foolish system, I would never take command."

April brought no alleviation of the crisis. In the middle of the month, Pilsudski once again strove to clarify the issue in general terms. His contribution took the form—as it proved, for the last time—of a lecture, delivered on this occasion to the Social and Political Club in Warsaw. From childhood, he explained, he had been attracted by questions of the working of the human soul in difficult circumstances. Thus he was led to the subject of his lecture, "On the Commander-in-Chief and the State". The Poles, he said, in time of peace judged war wrongly, and in time of war did not study it, so much did they long for the return of peace. Hence to them the phenomenon of war remained unintelligible.

Yet it was so universal as to be inevitable, and when it came, it transformed all civic life. In 1914, the military seizure of the railways had brought all industry in some regions to a standstill. Money, too, must be apportioned between the army and the civil population. A few days after mobilization, an army of 200,000 has grown to over 1,000,000. Such simple facts as these showed what a weight rested on the Commander-in-Chief. Napoleon, moreover, had declared that success in war depended as to three-fourths upon morale. It was lack of morale that had brought defeat to Germany and Russia. The Poles, at the same time, had influenced not a little the commanders of those Powers and of Austria.

France had been concerned with many fronts, and the

PILSUDSKI AND THE GOVERNMENT

division of her efforts between them had depended on the Commander-in-Chief. Military *attachés* attend him, rather than the government, in the interests of their respective countries. Upon his own nation his influence is so immense that victory is thought of rather as his than theirs, and Caesarism comes within sight. If a country in time of war can find a leader of adequate talent, its chance of victory and of national strength becomes overwhelming. But, since it cannot create such a man, it is safer to rely upon the work of the average citizen, and not to think of war in terms of the exceptional commander. Sound sense concedes to the Commander-in-Chief a predominant influence in time of war, and devises means by which he can collaborate with others. The present project so fetters him as to suggest that it originates in folly and unworthy motives.

The simplicity, intelligence and calm of this pronouncement suggest that, amid the general tension, Pilsudski retained his self-control. In passing without effort from the ring to the professor's chair, few men have ever been his rivals. Three days later, on 18 April, 1926, he was summoned to attend on 21 April at the Belvedere. The "muddled dawdling" of the last two months had given occasion for a new conference with the President, the Premier and Zeligowski. At that moment, however, the ministry began to crumble. On 18 April, the P.P.S. declared that its support would be withdrawn, thus inaugurating a new crisis. The programme of the Finance Minister, involving further increase in taxes and decrease in salaries, could not be popular, while the prevailing depression was deepened by suspicion of the negotiations between Germany and Russia, which brought those dangerous Powers into a new *entente*.

After attending at the Belvedere, therefore, Pilsudski

notified the public that his visit had no connection with the crisis. The subject of discussion, he declared, had been the project and the interpretation of the constitution with regard to the President's military powers. In this he had taken no part, but at its close he declared that he disbelieved in the possibility of a speedy settlement of the project by the Seym, that he could not seriously discuss military work until it was withdrawn, and that he had warned the President against employing Sikorski, either in the central army administration or as Minister for Home Affairs.

In a subsequent interview, he pointed out that, when the constitution was drawn up, Poland had never had an army in time of peace, and that, therefore, its terms must be interpreted as primarily referring to a state of war. To war the President stood in a different relation from that which he occupied towards railways, education and the like. His was the highest authority in questions of national defence. In accordance with the spirit of the constitution, the War Minister must answer for his work, first, to the President as his superior; second, to the Cabinet; and third, as a member of the Cabinet, to the Seym.

The ministry, meanwhile, at the President's request, was continuing its harassed term of office. As usual, the budget was for months the grand parliamentary business of the financial year, and a change of ministry must delay and even jeopardize its forthcoming final stage.

The Premier, therefore, installed two makeshift ministers in the places vacated by the P.P.S., and negotiated with other parties, in the hope of regaining a majority. On 28 April, the budget for May and June was voted by the Seym. On the same day, Pilsudski engaged in a lively verbal tussle with an interviewer who sought his opinion on the crisis. This, he said, he had foretold in 1924. It arose largely because the principle, "the government governs, the Seym judges", had been infringed. Whenever the accused were the judges, demoralization had set in, and Poland felt this more keenly than the rest of Europe, because, being inexperienced, her hopes from parliament had been higher. The remedy lay in a clear-cut, responsible government, abandoning the attempt to bargain with every group among several hundred deputies.

"Don't you think that dictatorship is simply a question of the man?" asked the interviewer. "That I will not decide," replied the Marshal. "But don't you agree, Marshal, that a strong man who grasped power would easily overcome the difficulties?" "With the Seym, or without?" cried the Marshal. "That would be his affair," said the journalist. "You are trying to trap me," smiled the Marshal, shaking a warning finger. "Dictatorship . . ." the journalist began. "And what do you find wrong in that?" broke in the Marshal. "Is it not simply a question of the man? Would you undertake it?" was the rejoinder.

"An unconstitutional question," said the Marshal, with a grim smile; "you ought to go to gaol for it." "As you please, Marshal," said the journalist, "but may I have your answer first?" "But I won't answer, for I don't want to go to gaol," smilingly replied the Marshal. "I have often considered the problem of dictatorship, but I maintain that a strong government can do its work within the limits of the constitution. Every effort must be made, however, to put an end to the evil customs of the Seym, for these are worse than an evil constitution."

The almost judicial tone of this interview strengthens the impression which the preceding documents produce—that during April, 1926, Pilsudski remained relatively calm. The continued presence of Zeligowski at the War Office was a guarantee against subversive changes in the army, while Wojciechowski was a President of whose fundamental loyalty the Marshal was well aware. May opened well, for Labour Day brought almost no disturbance. On the 3rd, the nation celebrated the constitution of 1791 with the accustomed unanimity and pomp. Next day, Zeligowski at last withdrew the Sikorski project, and substituted a new one for consideration by the Seym.

In many respects, the new proposals embodied Pilsudski's views. The position of the President as the highest authority in regard to war was emphasized, although when war broke out he might not take the field. The War Minister served as his lieutenant and was not responsible to the Seym. The lieutenant of the War Minister during peace was the Inspector-General, whose influence in preparation for the war in which he must command was guaranteed by his control of armaments and of the General Staff. In addition to these three, the government proposed a National Defence Council with the Inspector-General as a member. Next day (5 May), however, finding an assured majority unattainable, the ministry resigned.

The President must now endeavour to find out from the party leaders what successor could secure enough support. After Witos and another had failed to justify their nomination, Ladislas Grabski made the attempt. On 9 May, he conferred with Pilsudski at the Belvedere, but in vain. Next day, a new *communiqué* was published. In this the Marshal stated that he had told the President that every War Minister must find his situation difficult in consequence of the economies that the previous Grabski Cabinet had effected. He would, therefore, probably seek from the Premier some guarantee safeguarding the moral and material interests of the army. As for the new project, he stated that he had not studied it, and therefore could say nothing positive about it.

On this, Ladislas Grabski had abandoned his attempt to form a ministry, and next day (10 May), Witos succeeded. It was calculated that, with the National Democrats, Christian Democrats and National Workers in addition to his own Populists, he could command a majority of thirty in the Seym. Such a majority, the fruit of hard bargaining in a parliament elected three and a half years before, offered little prospect of successful dealing with the economic crisis. Its foes might well believe that Witos did not represent the Poland of 1926. He dared, however, to choose a War Minister whose name was a challenge and a threat to the Pilsudski section of the army.

On the same day, the Marshal gave an interviewer his unreserved opinion of the situation. The crisis, in his judgment, was not over, for Witos had shown himself unable or unwilling to respect the moral interests of Poland. Foreign relations and the army could not endure the fluctuations of the party game. The Premier was notorious for his unceremonious conduct, his encouragement of corruption, especially in the army, and his misbehaviour towards himself, even to seeking his death. He had begun the system which Sikorski followed. The Witos and Grabski ministries had impoverished Poland and halved the budget of the army. They held that, as soldiers are not electors, they have not full civic rights. Neglecting the honour of the service, they had often stretched out dirty hands to trouble the conscience of the army. But their dishonesty, corruption and spying were no secret, and he doubted whether any soldier would risk his life for such as they. The deputies imagined that the servants of the State could be changed about in consequence of buffet conversations between Witos and party leaders like himself!

"Mr. Witos", observed the interviewer, "has announced that the War portfolio would be disposed of in agreement with yourself. Has anything of that kind happened?" "Far from it," cried the Marshal. "I would never have chosen the candidate whom the papers name. It would be absurd to suppose that Mr. Witos, who thinks more of the elections than of anything else, would renounce his principle of using military influence only for his party aims." For these he had formerly made unauthorized use of Pilsudski's name.

The Marshal, however, declined to take up a suggestion of the interviewer with regard to the disposal of the portfolio by the President. Then came the final question. "Will your return to the army be delayed?" "Of course," replied the Marshal. "I shall do nothing to support such a glaring transgression of the moral interests of the State and of the army. I shall, as of old, make war against the chief evil of the State, the mastery over Poland by ungovernable groups and parties, which remember only pence and profits, and forget the imponderables."

Chapter XXXI

THE "EVENTS OF MAY" (1926)

THIS scathing denunciation by a soldier too irate to mince his words was met by the confiscation of the newspaper and by hints of the Marshal's prosecution. At the same time the tension in Warsaw and in the army was heightened by the news that at Sulejowek an attempt had been made upon his life. This news, and no premeditated manœuvre, brought troops from barracks some five miles distant to their champion's side, while his civilian admirers in Warsaw called on him to save the State. On 12 May, after a struggle as terrible as that before his march in August, 1920, he resolved to cut away the gangrene from the body politic, and led three regiments to Warsaw.

Three bridges over the broad Vistula formed the chief connection between the Praga suburb, on the east bank, which he first seized, and the main city on the western side, whose vital spots lay roughly parallel with the stream, at no great distance from it. The northern bridge carrying the railway approached the Citadel; the next led to the Castle and the Old Town; the third, renamed after Napoleon's Marshal, Poniatowski, to the chief railway station; while on the southern outskirts, more than two miles from the Castle, was the Belvedere. Having secured bridge-heads from the east bank into Warsaw, Pilsudski met the President on the Poniatowski bridge. Wojciechowski, though no soldier, was too brave a man to yield to threats of force. He commanded Pilsudski to desist from his rebellion, and refused to bargain at the new Premier's expense. Pilsudski, for his part, had not gone through the agony of decision only to abandon, after an official admonition, his duty of saving Poland. His position, indeed, was critical, for a few thousand men had a city of a million souls before them, the Citadel on their right flank, and rail communication open with Poznan, the stronghold of the government. On 12 May, Pilsudski could do little more than offer to the army and the nation an opportunity of judging between Witos and a better Premier. Many hold that his march was a demonstration with no other object.

Before nightfall, the government troops counter-attacked, but in vain. Pilsudski, aided by important captures of material, occupied the government offices, and the heart of the city, pushing the enemy southwards towards the Belvedere. Inspired by his presence, the rank and file did wonders, though ill-provisioned and hampered by the Warsaw crowd, on which they were loath to fire. He then conferred with the Speaker, Rataj, who undertook to mediate between him and Wojciechowski. That night, the Pressmen sought him out at Headquarters, and received, from one who confessed himself physically and morally exhausted, a brief but memorable statement.

"Though opposed to violence," he declared, "as I showed while Head of the State, I have brought myself, after a severe struggle, to a trial of strength, with all its consequences. All my life I have fought for what are called imponderables—honour, virtue, manhood and, in general, man's inward forces—not for profit for myself or for those about me. If the State is not to perish, there must not be too much injustice towards those who give their labour for others." The utter sadness of his face haunted one who saw it. "Imponderables" and "injustice" were the watchwords which permeated the weary mind, and disclosed, as

THE "EVENTS OF MAY"

often with Pilsudski, what was dominating his action at the time. Had he thought out a manifesto in advance, he could hardly have drafted one more advantageous, for intellectuals, Socialists, Jews and rural workers desired social justice no less than did the army, and had little cause to expect it from the government.

On 13 May, when assailed at once from the Citadel and from the Belvedere, Pilsudski's position showed its weakness. The troops in the Citadel, however, came over to his side: his tanks cut the Poznan railway: and the arrival of Rydz-Smigly and the Wilno garrison enabled him to advance towards the Belvedere. One cavalry regiment, he was proud to tell, had ridden eighty miles, but insisted on going into action. No Witos or even Wojciechowski could evoke such zeal. On the morning of 14 May, a further advance drove the enemy from the Belvedere, and the arrival of fresh support from Pomerania did not reverse the decision of the President and Premier to resign. Although Poznan was far from content to follow Warsaw, 15 May witnessed the formation of a new government headed by the popular Bartel, an engineer, who had risen from a simple railwayman to be Professor and Minister of Railways. The Polish civil war had lasted three days, and the total casualties, many accidental, fell short of a thousand. To his opponents, none the less, Pilsudski became the man who had brought Poland near to overthrow in 1920, and who now drowned law in blood. As he remembered the murder of Narutowicz, so not a few remembered the events of May.

Technically, at least, there was no revolution. The President had resigned, and, in strict accordance with the constitution, Speaker Rataj became Acting President, as he had done when Narutowicz was shot down. Like Wojciechowski on occasion, he conferred with Pilsudski and then commissioned a Premier-designate, in this case the popular Bartel, to enlist a cabinet if he could. Many deputies refused to serve, but a cabinet, largely extra-parliamentary, was promptly formed, with Pilsudski as Minister for War. This ministry proposed to serve until the National Assembly of Seym and Senate could meet to elect a President. Juridically, there had merely been unauthorized manœuvres by the army, which no one proposed to punish.

Actually, of course, Pilsudski had ventured all to effect a moral regeneration of Poland, and was now free to guide her as he would. His first appeal was, naturally, to the army. On 22 May, he addressed his fellow-soldiers as one who, like them, had an omnipresent sister in death, with her shears ready for those at whom God's finger pointed. Let the most dear blood that had been shed for Poland sow the seeds of a new brotherhood between them! he cried. Let the contention in the streets of Warsaw be a lovers' quarrel! Himself they knew as their old comrade, and, if all did not love him, they must all honour him, both for his victories and because amid general corruption he had sought no private gain. "May God have mercy on our sins and stay His chastening hand!" was his prayer, and he bade them work together for the regeneration of their country.

Next day, a French interviewer found him at Sulejowek, resting and quietly considering the future, without fear of the "demoralized and partisan generals" who were his foes. He said little of public affairs, but insisted on showing off his daughters, chatterboxes of six and eight. A few days later, however, he gave important statements both to the French visitor and to a Polish colleague. He explained for publication in France that the existing powers of a President

THE "EVENTS OF MAY"

in Poland were far too small. He was expected to defend his country and its dignity, but without the necessary means. Poznan had been somewhat Germanized, but was far from desiring separation. Fascism would not suit Poland, a land of small local organizations. The country needed peace, but it lay in her nature and in his own to defend themselves when they were attacked. Although a strong man who loved to make his own decisions, he did not like dictatorships, nor did he believe that the Poles deserved to be governed by the stick. The next generation would be still better. The President, however, should be enabled to make swift decisions on questions of national importance. While it would be unwise for Poland to imitate the United States, a federation of units with great autonomy, she might well move in that direction.

He was weary, he said, of Lefts and Rights, who had failed to solve the social question. Poland had no desire to copy the subversive experiment of Russia. She was too new and poor for great adventures, as he had seen when he returned from Magdeburg. Not party, but a great effort of honesty, was what she needed.

For the Polish public he traced the origin and history of the *coup d'état*, stressing, perhaps for the first time, his desire to free Poland from the domination of "money barons", who, by corruption, had gained wealth and power. The final impetus to his decision, he declared, had been given by the formation once again of a government of the unpunished murderers of Narutowicz. These men tried to show their strength by confiscating the report of his interview. It was against them, not against the President, that he struck, and he regretted that the President had brought about the ridiculous meeting on the bridge, instead of refusing to represent those who dared not face Pilsudski.

It was to spare the President that he had attacked by the other bridge. He had made various attempts at mediation, but in vain. It therefore now remained to legalize with all speed the accomplished fact. Although he trusted in his own strength and internal worth, he abjured dictatorship, because the Poles too readily threw all the burden upon one man, while the co-operation of many was needed for a real reformation.

Aided by troops who had shown marvellous self-restraint, he claimed to have achieved something unknown in history—a revolution without revolutionary consequences. The enemy had committed many outrages, from attacking a hospital to sending aeroplanes to frighten his wife and children. As to his candidature for the Presidency, he would not be the sole candidate. He would like to see an undertaking by all the candidates that they would not bind themselves to parties in the Seym, or to banks, or to business concerns. It was shameful, moreover, that the President, the representative of all Poland, should be fettered by so many oaths as were imposed upon him by the constitution.

In supplementary interviews, he spoke of the handicap to Poland involved in the inheritance of antiquated institutions from three different empires. He would not be the candidate of Left or Right. The constitution, as he had said in 1922, gave the deputies so many privileges, and so much braking-power, that the President was doomed to boredom. He himself had a passionate love for such work as produced swift results, and he found long and fruitless discussions hard to bear. Public opinion might now be ripe for a better system, but parties and cliques were wont to cling closely to what they had secured. He wished for a non-party government, strong, as one based on "long and involved discussions of clubs, parties, cliques, cliquelets and conventicles" could never be. In the army, attempts to gain allowances by self-mutilation were severely punished, and nepotism in State service should fare no better. The President, not the Seym, should make the government.

On 29 May, two days before the momentous election, Pilsudski addressed a meeting of the spokesmen of the chief parties in the Seym, the National Democrats excepted. He explained that he spoke not as a candidate for the Presidency, but, at Bartel's request, to explain his own views on the *rôle*, hitherto a hard one, which the President must play. He would not discuss the events of May, for which he was answerable only to his conscience. Poland had been made poor and weak by the unpunished wickedness of selfish men and parties. National regeneration had not gone beyond the army. As a democrat, he was saddened by the rise of parties so numerous that the public could not understand them, which united only to oppose the representative of Poland. He himself had not succumbed, because he was stronger than them all. His first successor had been murdered, and the next collapsed under the torture caused by the parliament.

They could choose a President freely, but he warned them against party arrangements to this end. The candidate must stand above parties and represent the whole people. Failing this, he would not protect the deputies when they ventured into the streets. The President must be free to choose his ministers without party pressure. They must elect a non-party man worthy of his high position. As for himself, they might make him a candidate if they pleased: he cared not how many or how few votes he might receive. The President should for a time be unencumbered by Seym and Senate. His own programme, he said before dismissing them, was to reduce rascality and to trace out the path of honour. He would wait, but he warned them that he would not change. "I will pursue the thieves" were the last words of an allocation perhaps unique as addressed to the party leaders of a democratic country.

On 31 May, Pilsudski was elected President by a majority of 3 : 2 against the candidate of the Right. He had consented to stand, but had stated unequivocally that he was by temperament ill-fitted for the office as it stood, and that, whoever was elected, the rules needed drastic change. If, then, he accepted, it would be in the expectation that the constitution would at once be revised at his dictation. The fulfilment of such an expectation, however, would be an unimaginable breach with the whole of Poland's past. Only war or the threat of war, foreign or domestic, could induce the deputies to reduce their own power and to resign the actual sovereignty to a fellow-official, chosen by an unstable majority among themselves. If Pilsudski would achieve his programme, it must be by exerting influence from outside the Belvedere. When the result was announced, he said at once that he had no intention of accepting the office. The vote, indeed, justified in a considerable degree the march on Warsaw. If the senile parliament endorsed an act of violence directed against its own misuse of power, it was probable that the nation viewed it with still greater favour.

Later in the day, in a letter of thanks addressed to the Speaker, he carefully explained his position. As in February, 1919, he wrote, his action had received parliamentary approval. He was grateful to the electors for not making it unanimous: there might be less falsehood and treachery in Poland. But he could not forget the murder of Narutowicz, nor the brutal attack upon his own children. He must repeat that he could not live

THE "EVENTS OF MAY"

without immediately fruitful work, and that the office needed a man of a different stamp. He asked the forgiveness of his supporters, within the Assembly and outside, but his conscience would not allow him to comply.

Next day, on 1 June, 1926, the parliament again assembled for the election. By a somewhat smaller majority, Pilsudski's candidate, Professor Moscicki, was elected, with the happiest consequences. An exact contemporary and a revolutionary colleague of Pilsudski in London thirty years before, he had gained great distinction in the world of electricity and chemistry as a teacher both in Switzerland and in Galicia. Combining rare powers of research with a real talent for organization, he gave Poland a high place among the producers of artificial fertilizers—a notable boon to an overwhelmingly agricultural country. Modest, kindly, dignified and athletic, he made an ideal representative of the Republic, and, for the remainder of Pilsudski's life, a collaborator whom he could both respect and love. Moscicki, for his part, recognized in the Marshal the supreme Polish patriot and benefactor, a friend and a fellow-servant with whose asperities he was content to bear.

The advent of Moscicki coincided with a sudden development of Polish trade, favoured by the coal strike and general strike in England. The new President, moreover, brought into the service of the State an energetic assistant, Kwiatkowski, who developed factories, and once again pressed on the construction of the new port at Gdynia. Aided by American advice, Poland acquired a modest degree of economic freedom, and this at once improved her status among the Powers. Pilsudski could set out upon his new mission with more reason for hope than had existed eight years before.

CHAPTER XXXII

THE PILSUDSKI *RÉGIME* (JUNE, 1926–1927)

THE early days of June, 1926, were spent in the usual formalities of installing a new President and a new ministry. Bartel, of course, returned, but could he prevail upon Pilsudski to serve as Minister for War? The Marshal, since Sikorski and his friends were now disposed of, consented, on conditions which he carefully laid down. To combine the letter of the constitution with that clear commission which the army administration needed, the President was to declare that he understood that the Command-in-Chief should be vested in a single person. Pilsudski's resignation was to be placed in the Premier's hands for use at any moment, and an official spokesman for the army was to be appointed.

When, in the usual August celebrations, he addressed the Legionaries at Kielce, where a few hundred of them had first invaded Russia, he found in the retrospect of his "whole long life" no little ground for hope. The Legions, he maintained, in 1914 had far less reason to expect success than had their predecessors in the risings of 1830 and of 1863. Yet they had fared much better. Their example proved to all men that to be bold in thought and action was sometimes better than to cackle in a marsh.

The summer of 1926, indeed, may well have ranked among the happiest of Pilsudski's life. His health was good; his domestic happiness, unclouded; his fame, secure. A revolution which no enemy could ascribe to any other man had opened the way, as he not unreasonably believed, to the regeneration of Poland. Hard work in plenty lay to his hand, and his thoroughness in every detail made it harder. President and Premier were his friends, and in his hands the army must be safe. Early in August, his plans for strengthening the executive and for reorganizing the army administration acquired the force of law.

Economy, it is true, must still be rigid, and taxation high, but times had perceptibly improved; while Poland, like Spain, with the ultimate assent of Germany, gained a seat on the Council of the League and a special possibility of re-election. The one cloud on the horizon was the hostility of the Seym to his *régime*. Though forced to abdicate its predominance, it could still obstruct the government, and it did. To appeal to the country, as the President now had power to do, might not improve the situation, for regeneration meant present hardship, and most electors are careless of the future. Except in a national emergency, their well-known "partyism" was more attractive to the Poles than was stern discipline by Pilsudski.

In September, 1926, the Seym drove Bartel to resign, but he received a new commission from the President, and the same ministers returned to office. The National Democrats, however, attacked the budget, with marked success in both Houses. In the Seym, their victory was overwhelming, and Bartel was swept away. Pilsudski's remedy was to become Premier himself, with a cabinet of efficient supporters from all parties, and with Bartel as Vice-premier.

One consequence of the Marshal's decision was that the man who was destined to become his Boswell, and, later, Premier of Poland, gained frequent access to his person. This was the army doctor and ex-Legionary General Skladkowski, the humblest of hero-worshippers, simple, self-sacrificing and effective. The events of May had left him

Government Commissary in Warsaw, and the Ministry of the Interior learned his value.

On 1 October, he was summoned to the Belvedere. The Marshal, whom he affectionately thought of as "the Commandant", though he was not of the small circle that could so address him, to his joy looked well and flattered him with an unceremonious reception. He shook hands across the patience-table, pointed to a chair and said, "Well now, you are to be Minister of the Interior, for M— won't work any longer with this . . . Seym." As the Marshal had ceased to speak, Skladkowski uttered modest murmurs about his ignorance of politics, and the like. "Politics are not necessary in this case," replied the Marshal, smiling. "They all praise your administration, so you will be Minister. Report to Mr. Bartel. Good-bye." And, as though bored by the conversation, he bent down his head and dealt the cards, without shaking hands, giving the impression that he shared Skladkowski's own modest estimate of his powers.

This fear, however, happily vanished in the following month. The Marshal, in radiant humour, then surprised the Cabinet by attending their meeting, and asked Skladkowski why he wore no sword. "To be the only armed man would give me an unfair advantage," was the reply, received so jovially that thereafter he felt sure of his ground. As a medical man he had another line of approach to Pilsudski, whose zeal for physical education was often evident, while as a general he could speak familiarly with the Marshal's adjutants. He thus gained a rare knowledge of his moods and methods, and when those old comrades whom the Marshal loved were present, Skladkowski often saw or heard of it. Even before his sixtieth birthday, however, the Marshal's testy humour was more often visible than his enchanting sunshine.

THE PILSUDSKI RÉGIME

Three further glimpses of Pilsudski during the autumn of 1926 suggest something of his variety and of the Poland with which his "disguised dictatorship" had now to deal. In the campaign of 1920, one of his adjutants, a member of the historic house of Radziwill, had been killed. On 25 October, the anniversary of his death, the Marshal journeyed to the famous seat of the family to lay a military Order on his tomb. "Beyond doubt," he said, "his spirit is with us, while his Commander is your guest." The chivalry of Poland had gathered to meet him, and two of his ministers were in his train. The visit had political importance, as it gave evidence of his avowed purpose of uniting men of goodwill from every party in the service of the State. It occasioned the rumour that he was aiming at the crown of Poland, a twin brother to the rumour that he would make Poland the vanguard of a great anti-Bolshevist crusade.

Soon afterwards, the approach of the anniversary of Polish independence on Armistice Day brought a request that he would broadcast to the nation. His theme, eight years after the Great War, and six months after the events of May, was naturally Poland's emancipation, and the need for her regeneration. Its development reveals so much of his mind and art as to claim at least a compressed translation of almost half its length. This may suffice to indicate how the memories of the retreat from Kielce and of later triumphs could be treated by a Polish father.

"Two dear little ones", said the Marshal, "are sitting by me and begging for a tale. So I will tell the ladies and gentlemen a tale for children and grown-ups alike. 'As much happiness as in a dream, as much truth as in a song.' So one man wrote, and we who read sometimes believe him and sometimes not. But today I tell you truly that there are charms and spells, so long as we are happy. Once I saw a crowd of children bending over something on the ground. Wondering what they could find to look at in a dirty courtyard, I espied a little frog. Filthy and frightened, the frog hopped clumsily on its long legs and glared at the children with its goggle eyes.

"'What are you gazing at?' I asked the little ones. One lad answered that he had read of a frog which was jumping about in the dirt, but suddenly, by charms and spells, there came a great golden chariot drawn by six big horses. Six big lackeys held their bridles, and from the chariot ladies alighted dressed too gorgeously for words. They took a box from the chariot, and—oh! charms and spells!—the frog turned suddenly into a magic maiden, with lovely eyes and countenance.

"The maiden looked at herself and marvelled. For her robes were gleaming with pearly-white and rose colour shot with gold and silver. Snow-white stockings covered her legs, which had been red with cold, but now were so warm that they gleamed like white marble through the silk. The dirty frog, transformed into a charming maiden, took her place in the chariot and drove to a great white palace. The parquet mirrored her beauty, and maidens, yellow with envy, whispered that she was an evil changeling. So there are charms and spells when a maiden is happy. They say that on earth there are no such tales.

"'I do not know if fairy-tales are true, but it is true that there are charms and spells when one is very happy. I have heard with my own ears, I have seen with my own eyes, I have touched with my own fingers such charms and spells that of them I fear to speak. None of us, indeed, may have seen the dear child who was picking strawberries and suddenly espied a forest where, instead of branches, the trees grew cakes, ready to break off and eat. Who has seen the child who, as he hopped, found himself in an enchanted garden where magic birds chirped joyously between themselves? Or the dear girl in that garden where big juicy pears came of their own accord to her lips, and red apples dropped into her pocket? Such, I believe, exist, and I will tell you about the wonder of wonders that I have touched and seen.

"On a bright November day, not many years ago, along a road drowned everywhere in mud, a short grey serpent of lads big and small pressed forward. Like the clumsy frog, they wearily stumbled on, often stamping with frozen legs on the grey and marshy track. Poor fellows! they were hunched up and trembling with cold, their eyes dimmed by a toilsome night and many toilsome days. Their feet, soaked through their worn-out, mud-caked shoes, stumbled over the ground, lingering as though they clung to it for a moment's rest. On the eleventh of November, they found themselves somewhere under the walls of Cracow. Before them rode another lad—rode on a young chestnut with a white-starred head.

"The chestnut, daughter of the meadows, went mincingly into the town whence came those ragged lads, who now, as dirty as the earth itself, marched in. They had marched the whole night long, with death always staring them in the face. They had marched through the gate of death, through its strait and stifling portal. Like the frog, they longed to stumble into safety—safety within the walls of Cracow. But the country chestnut with the hairless head gazed on the city with disgust. When she reached the first houses, a scarecrow lorry came along, groaning and hissing, and she jibbed in terror. The lad upon her back caressed her and began to tell her of charms and spells. 'Fear not, chestnut,' he murmured, 'you are going into the capital, where thousands will gaze upon your lovely neck and golden hair.' For in Cracow there are charms and spells when a lad is happy, whether they be in the twin-towered church, or in the mighty bell, or in the crypt where kings for ever sleep, or in the hero's or the poet's tomb.

"Not many years passed by, and the same chestnut gazed upon the same city on a new eleventh of November. Charm on charm and spell on spell—where were the grey and dirty lads, and where their leader? The same leader, but see how he has changed! On his breast as many stars as there are countries in the world. Trumpets and drums sounded as the infantry, in their steel helmets, marched firmly by, and the heavy guns made the windows rattle as they passed. An enchanted world, transformed!

"But my time is up, and I must close with a wish for the next eleventh of November. Even if the month brings storms which roar in the chimney and shriek of death and terror, I know that restoration of the body and the soul's rebirth give strength and beauty. In them we find an inward warmth which baffles the damp and poison. And may you smile then as on the magic eleventh of November in 1918! May the autumn sun burn your cheeks and a gentle breeze cool them, and may we laugh together from happiness at being great-souled and reborn! This, men and women and dear children, I wish you all."

In mid-December, 1926, the Marshal gave a memorable proof both of his desire to collaborate with the Seym, if possible, and of his powers of self-control. In its struggle with the executive, parliament could still dispose of two formidable weapons, votes of no confidence and budget cuts. These had driven Bartel from the helm and compelled Piłsudski to take his place. With Christmas in sight, however, it voted the sum proposed by the government. On this, Piłsudski joined freely and fully in the debate on army administration, and took the Seym into his confidence. As usual, his speech was marked by originality and width of view, as well as by expert knowledge. Confronted with such rough-and-ready prescriptions as "Halve the men, and double the money spent on equipment", or, "Introduce the Swiss system", he pointed to the real weaknesses and needs of Poland.

The Poles, he said, unlike the Ruthenes and White Russians, learned the rudiments of soldiering quickly, but they were slow to become efficient. They had not, like the Swiss, an inclination to join the army. Each regiment must provide recruiting agents. The number of illiterates was a great handicap. The country was poor, and the Swiss system the most costly of all. Poland had a general bias towards over-administration, which meant that the number of officers employed was disproportionate to the number of those who could lead troops and train them. The army was also hampered by the system of monthly budgets—an evil aggravated by the sudden rise of prices. He was arranging that the monthly expenditure should be uniform, and that the pressure of the administrative officers on the army budget should be reduced. Given universal military service, he would produce a plan for adminishing the length of service. He must stress reserves and armament.

Next day, the need of an efficient and contented army was emphasized by a sudden outbreak in Lithuania, which resulted in the ill-fated Premiership of Waldemaras. Good relations between Poland and Lithuania were Pilsudski's constant aim, but one which always escaped him. On Christmas Eve, 1926, he gave an interview on the subject. Lithuania, he said, in a fashion unique in Europe, refused to recognize a state of peace with Poland, and any unbalanced Lithuanian might perform some act of war. He knew the frontier lands too well not to realize the misery which the Lithuanian attitude caused to their inhabitants. He would never do more than order the utmost readiness and observation. All Press reports to the contrary had no foundation.

For more than a month, he declared, Poland had known that a *coup d'état* in Lithuania was imminent, but more than one group was concerned, and it was difficult to forecast the outcome. The deposed government rested on a majority in the recently elected Seym. The present situation was provisional, but provisional situations sometimes proved the most enduring. He saw no probability of fresh complications, and only hoped that, under Waldemaras, their unquiet neighbour would turn towards moderation and peace.

Throughout the new year, 1927, Pilsudski followed in the main the formula of "Work, not words", which he prescribed for Poland. Both at home and abroad, the situation was easier, though as yet by no means easy. The factors of unrest were scotched, not killed, and while a strong *régime* relieved distress in Poland, it thereby strengthened the people to cry out for more. The deputies soon showed renewed impatience with the executive, especially when, having voted the budget, the parliament found itself adjourned. Bolshevist intrigues were traceable even in the Seym. The name of Waldemaras became a synonym for Lithuanian intransigence. Germany, which in the east

THE PILSUDSKI RÉGIME

had evaded the prescribed disarmament, seemed almost as hostile as Lithuania, and far more dangerous.

On the other hand, rocks ahead made the Poles less willing to drop their pilot, and their frontiers grew stronger by mere lapse of time. Meanwhile, the *régime* worked with energy and success to achieve regeneration. In the first days of the year, Pilsudski himself initiated a new Council of Physical Education, which at once set several sub-committees to work. Other new councils promoted economic progress, financial reform and national defence. Pilsudski's name was a pledge of the efficiency and enthusiasm of the army. Never provocative, he spoke plainly and firmly to both his great neighbours, when they appeared to menace Poland. Germany, in particular, was forced to hear that Poland would never consent to frontier revision, and was constrained to abolish her illegal fortresses.

On the side of foreign affairs, the year 1927 was brought to an appropriate end when, in December, Pilsudski appeared in person at Geneva, to end, if possible, the dispute with Lithuania. Thanks to Lithuania, this had reached the stage of a mutual persecution of minorities, and the League found it hard to establish tolerable relations between the two States. Face to face with Waldemaras at the Council meeting, Pilsudski insisted on learning from him whether he would have peace or war. The Lithuanian could only answer "Peace", and on this, Pilsudski straightway shook hands with him and returned to Poland. In the eyes of the world, the *régime* was gathering credit by its policy of vigorous peace.

The Seym, meanwhile, had been playing an uphill game against the government. Pilsudski and his friends, keeping strictly within the rules of the newly revised constitution, were legislating by Presidential decree, and adjourning the dissentient Seym by Presidential order. They thus prevented their critics from dissolving when this seemed opportune, and secured an interval in which to prepare for an election in March, 1928. By that time the rising prosperity of the country might well have brought them an electoral advantage.

In such circumstances to improve the army and to regenerate the State were tasks which pressed heavily upon Pilsudski, the main motor of the *régime*. From this time forward, except when travelling for his health, his private life may almost be said to vanish. Soon a foreign journalist could declare that the peace of Europe lay in the hands of a recluse. Like Narutowicz, he came more and more to exist only for the State. Even the famous patience-table was merely a contrivance for giving his eager brain a little necessary rest. Chess became an unattainable delight. At midsummer, however, when the bones of his favourite poet, Slowacki (1809–1849), were brought from Paris to the Wawel, the Westminster Abbey of Poland, the Marshal went to Cracow, and rose to the height of the occasion in his address. "Let us not weep for Slowacki. Throughout all Poland, as his coffin is borne along, men greet him as a living man, uttering no farewell, and bells ring out, not in grief but in joy and triumph. . . . I dare to say that for some men the gates of death have no existence." In servitude Slowacki had striven to make strength of soul prevail over the power of the sword. A king of men, he now rested in the burying-place of kings. Such was the tribute paid by his lifelong disciple to the poet, whose work had done much to keep Poland's soul alive.

On 7 August, 1927, the Legionaries met at Kalisz, near the western boundary of Russian Poland, some sixty miles from Warsaw. There they celebrated the tenth anniversary of their confinement in a concentration camp by unveiling a memorial on its site. Pilsudski closed his own address with a strong denunciation of Polish proneness to accept fees from foreign sources, so that a magnate with a palace on the scale of the Vatican took 150 ducats yearly from Catherine II—a sum that he could well afford to stake upon a losing card. "Abhor those Poles who serve foreign Powers" was the Marshal's final word to his old comrades.

Meanwhile, in Lithuania, the Waldemaras government was moving towards that conflict with Poland which occasioned Pilsudski's December journey to Geneva. At the end of November, he had given an extremely frank and pungent interview of no little biographical interest. The beginnings of Lithuanian mobilization, he confessed, had caused him to spend a whole night in seeking to decide on his own course of action. If he mobilized, and war followed, victory would be certain, but the border regions might suffer before aid could come. If he delayed mobilization, every hour gave the enemy an advantage. Following the highest dictates of State necessity, he decided to appeal to the League of Nations. Waldemaras, long a Russian, and then a German before he became a Lithuanian, seemed to be irresponsible for his actions. When Pilsudski went to Wilno in October for the anniversary of its occupation by Zeligowski, Waldemaras had proclaimed that this was a threat against the Lithuanian State. As the price of peace he had proposed that Poland should undertake to send a quota of goods through Memel, exposing them to Lithuanian confiscation on the way.

Pilsudski now appealed to his fellow-countrymen to show the utmost calm in the face of threats made while the sword was wielded by a madman, and of the false news that would doubtless circulate. They would thereby disappoint their enemies. They should receive with kindness fugitives from Lithuanian persecution. Poles had known the bitterness of exile, and to their exiled poets they owed the strengthening of their nation's soul.

Thus the Marshal spoke with no less firmness to Lithuania than recently to Russia. Even by appearing before the Council of the League, however, he did not terminate the Lithuanian question. Ten years later, the Polish-Lithuanian frontier was still closed, and Poles complained that it was used for smuggling into their country vast quantities of dutiable goods, including some that debauched the population. But Waldemaras had at last uttered words at least negativing war, and the grateful Pilsudski could order a *Te Deum* to be sung in every church in Poland. If the two nations were at peace, they must in time acknowledge a common frontier.

To a French interviewer on the same day, he admitted his debt to France for her share in this joyful success. "What is your impression of the League?" was the rejoinder. The Marshal paused, perhaps seeking the exact equivalent in French for what he thought. "There is much good in it," he answered in effect, "and it has done good work. But I think that, in its decisions, realities are somewhat lost in formulae. And, while undoubtedly it is easy to settle questions in friendly talk over breakfast or tea, the importance to those represented may be forgotten. Men who meet several times a year may arrive at a common view on points about which their nations still differ." While delighted with this visit to Geneva, he did not like journeys with no set object, and he hoped that he would not be called upon to make another. That hope, as it proved, was realized.

Chapter XXXIII

CONSTITUTIONAL FRICTION (1928)

FOR the first half of the year 1928, Poland and her Premier were mainly concerned with questions of internal politics. In face of the revised constitution and Pilsudski's clear-cut programme of moral regeneration, parties regrouped themselves and left no stone unturned to attract the largely illiterate electors. A non-party *bloc* for collaboration with the government was formed, and the government saw to it that local officials recommended it to the countryside. A significant proof of Pilsudski's hold upon the people was the attempt of many among the 34 parties to claim that they had his support. When the votes were cast in March, he gained an undoubted victory. The *bloc* polled nearly 2,400,000 votes, while the Socialists did not reach 1,500,000. The National Democrats and the followers of Witos combined fell a little short of 1,700,000. About one-half of the valid votes were given to other groups.

All that could be said with confidence was that the Right and Centre had suffered a disaster; that, since Left and Right were unlikely to co-operate, the government should have a reasonable prospect of survival, provided that it did nothing violent and that prosperity continued; and that a *régime* which meant to dominate the Seym would find it an awkward instrument to handle. The National Minorities held 81 seats out of 444. While the German and White Russian representation remained stable, the Jews had lost heavily and the Ukrainians increased to 43—a welcome indication that more of them were willing to vote in a Polish election. In the Senate, the *bloc* was stronger, holding almost one-half of the seats.

Pilsudski, hoping for further changes which would strengthen the President and give the government more initiative in the Seym, set out once again on the path of collaboration. But, as he plainly told his supporters, the Seym did not exist to torment the government, and, if it would not collaborate, it must go. Cromwell, he reminded them, had cut down the power of parliament and saved his country. Poland should have a parliament, and not take up an exceptional position, like Italy or Russia. But parliament should meet only when there was something for it to do. The government needed fuller powers, especially for making treaties. Most Polish trade was with Germany and Russia, and smuggling was rife. Yet they could not come to terms with Germany until her elections were over, and then lack of full powers would hamper them.

On 27 March, 1928, the newly elected deputies assembled for the formal opening of the Seym. Pilsudski himself, in sky-blue uniform with Orders, began to read the President's inaugural address, which he himself and an assistant had composed. To guard against accidents, he had commissioned Skladkowski to attend him throughout the session, and that "administrator" had carefully surveyed the unfamiliar ground. While the Marshal was unrolling the address, the stillness was broken by a cry from the few Communists on the back benches, "Down with the Fascist government of Pilsudski!" "You will be turned out of the room," growled the Marshal. The cries grew louder. "Turn them out," said the Marshal to Skladkowski, who left his side, and re-entered behind the Communists with ten policemen. Then, while the Marshal, leaning on his sword, impassively surveyed the scene, the Left rushed at

Pilsudski and his family in 1928, during his virtual dictatorship.

CONSTITUTIONAL FRICTION

Skladkowski and his policemen in an overwhelming mass. Ten more police with rifles then appeared; the arrest was carried through; and the Marshal, who had commanded silence on pain of adjournment, read the address.

This touched on the vast improvement in the State of Poland, now allied with France and Rumania, and on her ardent wish to work for the preservation of peace. Collaboration with the government, and the remedying of "the universally felt defects of our constitution", were specially commended to the Seym. The Marshal then summoned the oldest member, a village teacher, to preside, and helped him out with a name that he found it hard to read. While the deputies were being sworn, he left the hall, significantly exhausted by the experience.

There followed the defeat of Bartel, the government candidate for the post of Marshal of the Seym. The old revolutionary and Legionary, Daszynski, was elected, and the Seym immediately plunged into the budget for the year beginning on 1 April, 1928. The government, meanwhile, was vainly endeavouring to profit by the negotiations with Lithuania. The proclamation of a new Lithuanian constitution, which claimed Wilno as the capital, was hardly a good omen for their success.

At midsummer, 1928, Pilsudski suddenly declared that he must resign. He was obviously feverish and exhausted, worn out by the incessant demands from all sides upon his attention, and irritated beyond endurance both by the unremedied defects of the constitution and by ceaseless friction with the Seym. The manner of his resignation was characteristic. The ministers were summoned to the presence of the President, and there informed by Pilsudski that they had all resigned. He was prepared to go on until the President named his successor, and to remain Inspector-

General, with a prospect of returning at a later date to the Premiership, if so desired.

His grievances, as reported by Skladkowski, found vent in a series of feverish interjections. The Premier, he declared, was said by all to be omnipotent, which meant impotent. There should be several heads of the Cabinet serving in rotation. If he were to serve further, the War Minister's budget must be made a reality. When his strength failed and he ceased to speak, the President expressed his pleasure at hearing that he would take the needful rest, and his hope that he would then return to harness. He then called on the ministers to do honour to the Marshal's services as Premier by rising from their seats, and the painful scene was over.

Five days later, when Bartel had become Premier once again, with only two ministerial changes, Pilsudski gave one of the fullest and frankest of his interviews. The tone and texture show that the prospect of freedom had already raised his spirits, while the repetition of phrases uttered at the meeting of the Cabinet suggests that on both occasions he was speaking from well-ruminated thought. Before consenting to say anything, he stipulated, first, that his exact words should be printed without abridgement, and, second, that the newspaper should contribute handsomely to a private charity of his own. He then revealed that the doctors found his health undamaged except for overwork, a danger which he had courted all his life.

The prime cause of his resignation, he said, was the grotesquely exacting character of the Premiership as prescribed by the existing constitution. The President, no less absurdly, possessed so little power that he must feel himself a mere foundling. The man who, by his victorious war and strength of character, had rescued Poland from chaos and given her far wider bounds than the world intended—for him the Constituent prepared so bitter and despicable a life as only savage and monstrously stupid minds could devise. He himself had stepped aside with a contemptuous smile, but his successor they had first insulted and then done to death, as a lesson to their rival for the sovereignty. On the other hand, they had given the Premier great power, but so many duties that, if he performed them conscientiously, he could originate nothing of his own.

What little he himself had effected in almost two years as Premier, had been made possible by deputing much of his "omnipotence" to Bartel. The Premier's energy was spent in suckling the offspring which his colleagues had abandoned, and in composing the quarrels in which they, as true Poles, engaged. The "harmonizing" process expressly enjoined by the constitution involved such masses of typescript that he had never once attempted it, for fear of being driven into a madhouse. The ludicrous passion of the Poles for centralization caused his time to be frittered away over trifles, such as permission to enter the French Foreign Legion, while the widespread belief in private influence brought him appeals for all kinds of intervention. He agreed with his doctors that the inner tension due to the fulfilment of so many duties was damaging his health.

The worst of all was the dismal task of collaborating with the Seym. When he saw his small daughters solemnly giving orders to their dolls, which they themselves fulfilled, or, at dinner, putting spoonfuls to their porcelain lips, he looked on smiling, but confessed that he could not join in. But when the would-be sovereign deputies did the like in their work, he could not endure it. It was absurd to make work depend on speeches. He himself could stir an audience, turn a phrase, and make his hearers hang upon his lips.

But if he were bidden to speak daily for weeks together, he would regard himself as a scarecrow. Yet deputies did this for months, while the audience behaved as though they were in a public-house. Only the ministers preserved any decorum. While the deputies hurled insults at them and at each other, they, receiving a pittance for their frantic labour, must make a show of reverence for the Seym. The deputies were free to make speeches without a word to the point, and dull enough to cause stomach-ache.

In the last Seym, which he always called the Seym of corruption, he had to make the closing speech, and found the atmosphere of accumulated boredom poisonous. "Even the flies", he quoted, "cannot bear your prattle, gentlemen, and, when they try to spread their wings, they fail, half dead from boredom." A great French parliamentarian had compared such work with that of a heavy railway-engine under full steam drawing after it a pin. In Pilsudski's eyes it resembled the treadmill, which, to please the Chartists, who objected to the competition of prison goods, had been made the penalty of Hard Labour. "I will add," he continued, "to avert any misunderstanding, that I myself, as dictator of Poland, summoned the Seym; that when, after a victorious war, I could have crushed the Seym of prostitutes like vermin, I refrained; that, as Premier, I always acted more constitutionally than the Seym; and that, therefore, no one can accuse me of lack of democratic convictions." The Seym should not identify its methods with democracy.

When the third Seym also proved incompatible, he had the choice between standing at the disposal of the President to proclaim a new order in Poland, and leaving it to others to collaborate with the Seym. He chose the latter, advising the President to look beyond Bartel and himself. In any severe crisis, he would serve again, and, at the wish of President and Premier, the direction of Foreign Affairs was to remain in his hands.

It was unfortunate that a prominent version of this interview in *The Times* should have formed the chief source from which the British public was likely to derive its notion of Pilsudski. With every allowance for the indiscretion of a soldier and patriot brought near breaking-point by overwork, calumny and perhaps deep-seated physical disorder, the violence was not hysteria, and the personality revealed was unattractive. When a statesman proclaimed himself an orator and a hero, and his opponents vermin and assassins, much previous knowledge of himself and Poland was needed for a due appreciation of his real character.

Reading of ministers and parliament, a British reader could hardly fail to picture a body built up by centuries of experience, chosen by literate electors, itself empowering some of its own best members to fill offices with the aid of skilled and incorruptible civil servants. For Poland, this picture was almost wholly incorrect. Pilsudski, again, as self-drawn in a single utterance, was equally unreal. What in all this outpouring could suggest that the speaker was normally a man of distinguished humanity and courtesy, a leader so inspiring that a trooper rode with a broken leg rather than fail to ride before him, and that Skladkowski was proud to publish, so far as they were printable, the censures of his Commandant upon himself? Like Napoleon and many a lesser man, Pilsudski looked with wonder and awe upon the long miracle of his endowment and career, and, to homage truth and benefit his country, was ready to act as his own prophet. The critic who, none the less, sometimes finds his invective indecent and his boasting intolerable, may at least remember that he was struggling to keep Poland parliamentary in a world which was turning towards easier forms of rule.

The thunderer against the Seym soon departed to take his little girls to the seaside. August brought its accustomed celebration of the Legion's march in 1914, and at Wilno, for what proved to be the last time, he addressed his "dear colleagues". In Wilno, he said, where he had learned to fall in love, and whither his longing thoughts had turned from Magdeburg and from the Belvedere—in Wilno he could utter no jarring or angry word. He therefore turned to analyse the meaning of an adjective (miły) with much of the significance of "sweet" or "gentle", showing the place held by the notion in the minds of children, and how men clung to it until their death. Their own meetings, he said, were merry through and through, and, from the first outbreak of war, theirs had been the joy which comes with the thought of national regeneration. Among his own memories of the campaigns there stood out some of the Legionaries' peculiar kindness to himself, and of such he told several stories: the first, that of a sentry with the face and heart of a child, whom he found weeping because he could not give the Commandant a treat.

In Wilno as a boy he had dreamed much of Napoleon. When he returned to the Belvedere, he remembered how ill Napoleon rode, and how once he called one of the Guard clumsy for falling off his horse. "But God", he said, "chastised him, for after riding sixty yards further, he too fell off, and the guardsman at full gallop caught up with him and asked, 'Who is clumsy now?'" A moving tribute to Wilno, where his heart dwelt (and dwells) in the burying-ground amid the ranked battalions of those who fell for Polish freedom, a tender farewell to the Legions, and the speech was over. It had proved that the man who flung insults at the Seym was at heart a poet.

A week later (19 August, 1928), Pilsudski set out for a six weeks' holiday in Rumania. So long an absence showed that both Poland and her foreign politics were fairly tranquil. Employment and trade were, in fact, advancing, and, while Danzig dealt with an unprecedented tonnage, the rising port of Gdynia handled almost one-fourth of that amount. The dispute with Lithuania, indeed, dragged on, and Germany from time to time showed that her wounds still ached. Every month of peace, however, continued to strengthen Poland's prescriptive right to her possessions, and her tradition as a member of the European circle. In August, she joined in signing the Kellogg Pact for the outlawry of war. Pilsudski's visit to Rumania helped to confirm the second among her alliances, and her relations with the Baltic States continued intimate.

For some six months after he laid down the Premiership, Pilsudski departed but seldom from the ordinary routine. In November, he appears to have been somewhat seriously ill, and winter always tried him. Occasionally, however, he published a brief essay, which showed that his powers of thought and expression were unimpaired. He continued his unquestioned domination over President, Premier and Cabinet alike. To a discreet colleague he might say that in Poland power came from three sources, the President, himself and Bartel, and that no one should seek it in the Seym. Such, it was widely understood, was his theory of the government, and in practice his mastery of the two remaining sources was well known. This, however, was no novelty, and no public proclamation of the fact took place. The sharp clash between Seym and government in February, 1929, was in no other sense provoked by him.

Chapter XXXIV

RÉGIME v. SEYM (1929)

EARLY in February, the *bloc* embodied Pilsudski's well-known ideas in a new constitutional project, which they submitted to the Seym. In place of election by parliament, the President was to be installed for seven years by a *plébiscite* of the whole people, whose power he then would obviously embody. When parliament was sitting, he could introduce and veto laws; at other times he could issue decrees. His control of the government was qualified only by the power of an absolute majority of the parliament to drive it from office. Such a project would have been more appropriately introduced when the political sky was darkening, than when the progress of Poland was still unchecked. The Seym, it was clear, would struggle to escape self-mutilation. Even the *bloc* showed signs of splitting, and the extreme Pilsudskists, under Slawek, received the nickname of "the Colonels' party". The latent antagonism between Seym and government found vent in a motion to impeach the Finance Minister, despite his distinguished service, for spending large sums without parliamentary consent.

Pilsudski's impulse in his warmer moments, as he confessed to a trusty friend, was to have one or two hundred of the scoundrelly deputies hanged or shot; then, he growled, there would be order and peace in Poland. But he knew the lifelong strength of his own passions, avoided violence in deed, and strove to be as parliamentary as he could. Although he sent no representative of the War Ministry to the budget committee, or to the Seym, when it debated the war budget, on 28 February he complimented the more moderate Senate by himself taking part in their discussion. To them he explained that the procedure in the Seym on budget questions was antiquated and unsatisfactory, and that his officers could not appear there because it was incompatible with their honour to listen to insults without resort to action. He then asserted that, in comparison with 1924, the army budget had been cut down by one-third.

Reviewing the heads of expenditure and the reductions made by the Seym, he showed how the cost of military display had been much reduced by his own distaste for it, how a great part of the expense of entertainment fell on the officers, and how spying was nowhere so much practised as in Poland, "the spy's paradise". The "Funds at disposal", which the Seym had reduced by one-fourth, should, he contended, be voted in full. This, by a majority of two votes, the Senate refused (11 March, 1929). Next day, a patriotic society appealed to the public to contribute the amount of the deficiency, and subscriptions began to come in. On 20 March, the Seym resolved by almost two to one to impeach the minister. Their action was tantamount to the impeachment of Pilsudski for applying public funds to influence the elections.

The Marshal's rejoinder took the form of an appeal to the masses in their own vernacular. On 7 April, during the recess, a newspaper published his article, "The Bottom of the Eye, or the Impressions of a Sick Man on regarding the Budgetary Session of the Seym". Last year, he explained, when he fell ill of a mysterious sickness and the doctors were struggling to find the cause, one of them said to his colleagues, "We have forgotten to investigate the bottom of the eye; we will do it tomorrow." This left a patient, who did not know that his eye had a bottom, fearful lest he should play the coward before the tortures which might be in store. When the operation proved to be a painless trifle, he wondered whether it would not be more reasonable to frighten people less.

He told this absurd story, he declared, because the majority in the Seym had such a "bottom of the eye", in their proposed impeachment. They were impeaching a most successful minister for what was done when Pilsudski was too ill to be fully cognizant of transactions for which he, like Bartel, was ready to assume responsibility. No tribunal in the world could reject the testimony of a witness that he, not the accused, was guilty. So stupid were the deputies, that he had thought of providing tutors to teach them how to put intelligible questions when ministers were being heard. But he could not doubt that the deputies would have grudged the expense, and that the tutors would have needed canes. One of the most intelligent of ministers quitted the Seym with the feeling of quitting a menagerie of spiteful apes.

When so ill as to be indifferent to everything except his children, said Pilsudski, he had advised that the Finance Minister should not resign, and that, if the budget were rejected, he himself would lead the Cabinet. But the minister insisted on standing trial for his honour's sake. Finally, on 29 March, the hostile deputies, whose leaders were caricatured without mercy, assembled a band of party warriors at the Seym. He much regretted that his illness kept him from attacking these bandits. But all had ended with an impeachment as farcical as the "bottom of the eye".

The article, written two days before, appeared on 7 April. Next day, the Marshal, through his attendant doctor, summoned Skladkowski to a meeting, of which the record is unsurpassed in characterizing both participants. The Marshal looked well and seldom coughed. The summons, he said, was to talk over Skladkowski's office. Either he himself or Switalski would be Premier. He would be glad to serve, but the President had warned him to take care of his health, and, as always, he had had the hard task of controlling his nerves. After an illustrative outburst against the Seym, he added that the weather was so bad that he might not be able to leave home, and so it must be Switalski. Would Colonel P— suit Skladkowski as Vice-minister? "It is an order," the ex-Legionary replied, but his astonishment showed in his face. A safe man as lieutenant was necessary, the Marshal explained, because the minister was, quite rightly, often absent. After a pause he added, "I am no Austrian swine to cheat you, but so it must be."

Years afterwards, Colonel P— confided that the Marshal had directed him to restore order in the office, as Skladkowski did nothing but drive about—a calumny which its victim ascribed to his false friends. The Marshal next nominated the head of the Border Defence Corps, and again Skladkowski replied, "It is an order." The Marshal's face then cleared and he interjected, "What do you think of my article?" "That it is shattering," answered Skladkowski. "The opposition dailies sound the retreat. Opinion in the Seym is surprised by your new attack. . . . They declare that they cannot do battle to harm Poland, or they fall back all along the line."

On this, he retired—dismissed, indeed, with cordial thanks, but humiliated by the arbitrary nominations.

The blow was shrewd and unexpected, but after a night of agitation, his ingrained loyalty prevailed. The Commandant remained the Commandant, and by hard work and loyalty, Skladkowski regained his confidence and kept it to the end. A week later, when Bartel took leave of his former colleagues, Pilsudski's gracious and cordial good humour relieved the pain of parting. He declared that the ex-Premier had notably improved the technique of government in Poland, and bade him stay away only so long as was necessary for his nerves and kidneys to be healed. Bartel was visibly moved by such gratitude.

Although the impeachment still lay ahead, victory in the struggle with the Seym plainly inclined towards the Marshal. The Left were meditating co-operation with the *bloc*. An agitator against the government heard from his peasant audience that the best reform would be to halve the salaries of such deputies as himself. In every department Pilsudski spoke as a master. His instructions to the police for May Day were to ignore shouts, songs and even fights, though if shots were fired, they must react with vigour. As War Minister, he decreed that the papers of the outgoing head of a department should be sealed, publicly charging those who succeeded himself with having stolen his papers and forged his signature.

In framing the budget, he addressed his colleagues for more than half an hour, deprecating fits and starts, either of optimism or the reverse, and strongly urging economy. Then, in mid-May, he took a few days' holiday in Wilno, and returned sunburned and radiant, stepping quickly along the platform and chatting with those ministers who had come to meet him. The waiting crowd, probably from their Russian training, largely forbore to cheer, but their earnest gaze showed how large his figure loomed in their minds.

Pilsudski's greatness, indeed, is attested by the stature of the men over whom he ruled with such easy domination. The President and several of the ministers, notably those of

The Patience-Table, said to be the instrument of much unconscious thought on policy.

RÉGIME v. SEYM

Foreign Affairs, Finance, the Interior, and Commerce, were men of marked ability. Yet Pilsudski towered over all to an extent which perhaps only Bismarck, Gladstone, Lenin and Mussolini have approached in post-Napoleonic Europe.

His conscious superiority was never more apparent than in the long-delayed impeachment of the Minister of Finance. At the end of May, he was addressed as a future witness. This he declined to become, contending that a Premier fulfilled a dominating and decisive *rôle* towards his ministers. On 1 June, however, he drew up for the State Tribunal a declaration on the subject of the extra-budgetary expenditure.

First among the causes which he assigned for this, came the corrupt practices of government which were based on parties in the Seym. Another was the inexpediency of keeping idle in the Treasury the proceeds of the Stabilization Loan of 1927, which he, by personal pressure, had obtained from the United States. He had ordered that supplementary credits should be raised for public works in order to safeguard them against the bungling preliminaries of the Seym. His illness had intervened, but he could say that Bartel had raised the constitutional point; that the accused minister, who was the most constitutional of men, had made a written reservation; and that the responsibility rested upon himself alone. His action had been dictated by the hopelessness of the Seym—the last "so befouled with corruption and want of honour in relation to the work of the State, that it was impossible to give it questions of the greatest public importance to decide", while the methods prevalent in Poland subjected every question to such absurd formalities that it could never be decided at the proper time. The majority of the present Seym was plainly incorrigible.

Pilsudski had reached the conviction that parliamentary government, as ordinarily understood, was impossible in contemporary Poland. This he proved by declining the proposed co-operation of the Left. It was difficult, however, to see how a tribunal appointed by parliament could admit that parliament was incapable, or, on the other hand, how it could condemn one man for an offence which he obviously committed as the tool of another, while that other was suffered to go free. Pilsudski himself intended that the Tribunal, a novelty in Polish procedure, should merely enable the witnesses to decline to give details of the Cabinet deliberations. They, like the impeached minister, had acted as one body under the Premier's direction. In seeking the offender, all roads led to Pilsudski.

He himself, it may well be, was enjoying the summer and the Seym-baiting alike. He presided with no little energy over a long meeting of the Physical Education Council on 22 June. Of the cadets, he said, one-third proved unfit for service; and, among students, the same proportion. Compulsion was necessary, if these were to be properly trained, but there were many difficulties. He knew something of the youngest classes, for, as he confessed, he egotistically thought always of his daughters. And, with them in mind, he discussed, with his usual ability and insight, many proposals and ideas.

Next day, he presented himself before the twelve whom the Seym and Senate had placed on the Tribunal, all save the judges rising when he appeared. With all respect to its members, he confessed himself unable to speak of the Court without derision. He had read the act creating it only the day before, and found it a bungled piece of work, containing everything but sense, resembling journalism rather than law. The minister was charged with neglecting the Seym, a body which the act did not mention. The constitution likewise seemed to have been so drawn up that everyone could find in it what he pleased. He, as they knew, had resolved to work and rule in conflict with the infamy of a Seym which made itself sovereign instead of the President. He did this without transgressing the constitution, for he could always find paragraphs allowing him to neglect it.

When he turned to the indictment, as yesterday for the first time, since he disliked the Seym's nonsense, he found that the first paragraph related to the former Seym, whose rights ended with its decease. To accuse the minister instead of himself was to falsify history, and to attempt a ritual murder of an innocent substitute. He had noticed that many of his friends who entered the Seym soon lost their mental clarity, so that they came to think that the cackle of its members was important. He urged the Tribunal to listen for a short time to their debates: they would soon forget their own names. The mental confusion of the Seym accounted for this comic situation, in which a government, led by the greatest man in Poland, whose hands, unlike those of the prosecuting deputies, did not stink, was the accused. He it was who had prevented the Finance Minister from paying heed to the Seym.

As Zeligowski and the father of Colonel Beck, the Marshal's own chief secretary, were members of the Tribunal, Pilsudski's baiting of the Seym was not wholly unwelcome, even within the Court. On the fourth day the impeachment collapsed, the Tribunal indicating that the indictment had been made without sufficient study of the question.

During the greater part of 1929, the Pilsudski *régime* derived prestige from the unquestionable progress of Poland, at home and abroad alike. A State only ten years old then displayed its products to more than four million people at the great national exhibition at Poznan, while relations with neighbouring Powers improved, and the Polish seat on the Council of the League bade fair to be permanent. Germany being still disarmed, while Russia was embarking on a desperate struggle with her own peasantry, the army in Pilsudski's hands gave Poland something of the status of a Great Power.

Before the year ended, however, there were signs that, from causes beyond her own control, her economic progress had been checked, and that the world-crisis, bearing hardest upon the poorer States, had already begun. World-prices of agricultural produce fell heavily, and, in an agricultural country with few reserves of wealth, the reaction upon industry swiftly followed. If a poor peasant farmer could not sell his surplus at a profit, how could he buy manufactures? If the manufacturers lost orders, they must dismiss workmen, for they had neither the capital nor the credit to enable them to produce for stock. Who, then, could pay taxes? and, failing taxes, how could government support its many employees?

Meanwhile, the energies of Pilsudski and of Poland were being taxed by the unending strife between the *régime* and the majority in the Seym. Early in September, by Pilsudski's desire, the Premier conferred with Daszynski on the method of voting future budgets. He proposed for its improvement a conference with the representatives of the parties, which Pilsudski would attend. The National Democrats, however, declined to discuss budgetary questions except in the whole House. On this, Pilsudski published, on 22 September, 1929, an article dedicated to "A Dying World". It followed immediately upon an official statement which insisted that severe retrenchment was inevitable.

RÉGIME v. SEYM

Pilsudski had no difficulty in showing that in Poland, where some German laws had been in force in Poznan; Austrian law, in Cracow; the Napoleonic code, in Warsaw; and some Russian laws in the Borderlands, the whole administered by sluggish and incompetent officials—that there the cast-iron budget system was a most formidable obstacle to progress. If the army were assigned a reduced sum, payable in equal monthly instalments, he must work out everything afresh, and the army took one-third of the whole revenue. The secret of the system, he declared, was that it was constructed only for officials, not for the needs of the country. Unassigned funds were indispensable, if any regard was to be paid to the national interest. He had invited the deputies to confer with him about the budget, since it was they who convinced the world that the Poles were incapable of self-government. To avoid contention, he had merely copied his own estimates for the preceding year. But, for reasons which showed that they belonged to a dying world, the deputies refused the conference.

This article, beginning with contemptuous reference to Daszynski, and continuing with still more contemptuous references to the Seym, was probably justified by the facts of the case. It could not, however, improve the prospects of collaboration with the government in the coming session, which was summoned for the last day of October. Meanwhile, the economic depression had had time to deepen. In a land where a majority of the inhabitants might count themselves fortunate if their rye held out beyond Christmas, and if they ate meat six times in a year, depression and starvation were not far apart.

The ordinary session of the Seym was to be opened at 4 p.m. on 31 October, 1929. Pilsudski arrived a few minutes before the hour, and sent Beck to inform the Speaker,

Daszynski, that he was attending as the sick Premier's representative. In the public lobby of the building a number of officers had assembled to greet the Marshal, whom they saluted in silence. The Seym officials and Daszynski resented their presence as an attempt to intimidate the Seym, and an official twice ordered them to withdraw. They, singled out and ordered by civilians, held their ground in angry silence. Daszynski thereupon wrote to the President, refusing, "in the presence of more than ninety armed officers", to carry out his instructions to open the session.

After waiting more than an hour, Pilsudski, accompanied by Skladkowski and Beck, entered Daszynski's room. The Marshal declined the suggestion that his witnesses should withdraw, since, he said, Daszynski misinterpreted everything. When the two men had shaken hands and seated themselves, the officers standing, Pilsudski asked why Daszynski did not open the session. What was this freak? "Do you mean the presence of officers?" replied Daszynski. "No, no," Pilsudski said; "I mean, why don't you open the session?" "Not under the menace of bayonets, rifles and swords," loudly declared Daszynski. "There are armed officers in the lobby." "How do you know?" Pilsudski asked. "My officials told me," was the answer. "Oh, your officials!" rejoined Pilsudski. "If you don't want the public there, you must announce it betimes. Otherwise you will always have a crowd in your narrow lobby." And then some servant or deputy orders officers out. Why this stupidity?"

"You are my guest," replied Daszynski, "therefore I will let it pass——" "Let what pass?" "You say I do stupid things." "I am not your guest, I am here officially——" "So am I." "Then please hold your tongue," said Pilsudski, banging the table, "and I ask, will you open the session?" "Under the menace of bayonets, revolvers and swords, I will not," replied Daszynski. "Is that final?" "Yes." "Is that final?" "Yes."

At this, Pilsudski bowed slightly and left the room. In the anteroom he exclaimed, "The fool!" That "fool" was an insult indeed, the historic word which a Russian tsar hurled publicly at his consort Catherine the Great and shortly perished: the reproof addressed by his superior to the soldier who dashed out Pilsudski's teeth. It became a deliberate insult, for the whole dialogue was recorded by Skladkowski and Beck, revised by Pilsudski, and published. After quitting Daszynski, the Marshal hastened to the President, finding there Daszynski's letter with statements which he believed to be unfounded. The President thereupon suggested to Daszynski that the opening of the Seym should be postponed until the discrepancy could be cleared up. Daszynski, however, refused to meet Pilsudski, and conferences and *communiqués* followed in swift succession.

On 7 November, Pilsudski sent to the Premier a pungent commentary on the statements made by Daszynski at and after their interview. The statement that the officers who peacefully saluted him were a threatening armed band, he said, had suggested to him that Daszynski must be out of his mind. That they had occupied any part of the building by force was a falsehood. The bayonets, rifles and revolvers of which Daszynski had spoken, reduced themselves in his printed statement to swords, which had long ceased to be service weapons. Thus the assertion that the officers were armed was untrue. So, too, was the printed statement that they numbered well over a hundred. Including those on duty in the building, there were less than eighty. He had issued an army order declaring that the insult by the officials of the Seym to their uniform must be regarded as liquidated.

The Marshal's early remark that the Seym would make much of the event, but he would only mock them, may well have accounted for this last characteristic stroke. More than three months passed, however, before the document reached the public. The Seym majority, still busy in the new year with its investigations into these events, rejected a motion that it should be read in full, and only then did it appear in the Press. Unfortunately the strain of controversy appeared to tell on Pilsudski's health, which must henceforth take the foremost place in a biographer's consideration.

Two days after drawing up the pungent polemic against Daszynski, Pilsudski wrote his *Reminiscences of Grzybowski Square* for the twenty-fifth anniversary of the first armed demonstration against Russia (13 November, 1904). This brief historical sketch has a threefold biographical value. It proves that within a month of entering that sixty-third year which is traditionally critical for mankind, Pilsudski was still essentially himself, terse, lucid, racy, vigorous, with sense of scale and memory for detail unimpaired. The conflict in Grzybowski Square, he said, in that age of small-scale conspiracy, when letters, telegrams and telephone messages could not be sent, seemed as distant as Australia, but he showed that it remained fresh in his mind. Second, and perhaps less welcome, his declaration that in that event and many others he played a weighty part, though he was not so famous as at present, when his name was known throughout the world—this extends the area in which his later manner is apparent. Third, and most suggestive, is the fact that, as the representative of law and order, he could look back rather with pride than with disapproval at conspirators hoodwinking spies, printing subversive proclamations and buying fire-arms for use against the police. It contrasts with his subsequent tendency to say little of his exploit at Bezdany. The Grzybowski Square demonstration, he declared, did not rank among his dearest memories, and in it he did not himself participate. But he describes the preparatory work with zest, and rates high the work for Poland of those who fell. In history, he reflected, ingenuity is often of more account than strength.

After this, for a full year, his pen was seldom wielded save in connection with the dreary struggle of the *régime* against the Seym. Plan after plan was suggested for the revised constitution, but in vain. While Poland sank deeper into poverty, government and Seym made stroke and counterstroke without achieving or even approaching a decision. First, the *bloc* secured the appointment of a Commission to enquire into Daszynski's action in refusing to open the Seym. The Commission elicited from Pilsudski the fact that forty-seven officers, whom he named, had reported that they had been insulted by the officials. The individual reports, he said, he was not at liberty to disclose.

Chapter XXXV

PILSUDSKI'S TRIUMPH (1930)

THE Seym, meanwhile, had rid itself of the government by a vote of no confidence, and Bartel had once again returned to office. In mid-March, 1930, at the instigation of dispossessed Socialists, the Seym voted no confidence in Pilsudski's friend, the famous Legionary, Prystor, and on this, Bartel resigned. The President officially declared his surprise that the Seym should create a crisis while the budget was not concluded, and invited Pilsudski, as the most experienced person, to advise him. He then desired the Marshal to succeed Bartel.

Pilsudski thereupon appealed to the public in an article, giving his reasons for declining, which appeared on 19 March. His memory of his own loneliness as the Head of the State and army, he said, strengthened his natural desire to help the President if he could, but the Premiership was beyond his strength. The Seym's method of work, though contrary to conscience and reason, was not the chief deterrent. First came its habit of calumniating friend and foe alike, not sparing children or woman's honour. His own practice, on the other hand, was to tolerate no word of calumny, even against his most distant acquaintance, and he had made hundreds of calumniators speechless by his rebuke. Second came its habit of chattering on all subjects without relevance or knowledge.

Why, he asked, should a conscientious man like himself who knew realities and spoke to the point—why should he waste his time and strength in listening to pompous nonsense? A stupid and unlearned man often had great beauty of soul, and, in some sections of work, might be far more skilful and intelligent than himself. But a deputy, irresponsible and fleeing responsibility, could change his mind on questions every moment, and attack people like a common cur. He himself had invented the Seym, but the first Seym had taught him that the deputy was the most worthless acquisition made by independent Poland. Where the President and all other officers must swear an oath, the deputy only consented to make a vow. He had seen them muttering it unintelligibly with unbuttoned trousers. Their affectation of superiority showed an aspect of the Polish character which he simply could not endure.

Thirdly, alas! the deputies had, from the first, erased from their vocabulary the word "honour". Virtue, indeed, was beyond most men's reach, but honour was its necessary substitute. Within his recollection, he had never been dishonourable, and therefore he was specially sensitive to offences against honour. The Seym, however, sheltered behind privilege, and only in the third Seym had the *bloc* renounced this immunity for themselves. Until this was the case with all, his position as Premier would be intolerable. For all these reasons, he had told the President, compliance was beyond his strength. Yet to flinch shattered his childhood's dream that his will-power had no limit, even to devouring filth. He had, therefore, assured the President that, if the other attempts were unsuccessful, he would serve.

At the same time the Marshal of the Senate was setting to work to negotiate a ministry of reconciliation. After a week of interviews, he reported to Pilsudski that he had found a widespread wish for peace and co-operation, and that only one party raised the question of appointments.

This drew from Pilsudski an answer stating that, since the *régime* began, Poland had become known abroad for her exceptionally excellent system of transacting business. What formerly took ten hours could now be accomplished in ten minutes. If the deputies began to interfere in the government, they would intrude into the administrative departments and upset everything. They wanted agreement because they were driven into a blind alley. The Marshal of the Senate would like to get them out of it, but Pilsudski desired guarantees that the work which had cost him so much labour would not be destroyed. Therefore, he insisted that, as the price of his collaboration, four points must be conceded:

1. No intrusion into administration and appointments.
2. No interference with an enacted budget.
3. Security against undue limitation of supplementary credits.
4. No summons to the Seym for at least six months.

So speaks the victorious general when the enemy sues for an armistice. The Seym, not unnaturally, preferred to fight on. They passed the budget in half an hour, thus anticipating a dissolution. Then, on 29 March, the President secured Pilsudski's old friend, Slawek, as the successor to Bartel. Six weeks later, the constitutional war-game was resumed. On 9 May, 1930, the majority requested the President to summon an extraordinary session. This met on 23 May, only to find itself adjourned for thirty days. Meanwhile, Pilsudski's thoughts turned towards a dissolution, but he was advised that "good" elections required three months' propaganda. At the end of the thirty days' adjournment, the President declared the session at an end.

The majority, as well they might, regarded such use of

constitutional rules as unconstitutional. Centre and Left united, and, at the end of June, their joint "Congress for the Defence of the Law and Popular Freedom" charged the President with breaking his oath to the constitution. The Public Prosecutor indicted the conveners of the Congress: they replied by convening others. Slawek resigned, on the ground that he could not fulfil the duties both of Premier and of leader of the *bloc* (23 August, 1930).

Pilsudski himself stepped into the breach, declaring, however, that he could not be maid-of-all-work, and that he proposed to leave much to his colleagues, especially in finance and cabinet councils. On this he would consult the President. He designated Lieutenant-Colonel Beck Vice-Premier, determined to appeal to the country, and, within three months (26 August–24 October, 1930), gave seven interviews designed to influence the electors.

His task was made easier by aggressive words and deeds from across the German frontier. At a time when elections showed that Polish Silesia was overwhelmingly Polish, indiscreet words were uttered regarding the Corridor, and the growth of Gdynia was said to threaten the interests of the Danzig Germans. Worst of all, as heightening the agricultural crisis in Poland, Germany took away by tariffs what she had just granted by treaty. In the autumn of 1930, the distressed Polish masses turned towards the hero who had saved them ten years before. They received a lead from the August Legionary convention, which, roused to the utmost enthusiasm by a flying visit from Pilsudski, declared that they would defend the frontiers to the last drop of their blood.

The first of Pilsudski's election interviews was given on 26 August. His health had suffered from attending the Legionary convention in heavy rain, and he was indignant that an enemy whom he despised should force him to break off his quiet work for Poland, in order to form a cabinet and go electioneering. His mood was dark, and he so overbore his colleagues that none dared to question Beck's promotion. Thus the interview began characteristically enough. "What is your immediate programme, Marshal?" asked the deputy. "You ask that like a deputy," was the reply, "that is, so that it is impossible to give an answer; for a deputy to the Seym is created to ask stupid questions and make stupid speeches. The duty of a minister is to concentrate on the chief anxiety with which he is confronted, and to ignore the rest." His own chief anxiety was the constitution—a slovenly document full of absurdities—a kind of Irish stew. All were forbidden to interpret it. Having discussed this thesis at length, he went on to declare, on the basis of several years' experience, that what the deputies wanted was money, money, money, taken from the taxes by the government and given to themselves. Above all else, the Treasury must be defended against their attacks.

Three days later, Pilsudski's election campaign was carried a stage further. On 29 August, a Presidential proclamation, countersigned by him, declared that the weightiest task before all Polish citizens was the rectification of their fundamental laws. The Republic was in a state of legal chaos, declared the President, and he could not extricate it with the help of the existing Seym. He therefore dissolved both Seym and Senate, fixing 16 November for the election of the former, and for the latter, 23 November.

On the preceding day, Pilsudski, a weary and surly veteran, had informed his Cabinet that he had been driven to think of a dissolution by the impossibility that he, a born lordling, should continue to wallow in deep dirt. The scoundrels who pretended to be sovereign were the Seym only during the session. When vacation came, they lost their immunity. "I am a man of war," he growled, thinking aloud before the meeting. "I may use force, but I may not whip one of these gentry in the street for shooting at the police. What immunity!"

All voted for dissolution, and the Presidential decree followed. Within a week, Pilsudski again discoursed to his interviewer, with a fresh and startling plan in immediate contemplation. He had already authorized the use of his name at the head of the list of the *bloc* candidates, and had marked with a green pencil, on a list presented to him, the names of those deputies who were to be arrested and shut up in Brest-Litovsk.

Another of the contemporary difficulties of the government consisted in the Ukrainian agitation. Pilsudski decided that terroristic acts were not to be treated as insurrection. If they received popular support, first, police repression, and then, if necessary, the quartering of troops, must be tried.

Such was the mental background to his discourse on 6 October. In this he spoke with great vigour of the ambiguities of the constitution with regard to the position of members of the late Seym. Daszynski and others were claiming that their salaries should still be paid. If the Seym were dissolved, Pilsudski maintained, it could not have members, and members of a non-existent body were phantoms such as gain for their creators places in a lunatic asylum.

On 10 September, 1930, the work of the green pencil was accomplished. A government *communiqué* declared that criminal and political offences by deputies had been discovered during the session, and emphasized the evil consequences of their intangibility even then. Daszynski had demanded the release of a former deputy who shot at the police. Now eighteen of the ex-deputies, including Witos, deputy since 1919 and Premier thrice, found themselves in Brest-Litovsk, where they were treated as ordinary prisoners. Korfanty, the leader of the Upper Silesian opposition, and other anti-Pilsudski notables, followed them, until the number of political prisoners passed fourscore.

Angrily inveighing to his Cabinet against these traitors, on the same day, Pilsudski cried, "I want them punished. I cannot endure that such a band of former deputies should be immune to corrupt Polish morals. If the tribunals will not judge them, I will have them shot like dogs." It was clear to his friends that the Premiership would grievously impair his health. Three days later, however, he explained the arrests to the interviewer in a notably breezy style. The precise charges, he said, were not in his department. Shooting at the police, swindling, corruption and blackmail were, he knew, among them. These were strange deeds in defence of freedom. Why not claim freedom to defile the streets? Prison discipline was strict, and when these gentry came out, they might behave better than when they so abominably "served Poland" in the Seym. He was now turning to the budget, relieved to be extricated from wallowing in dirt.

When asked whether he might not thenceforward dispense with parliament, he said that he had raised that question in his article on "A Dying World". It was indeed a weighty question, for parliamentarianism all over the world was sick, and on all sides efforts to find a remedy were being made. In Poland, the difficulty was particularly great because of the foul behaviour of the deputies. He had not changed his opinion, that an elected executive with a strong feeling of honour was necessary. He had proved this by resorting to elections, which, he hoped, might produce a cure.

Nine weeks before the polling day, Pilsudski thus re-emphasized the issue which the country had to face. Was Poland to be governed by the automatic operation of democracy, which in many countries led in practice to the tyranny of a corrupt majority in the Lower House? Or was she to aim at "the equilibrium of powers in a 'true' democracy", and their collaboration within the framework of the constitution? The Marshal, who had called Polish democracy into being, held above all else that the constitution must be Polish, and that no theories must obstruct honest work. He believed that at that time the sovereign Polish people would commission his *régime*, in preference to that of the late majority in the Seym. But he left no stone unturned—interviews, arrests, explanations to the mayors and leading peasants by officials, his own appearance as a candidate, and frequent conference with the police. "No state of siege", ran his instruction when informed of some disorders, "but prompt repression, and stiff fines for unlawful possession of arms."

The national revenue had shrunk by one-fourteenth, but as the *régime* and the majority were on different sides, the inevitable discontent might be turned against either. And, since in Poland the fame of one man far surpassed that of any other man or group, a democratic election would be in effect a *plébiscite* for or against Pilsudski. Daszynski plaintively expressed to the President the fears of his high-sounding union, that the elections would not be free and honest. Pilsudski at that moment was noting with satisfaction that, without the smallest governmental pressure, the courts were taking his view of the arrests, and that he might entertain high hopes of the electors.

After four weeks of preoccupation with the elections, the Marshal was compelled to plunge into the preparation of the budget for 1931–1932. The constitution willed that the parliament elected in November should find a government draft ready for its scrutiny. This must be prepared before either the revenues or the outgoings could be accurately estimated. In an agricultural country, the most vital factors were the harvest and the price at which a surplus could be sold abroad, and by the end of September the necessary information could not be complete. Again, the voting of one budget was followed by an immediate plunge into the next, and the work went on throughout the year. Pilsudski did not spare either the system or the "sick parliamentarianism" which had produced it, emphasizing first of all the increase in official salaries which had taken place, despite his disapproval, when he was out of the country. The budget also suffered from the financial aid afforded to the corn-grower by exemption from taxes and reduction of railway rates, and from the grants to the unemployed.

A week later (4 October), he could say that two-thirds of the interval had been spent in working at the budget and in considering how much "cheating" could be allowed. He had convinced himself that a more elastic structure was indispensable, and that the budget work of both government and parliament must be improved. The discovery of a plot against his life by extremists of the P.P.S. did not for a moment disturb his calm. Soon afterwards, the same party struck at members of the *bloc*, killing two officials, and wounding other persons. Pilsudski consented to an increase of police protection, and in the budget refused to reduce either the numbers or the pay of the police. To link parliamentarianism with the revolver, he sneered, was a triumph of Socialist stupidity. Arguing that the absorption of ministers in Seym debates threw their offices into the hands of officials, he contended for budget fluidity, which officials always disliked. All these labours found expression in the long and almost stormy cabinets in which the Marshal imposed his views upon his colleagues. Reductions everywhere, with liberty to individual ministers to construct their own budgets and defend them in the Seym—such was his specific for the crisis.

When the elections were still some three weeks distant, his interviewer approached him for the seventh time. The Marshal gladly embraced the opportunity to explain to the public why he had departed from his custom by lending his name to the *bloc*. Hitherto, he explained, he had disliked the Seym's mode of work, and had been unable to imagine himself as remaining permanently a member of any party. Parties, he declared, always exalted their own petty interests above those of the State. Their competition made politics a common sewer. But the formation of the *bloc* had united all others against it, and he felt that Poland's best hope lay in its triumph. He was also deeply moved by its renunciation of intangibility in questions of honour. Poland had too many sons who regarded his championship of the public good as excusing them from further effort. He was not aiming at Caesarism. The events of May, 1926, had been due to the fact that the Seym was preparing a situation resembling that which preceded the Partition. Now he had induced the President to dissolve, so that Poland might, if she would, break with the corrupt and ambitious Seym, and turn the page of history.

At last the great day came, and Poland gave its verdict on the *régime*. No one could find it ambiguous. The *bloc* received nearly 5,300,000 votes; while the Centre-Left failed to reach 2,000,000; and the National Democrats, to reach 1,500,000. Only about one-third of the 13,000,000 voters cast their votes outside these three groups. The *bloc* thus gained an absolute majority in the Seym, and, a week later, a two-thirds majority in the Senate. Pilsudski might hope to gain the voting strength to revise the constitution. Two days after the poll, Skladkowski found him, spent indeed, but grateful to those who had organized the victory. On 26 November, when its full extent was known, his interviewer reported him as rejoicing over what was then rare in Europe—a majority sufficient to correct old faults and to establish a solid and permanent basis of work.

Once again Pilsudski professed himself full of hope that President, government and Seym might be brought to work harmoniously. A changed constitution was necessary, but he did not propose to be its author. Like Napoleon, he said, he liked things to be done well, but was himself no drafter of documents with many paragraphs. His brother John had been appointed to draft a project for revision in the last Seym, and had forced him to go through an awe-inspiring mass of papers. His own notion was, that there should be a kind of contract between the three chief springs, President, government and parliament, which actuated the State machine. The principal change, in his view, should be the abolition of the immunity of deputies. Life was developing so fast that institutions soon became superannuated. The requirement that all ministers should approve what perhaps only one understood was a case in point. The sphere of interference of the Seym should be limited. This was a world-wide necessity.

Two days later, on 28 November, 1930, Pilsudski called together his Cabinet and surprised them by including Slawek in the meeting. In an agitated voice he declared that he must resign: he was too nervous to converse with people: he had gone all to pieces. Slawek would form a cabinet, but in the meantime his own hand would still be felt. It was winter, he said, a season that always brought him to the gates of death, and he could work no more.

None the less, since he was suffering rather from worn nerves than from any organic failure, the effort and the stimulus of his surroundings gave him strength, and he growled out in a disjointed fashion much that is worth preserving. Their first business, he said, was to deal with the question of officials. On these they spent enormous sums, three-eighths of the war budget, for example, yet their officials were not good. Indolence was Poland's bane. The Poles, too, were always working for personal advantage, not for the greatness of the State. To his own shame, he had not been able to deal with the question of officials. He had, however, ordered a changed contract of service to be drafted for the Seym.

Hitherto, he declared, there had been a conspiracy against the State, which paid the officials in order not to be disturbed. Pensioners for services rendered to Russia, Austria or Prussia had increased abnormally. These should be cut down; only good men, promoted; work, supervised; and numbers, reduced. After discoursing long in this strain, and giving kind advice to several of his colleagues, he again became sensible of his exhaustion. He was not the equal of his father, he confessed. His father had worked eighteen hours a day, but he himself had not maintained that rate beyond his thirtieth year. Now he must flee from the winter.

On 4 December, 1930, Pilsudski handed over the Premiership to Slawek, retaining the portfolio of War. Five days later, the new Seym met, and a Pilsudskist Speaker was elected by a large majority. The government designed to reform the constitution; the opposition, to champion their friends on bail from Brest-Litovsk; while all parties were preparing to discuss the budget.

Before sailing for Madeira with his doctor, Pilsudski, on 13 December, gave a final interview, urging that the President should be made a real ruler, though without the burden of technical details. In the thesis itself no novelty appeared, but the volume and the liveliness of the demonstration suggest that freedom from responsibility and the near prospect of a holiday had already done much to soothe the statesman's nerves. His comparison of President and Premier, under the existing constitution, to billiard balls for ever colliding and rebounding into different corners, is hardly the fancy of a shattered man. His final words may be cited here, for they proved to be almost his last general exhortation to his people. "I always link the whole of the questions raised by me with the election of the President otherwise than by Seym and Senate", he declared. "To make him, both by law and usage, independent on that side, he must be elected by the whole country. And may I announce the most comic truth—that the objections made against this as establishing demagogy, come from the most stupid and most foolish demagogues?"

CHAPTER XXXVI

PILSUDSKI IN MADEIRA AND POLAND (1931)

BETWEEN the end of December, 1930, and the end of March, 1931, Pilsudski rested quietly in Madeira. To honour his name-day, more than a million postal packets were despatched to him, but he had his own way with papers, especially with such obvious tokens of goodwill. The Marshal believed that worn nerves recovered during sleep, and that for this one month was necessary. General recuperation then began, requiring at least a second month, and an elderly man might well need three in all.

His sojourn in an island more than two thousand miles away rendered a threefold service to his country. At a time when the growing power of Hitlerism threatened Poland with most deadly peril, the only man who could hope to unite and to direct her gained fresh strength and clear perspective. Again, since he possessed the orderly military habit of refraining from administrative interference outside his own command, the ministry gained a chance of self-education by governing without the feeling that their master was at hand. Further, by thus absenting himself, he gave the lie to those who spoke of his autocracy. "A tsar", it had been said of old, "should seldom leave his country, for in his absence its social and political life stand still." In Madeira, Pilsudski proved himself no Polish tsar.

Rest brought new energy and a revived desire to work. What *hors-d'œuvres* could be more piquant than the memoirs of an eminent opponent whose swordsmanship was inferior to his own? Daszynski, the leader of the hostile coalition, had published two stout volumes of reminiscences in 1924 and 1926; Bilinski, once Austrian Minister of Finance, likewise two, with documents, in 1924. Pilsudski read them for the first time at Madeira, and dictated to his doctor fifty-eight pages of typescript criticism—the last of his substantial writings. Its style and volume point to his recovery, while, both as history and biography, the text has no small worth.

To these detailed "Historical Corrections" he added a preface which emphasized the fact that it was to August, 1914, that modern Poland owed its first and feeble origins. Some historians, he contends, falsify history by suggesting that the nation was then what it had become by the Armistice, or even later. Pilsudski insists that in each of the three empires in 1914 all the Poles obeyed, and that the military leaders, with powers far greater than of old, trampled on everything Polish. These historians and their generation, in 1931 fortunately dying off, he compared with a worm masquerading as a leopard or an elephant. In point of fact, he held, what influence the Poles possessed in 1914, they acquired by spying, and largely by spying upon Poles. Indubitably also, after a few years of war, Poland became an entity for which her sons could fight. But during these years, it was the empires, not the Poles, who took decisions, and the Poles whom the historians praise aimed, not at independence, but at *condominium*.

From 1914, the Marshal declares, until reborn Poland emerged, the central figure in her history was Joseph Pilsudski. As portrayed by the historians, however, he is unrecognizable, and sometimes a mere stupid ape. His life, unlike any other life, full of dangers, adventures, accidents and fairy-tales which were true, could really be known only to himself. And he cared not whether he was called a mere adventurer or the ablest and wisest among Poles, for the verdict upon such a central figure was reserved for distant posterity.

Contemporary Poland, he complained, made very free with his name. One man reminded him that he had not yet paid him for an overcoat supplied in his flight from the Russian police through Demblin, a place which, before 1920, he had never seen. Another asked for the repayment of two hundred roubles lent to ransom him from those who led him through the streets of Lodz, though prisoners were always transported in closed vans. He had long reflected upon possible ways of preventing people from heaping rubbish upon his name, and had condemned himself for indecision. As a beginning, he had resolved to read and to correct what Daszynski and Bilinski had written about him.

The consequent "observations" on Daszynski's work numbered twenty-five, varying between a brief paragraph and an essay. Pilsudski had laughed heartily, he said, to find that, when he had journeyed to Japan, it was to discover how the political exiles in Siberia could oppose the Tsar. It was equally false that he had endeavoured to organize the Militants into an armed force, that he remained in their ranks until 1914, or that he was responsible for "bloody Wednesday" in 1906 and a series of terroristic outbreaks. He was always against the Terror.

Again, it was Sosnkowski, not himself, who had formed the Z.W.C. Pilsudski had laboured hard to correct its faults. In connection with the attack upon a train in Bezdany station, Daszynski claimed to have tried to exchange some of the Russian money in western Europe. As the whole of it passed through Pilsudski's hands, and as he made no communication to Daszynski, he strongly doubts his accuracy. Pilsudski, again, based the security of his pre-war military work on his relations with some of the Austrian General Staff, not on the intrusion of Socialist deputies, who were strongly anti-military. Daszynski, moreover, wrongly claimed to have learned from him of military measures which he was bound not to reveal, and which he would not, in any case, have revealed to a man whose egotism made him careless of another's secrets. Daszynski, indeed, often fathered upon Pilsudski his own ideas and work. "His tasteless tone, always hectoring like a stupid governor, at once disgusted me with everything that he began," declared the Marshal. The outbreak of war, however, frightened him into better behaviour.

Pilsudski deals ruthlessly with Daszynski's many inaccuracies. Only an extremely naïve author, he affirms, could make such stupid statements as Daszynski's on the relations between the Council of State and the P.O.W. Writing in Madeira, and having, alas! no memory for dates, he found himself unable to refute in all details the misleading account of the formation of the first government of Poland. He therefore wrote a vivid outline of his return to Warsaw from captivity, and of the part played by Daszynski and his Lublin government. Daszynski, he said, has falsified history. The truth is, that Pilsudski appointed him to form a cabinet, and drove away a National Democrat who came to denounce him. He dismissed him, however, because it was clear that he would be slow in forming a cabinet and would end by denouncing everyone, Pilsudski included. Daszynski, indeed, accepted his dismissal quietly, only making the childish stipulation that the official notices which set him free and summoned his successor should both be countersigned by himself.

Bilinski, who had been Finance Minister in 1919 from the

Pilsudski, aged. (By 1931, " a veritable Grandfather.")

end of July to the beginning of December, could hardly rouse either in Pilsudski or the modern student the same interest as Daszynski. Pilsudski declares that he met him for the first time in the autumn of 1916, and classed him at sight among the many Poles who, knowing nothing of war, were afraid to speak about the army. Like other Galician statesmen, Bilinski regarded the Legions as a stupid toy invented to give them trouble. And these men, whose ignorance of Russian Poland was unimaginable, were chosen by Austria to guide her policy! Pilsudski passes by the many compliments paid in the *Recollections* to himself, but dwells on his single conversation with Bilinski in the Belvedere. He had insisted on the need for expelling the Russian rouble, which he then regarded as worthless, from Polish government calculations, and had emphasized the fact that Ladislas Grabski and the National Democrats would raise objections. This was the sole basis for the "weighty nocturnal conferences" of which Bilinski boasted. His statement that when, in 1920, Daszynski joined the Witos government, and desired to take charge of foreign propaganda, Pilsudski supported him against the Foreign Minister, was baseless.

Madeira, it was clear, had refreshed without softening Pilsudski. When his sturdy sunburned figure stepped from a Polish warship upon the quay of Gdynia (29 March, 1931), the Marshal found a country whose prestige had not suffered during his absence, but whose chief difficulties still remained unsolved. Every month of peace, indeed, continued to strengthen Poland by accustoming both her citizens and foreign Powers to the fact of her existence. Every month swelled both her difficulties and her potentialities by adding more than 30,000 to her population.[1] The

[1] In 1937, the population rose by 406,000.

continuance of the economic crisis kept society poor, while the rise of German nationalism made Danzig, the Corridor, Silesia and the racial minorities all sources of continued peril. Lithuania remained intransigent, but the obvious restiveness of Germany drew Poland and Russia towards a better understanding, aided by France, their common friend.

The trial of the prisoners of Brest-Litovsk, moreover, must still be faced, while the chief question of all, the reform of the constitution, had made little progress. Although, to the most enlightened contemporaries, a great victory at the polls seemed to have given strength to end the veiled dictatorship, the government still lacked the necessary two-thirds majority in the Seym. Without this, reform could not be voted, nor was it easy to draft a reform which would secure a wise and far-seeing government to an ignorant and discordant electorate. Patience, education, the crippling of traitors—such might be the best policy for the *régime*.

Pilsudski, with his invariable thoroughness, resumed his duties as War Minister and Army Chief. He tended more and more to live solely for official work and for his family. During this year, and, indeed, with one exception, for the remainder of his life, he wrote no essays, gave no interviews, and made no elaborate speeches. Yet, within his country and without, he, more than all other men, represented Poland. On 26 May, 1931, two months after his return, Slawek resigned, to lead the *bloc* and to advance the reform of the constitution. Colonel Prystor, another old revolutionary, took his place, and, as Minister of Finance, Pilsudski's brother John continued the necessary policy of economy. At this time, the Marshal was mainly absorbed in army administration, with its incessant problems of rearmament, finance and *personnel*. The fact that this, after a long absence, might well claim all his time and strength, however, neither prevented every kind of difficulty from being brought to him, nor himself from following army questions across the frontiers between the war department and any other.

He could also instil a certain fluidity into constitutional practice. "You understand," he said to Skladkowski, when arranging for his transfer to the army from the Interior, "we must have a cabinet to appoint an undersecretary, but I don't want it to tell me what to do with generals, so I will ask the Premier to make a concession to me, so that your nomination comes only from the President and myself."

Like his father, he confessed, he was no administrator, and it was inevitable that want of order should impose a heavier tax upon his energy and patience. Legislation, moreover, was in disorder, and he resented the patchwork methods of his government. Eight hundred Presidential decrees, he said, had been promulgated in its early months. Above all, there was the endless question of the narrowing revenue.

Skladkowski, with his usual fidelity, reports his harassed explanations, when the military budget had to be drawn up. "Last year we did not receive seventy-odd millions (of zloty). That upset several items. You must have these things itemized. I refused to pay for a lot of things: I don't pay if they don't give me money. Those must remain 'unpaid'. I won't include them in this year's budget. I refused to give accounts to the Comptroller-General, for I don't understand how I can have to pay out what I have not received. The range of monthly rebates must be prolonged, for in this chaos it is impossible to see anything. I will speak to the Premier about it tomorrow. Write down everything unpaid last year. (Hunting among his papers.) Perhaps I have it, but I have lost the note." On the question of reducing the army income below a certain minimum he was adamant.

Early in July, 1931, he joyously set out for his holiday in Wilno, whole families crowding the station approaches to show the children Poland's famous man. A month later, however, he wrote to the Legionary Congress that "as he could not speak to them," he did not propose to attend. On 4 August, on the other hand, he showed renewed energy and high spirits in discussing legislation with his staff, who had to prepare twenty-seven bills by the end of the month. Everything, he said, fell on the Seym, and the defect was the lack of distinction between acts and regulations. Bills were therefore necessary to deal with trifles. Polish legislation, moreover, was inspired by a desire to limit the State on every side, and its diction was remote from ordinary life, and often ambiguous. The President should have the right of issuing decrees.

This was the prelude to a month of army work, in which, besides the budget, questions of military education and of stimulus to local administrations were prominent. On one hot morning, the Marshal, who had not dressed, asked his visitor if it was right to report himself to a superior officer who was in that condition. He was delighted with the answer: "I don't know, Marshal, I only know that it would be very wrong not to report myself." The good humour which prompted the question lasted through the summer of 1931.

As the autumn drew on, the crisis gripped Pilsudski, like a thousand other leaders. "The pound sterling is torturing me," he cried, "I am buried in pounds sterling, so that I can think of nothing else." Dreading the winter,

IN MADEIRA AND POLAND

he wished to prepare for it by a visit to Rumania, but 15 October was his daughter's name-day, and he did not wish to slight her by going abroad. He was praying for rain, he said, for then she would give him leave of absence. He also remarked on the continual quarrels among the Legionaries over personal questions of their past. The same was true of the veterans of '63. Early in October, he found himself weakened by a chill, and confessed that he was irritable and out of hand. He then took occasion to remark on the lack of technicians in Poland. In Paris, one of his orderlies had been afraid to venture into the streets, such was his ignorance of motors.

In mid-November, 1931, the Marshal was hard at work on promotions in the army. Those of the year preceding had cost 450,000 zloty in augmented pay. The Cabinet had therefore resolved that, this year, no one should be promoted. To this, however, the Marshal could not agree. He held that annual promotion was an obligation of the State, and that a stationary army was the worst of all. Joffre, he said, would have lost the war if he had not changed two-thirds of his commanders. He himself had once been in a tight place because his cavalry had no lieutenant-colonels. Prystor, the Premier, had consented at least to some promotion. They should economize at the expense of the *emeriti* pensioned for service to Austria or Russia. If promotion were to be restricted, it could not go by seniority. Merit must decide. And so, bidding his colleagues work out their recommendations on those lines, he dismissed them.

Early in December, the army inspectors and the vice-ministers met to vote upon promotions. Pilsudski alone proposed the names of generals and colonels, and then left the room. The colonels, but not the generals, were then discussed, and unsigned voting papers filled up. These were taken to the Marshal by the Bayard of the Polish army, his genial familiar Wieniawa, and the final list drawn up. Before Christmas, but far less formally, the promotions in the Sanitary service were arranged. The Marshal then presided over four high officers, and, as his old friend General Rouppert was one of them, the proceedings were jocose. Pilsudski explained that it was necessary to halve the average annual promotion of eighty-four doctors, and that it would be best to promote few senior officers, but to make many juniors captain. As this cost less than the normal average, the number might exceed the forty-two. The old comrades bargained a little, but the business was soon concluded, and promotions in other branches postponed until after Christmas.

Then the demands of Skladkowski were indulgently dealt with by a chief who obviously wished to give him a good start with his subordinates. Soon afterwards, however, the army budget came under consideration, and Skladkowski's proposed economies were by no means welcomed. To cut down the monthly budget, explained the Marshal, might well lead to closing the year with a deficit. Two days later, he added that, in the meantime, he had fought over the ground with the Premier, Prystor, and had demanded an unchanged budget. The danger to the army, however, was not yet past.

At the end of February, 1932, on the eve of his departure for Rumania and Egypt, he warned his colleagues that the next two months, the last of the financial year, were likely to prove the most difficult of all. The State was facing a total deficit. In this he himself saw nothing sinister, provided that all was accounted for. They must defend the military budget tenaciously and always be on the watch against unforeseen expenses.

Chapter XXXVII

PILSUDSKI IN 1932-1933

PILSUDSKI returned to work on 22 April, 1932. Young as the year was, it had already witnessed some six developments of high importance. Despite the deliberateness of Polish criminal procedure, ten of the prisoners of Brest-Litovsk had received a preliminary condemnation and sentence. Witos, the most important, was released on bail, pending an appeal against a sentence of imprisonment. The still more protracted negotiations with Russia had at last resulted in an agreement for a treaty of non-aggression. At the same time, the wider question of general disarmament had been taken up by the League of Nations, and, in February, a formal conference opened at Geneva.

Next month, however, Briand died, and both the Franco-Polish alliance and the policy of European appeasement lost his powerful support. What this might mean became evident in April, when Hitler polled more than two-thirds of the vote by which Hindenburg was re-elected President. Shortly before this, the Polish budget, as Pilsudski predicted, had shown a deficit. The President called the leading Pilsudskists into consultation, and, by their advice and with the sanction of parliament, issued a number of decrees to combat the growing crisis.

The direct contribution of Pilsudski during his absence had been the perfecting of that collaboration with Rumania upon which Polish policy is largely founded. His contribution, impalpable but none the less real, during the remainder of his life was the influence over Europe of his name. Foremost came the belief, which Poland's enemies could not but hold, that if they dared her overmuch, the Marshal might make some bold and sudden stroke of diplomacy or even war. No other man in Europe could have dealt so effectively with the aggressive nationalism which in Germany was rapidly gaining power. So long as Pilsudski lived, the German leaders knew that Poland would not yield an inch of what she had regained from the old German Empire. But they felt that he was as nationalist as themselves, and no hide-bound Tory or *doctrinaire*.

Second only to the belief in Pilsudski's courage came the conviction, deepened by each successive year, that he was moderate as well as bold, and that his Poland stood for peace and co-operation. Instead of a hot-headed and unstable upstart, Europe began to see in her the future guardian, solid, pious and pacific, of the eastern marches, a barrier keeping Germany and Russia apart, and perhaps destined, in concert with Rumania, to link commercially the northern and the southern States and seas.

Thirdly—the foundation of the former two—Pilsudski in his declining years, though he lacked some characteristic Polish qualities, and could not, by rising above parties, extinguish faction, none the less was Poland incarnate as perhaps no other Pole has been. The various tribes within her frontiers lived side by side with a nearer approach to peace, the Slavonic Poles suffered less from inferiority complex, all classes bore their economic hardships more patiently, because the ageing hero dwelt in the Belvedere. To the army, and to the survivors and heirs of the Romantic generation, he was a prophet or an idol, evoking the last enthusiasm of their ardent Polish souls.

After his return from Egypt, until the days of bulletins and public intercessions, the biography of Pilsudski is sub-

PILSUDSKI IN 1932-1933

merged in the history of Poland. He toiled on, to the limits of his dwindling strength, but usually behind the scenes, while his pupils, the ex-artist Rydz-Smigly in the army, the inscrutable Beck in Foreign Affairs and, virtually, Moscicki in the Presidency, filled the stage. The health and vigour brought back from Egypt, indeed, enabled him for the last time to address a public meeting. On 22 May, 1932, midway through his sixty-fifth year, he presided during a part of the fourth plenary session of the Council for Scientific Physical Education, and displayed his unstudied self.

After the report had been read, discussion followed, discursive until the alert chairman intervened to avert a mere unfruitful conversation. Systematizing, as was his wont, he declared that, of six topics already introduced, two, sporting badges and the organization of a Central Institute, had their own place on the agenda. Some had spoken of academic physical training, others of training in the villages, others of juveniles, while a colonel had raised the question of sport, and a professor had condemned the mania for records and for sporting aces. On this last, said Pilsudski, observation of his daughters made him an advocate of play, but not of sport. He ruled that these four subjects should be separately discussed, the three last only when that of the student class had been exhausted. He later opined that, to preserve the results achieved in the middle school, physical training should be continued in the university.

As to physical education in the villages, the Marshal doubted strongly whether agricultural labour did not suffice. Better food and housing, he declared, was the real need. To speakers who urged that the villagers were maladroit and slow, he replied that to raise them in those respects to the townsman's level might be to sacrifice the calm nerves produced by rural quiet. For the sake of the nation, he was against such uniformity. In the Russian War, he had noted two Japanese divisions, one purely rural, the other urban. The townsmen lacked the staying-power of the countryfolk, though, unlike these, they could move as fast as cavalry. To urbanize the country would be to lose rather than to gain.

He had been surprised to see the influence of football—the countryfolk began to kick like the English, who would kick a piece of paper on the path. In the summer, at least, the men worked all day and the children herded geese. Hygiene, by all means, but he did not know whether gymnastics made for health. A professor replied that he wished to correct the villagers, not to urbanize them, and that the Danes had special exercises for the stiff. Pilsudski, however, was not to be convinced. He had once mowed for half a day and made himself ill for two days, unable to lie down: the villagers could mow for a whole day in burning sun: such endurance should not be jeopardized.

On the question of sport, Pilsudski revealed himself a resolute Tory. Sport, he said, possessed immense value as propaganda for physical education. But it was on the wrong road. Sport was always one-sided. He would never forget his astonishment at seeing a girl jump over a hurdle, and at being told that she had just finished her schooldays and was already a noted hurdler, being prepared for the international arena. "Poor girl," he thought, "can she do nothing but jump over hurdles? She must train, change her way of life, be weighed and massaged every day, and be always jumping over those silly hurdles, her only object to jump over one after another. She might rise to the stratosphere of sport, and make another minute or another millimetre the object of her life. A specialist in hurdle-jumping: what a destiny!"

PILSUDSKI IN 1932-1933

He liked to watch football, for there the element of working in combination and of solid struggle came into strong prominence. But to sweat for an hour and a half must in time damage the heart. In every sport there was one-sided effort, in disc-throwing, for example, and that went on in all of them—boxing, riding and so on. His daughters, and their schoolfellows, played for whole days at such games as net-ball, replacing their old hide-and-seek. He would have play, not litigiousness about centimetres and split seconds, and kicking the judge who had failed to see that a ball was out.

When, in August, the time came to write to the Legionaries assembled in the new port of Gdynia, Pilsudski's greeting was tinged with a feeling that, despite her triumphs, Poland had still much to endure, and that to achieve them he had in great part sacrificed his health. The struggle with the economic crisis and with disease was indeed to occupy the short remainder of his life. A subordinate, whom he knew long and well, telephoned in each of the three years, 1930, 1932 and 1933, for leave to see him once more. He first replied, "Later", then "Not now", and to the third appeal returned no answer. The stamp of sadness deepened on his face, and his waning vitality made him indifferent to former civilian comrades. At Michaelmas, feverish and dejected, he meditated reducing by one-half his working days. In October, he was oppressed by the bronchial disorders which thenceforward obstinately clung to him. Once again, however, he rallied, and in the winter months worked hard and not always without lightness of heart.

To this, Poland's progress, both at home and abroad, contributed. Although in 1932 the number of the workless rose by about 200,000, this was a far smaller percentage than that in several other countries, and the crisis itself had been chiefly caused by the superabundance of foodstuffs. Against the budget deficit, and the growth of unemployment, might be set the continued unification of the country, the growth of communications, and the increased efficiency of the army. French military tuition could now be dispensed with, and Poland thus gained greater freedom in her foreign policy. Perhaps more weighty still, that trend in German politics which brought Hitler to the Chancellorship in January, 1933, made an *entente* between Germany and Russia an extremely remote contingency.

Since the Germans seemed no less determined to regain the Corridor than the Poles to keep it, common prudence dictated the new pact of mutual non-aggression which Poland now concluded with Russia. At the same time, she secured almost unanimous re-election to the Council of the League of Nations, while with Danzig, which profited by her commerce, her relations notably improved. Pilsudski could look back with a smile to the outbreak of passion caused by his arrival in the port in March, 1931, escorted by a Polish destroyer, when, as his children said, "Papa landed and the world shook". In November, the appointment of Colonel Beck as Foreign Minister made the Marshal more than ever the dictator of Polish policy.

Pilsudski's unquestioned pre-eminence gives the remarkable decisions of the first months of 1933 a high place in his personal record. At that time the forefront of European politics was occupied by the problem of disarmament, the rise of Hitlerian nationalism and the question of the Polish Corridor. The contribution made by Poland was distrust of formulae and of pacific generalizations, together with firm insistence on her treaty rights. Believing that the Germans designed to seize a promontory at the mouth of the Vistula on which Polish munitions were stored, the

PILSUDSKI IN 1932-1933

Poles suddenly disregarded League procedure, and landed a small force for its defence. When the Danzig government undertook to respect Polish rights, the force was at once withdrawn, but the assertion of Poland's intention to claim what was due to her had none the less been made. What was more, the spirit of Hitler had been tested and found to be unaggressive towards Poland.

In the greater question of a four-Power pact for general revision of treaties, which Mussolini devised and Britain accepted, Poland declined to admit foreign interference either with her territories or with her forces. Early in May, Hitler proposed that Germany and Poland should work for better mutual relations. At a historic moment, nearly five and a half years later, he declared that if democracy had ruled in Poland, he must have failed, but that as she possessed a man, lasting good-neighbourly relations could be established. The "man", indeed, had made a truer estimate of the new force in Germany than had any of his compeers. He was aided, no doubt, by his own passionate resentment against the treatment of the Poles by their neighbours during the period of partition, while the thorny question of the Ukraine became more threatening as Germany drew apart from Russia.

At this juncture, on 6 May, 1933, Pilsudski, perhaps for the last time, performed an act of army discipline with something like the full force of his manhood. For a moment the setting sun pierced the clouds before sinking beneath the horizon. As General Skladkowski records, he himself, with a veteran general and an old Legionary officer, was summoned to attend the Marshal, who had been informed that the Legionary was at loggerheads with his divisional commander. He now stood before Pilsudski between the two generals, who received a courteous greeting and the assurance that the word of command did not apply to them. Then suddenly, like the swish of a cane, came "Attention!" "We were all turned to stone", declares the writer. "I felt as though my skin was too tight for my head and face." Such was the passion of the command.

Before they could compose themselves, the Marshal pronounced sentence. The correspondence between the two soldiers, he said, had been so unsoldierly and quarrelsome that he could not bring himself to read it through. But two generals had judged the Legionary guilty of lack of discipline and self-command. He was therefore compelled to punish, without regard to the offender's justification by the original facts or to his good intentions, and, without allowing him to speak, he directed an immediate transference to another corps. "Thus the Marshal taught obedience and discipline with all severity," observes Skladkowski, "even to his oldest and most trusty comrades. God preserve us from being punished by the Commandant "as an example". For then the man ceases to exist, and only stern, inexorable duty remains."

CHAPTER XXXVIII

PILSUDSKI'S LAST TRIUMPHS (1933-1935)

SOME six weeks later, in mid-June, 1933, Pilsudski assembled several of his generals and addressed them on military matters for about five hours in all. The excessive clerical work, inherited from Austria; the lack of uniformity in armament; guns so heavy that to transport them destroyed the streets, and so ill-found that they could seldom, if ever, be discharged; reckless expenditure on impracticable plans—such were a few of the military defects about which he unburdened his soul. The effect upon his hearers, both of the ideas and of the two orations, was immense. Deep feeling, it was clear, could still give him a temporary triumph over his infirmities, but those who loved him most were saddened by more than one assurance that he did not expect long life. He seemed to be offering a legacy of his ideas, rather than indicting the existing system. When, in August, he wrote to the Legionary meeting at Warsaw, he declared that he was always thinking that to live as he had lived was worth while, and also to conquer pain and weariness as he had done.

None the less, while certainly weaker and often more irritable than of old, his departmental labours remained unchanged until towards the close of the next year, his sixty-seventh. Through the second half of 1933, the economic crisis filled the foreground of Polish history and of Pilsudski's life. It had already lasted for some three years, and no way of escape lay open. Two-thirds of the population lived from agriculture. The amount of rye which in 1929 could be sold for twenty-four shillings fetched little more than eleven in 1932, and nine in the spring of 1933. The workless were struggling to maintain their families on an income of less than eighteen-pence a day, many living on bread, potatoes and a little tea. In three years, foreign trade per head of the population had fallen by more than two-fifths. Everywhere industry ceased to be profitable, debts remained unpaid, and businesses collapsed, while cut followed cut in the incomes of public servants. Pilsudski could only see to it that the army appropriations were not blindly sacrificed, and that the cuts in officers' pay for a forced loan were spread over as long a term as possible.

In the interest of Poland, he would still submit to no collective interference with her military forces. On the other hand, he desired to extend the area of the non-aggression pact with Russia, and joined with her and with many of her neighbours in formulating an agreed description of an aggressor. In the summer, moreover, a convention with Danzig attempted to cut the roots of strife. This provided for the unhampered use of that port by the Poles, and for an equitable division of Polish commerce between Danzig and Gdynia. Thus, by agreements with Germany and with the Free City, the palpable rise of Hitlerism among the population of Danzig became, at least for the time being, comparatively innocuous to Poland.

In home affairs, a great national loan palliated the effect of the decline in the yield of the taxes, while a scheme for constitutional revision was at least brought forward. President Moscicki had entered on a new term of office amid general goodwill, and the Pilsudskist scheme, if approved by the Seym, would make him something like a monarch, supported by a powerful Senate, composed predominantly of distinguished soldiers. When the year 1933 closed, it was evident that seven years of the *régime* had made Poland an important member of the European circle. Well armed, well organized and not insolvent, she stood for peace and for agreed collaboration with all the strongest Continental States. Poland and the outside world alike recognized that all this was mainly due to the work and influence of Pilsudski.

Through the year 1934, Pilsudski still fashioned and guided Poland. Although the peace of Europe remained unbroken, unrest continued, and on some sides even grew. Political instability increased in France, while in Germany Hitlerism became ever stronger, and in August the death of Hindenburg raised Hitler to the semi-divine dignity of the *Führer*. At the same time, Stalin's triumph over Russian peasant individualism seemed to be complete, and Russia, which had replaced Germany in the League of Nations, obviously intended to play a greater part in Europe. France strove to maintain her influence, and to stabilize the existing order, by an East European pact on Locarno lines—a policy to which revisionist Germany could not agree.

Poland, meanwhile, was confronted by many problems. Her budget was still unbalanced: her surplus population could neither emigrate nor find employment: her constitution remained unrevised: her Ukrainians and Jews were unassimilated: Lithuania continued to obstruct the Baltic League, to which Poland looked for prestige and safety: friction with Czechoslovakia regarding Teschen was revived: the old tendency to treat Poland as an upstart had not entirely vanished. But Pilsudski struck out manfully on every side. Although the Corridor and Polish Silesia still rankled, the Germans did not refuse to sign a ten-year declaration of mutual peace with Poland, nor the French, to condone this action by their ally. Constitutional revision was brought nearer by a clever parliamentary stroke which secured the passage of the government bill through the Seym when its chief opponents were absent. Pilsudski, however, declined to reap immediately the fruit which mere smartness had thus placed within his reach.

In September, 1934, Poland showed the same indifference to League opinion that, in making an agreement with Germany and in refusing the Eastern pact, she had shown to that of France. Pilsudski's henchman, Beck, who had been active in visiting foreign capitals, while his master received statesmen who came to Warsaw, denounced at Geneva those guarantees to national minorities which had been imposed upon Poland at Versailles. These minorities, he claimed, were fully protected by Polish law, and to endure international supervision degraded the Polish State. The representatives of Britain, France and Italy protested in vain against such one-sided denunciation of treaties. A few years later, Germany followed Poland in repudiating obligations imposed upon her when left helpless by the war.

Through this, the last year which he was destined to complete, Pilsudski more than ever lived for the discharge of his public duties. His strength was undoubtedly declining, and for the first time no greeting to the Legionary meeting in August came from his pen. From his summer quarters, in September, he sent a few lines of congratulation to a distinguished Polish airman, and of condolence to a Legionary's widow, but that was all. By strict economy of his strength, however, he was able to do his departmental work, and it was fortunate for posterity that in Skladkowski he had a subordinate who was both an experienced doctor and a faithful chronicler of what he saw.

In March, 1934, when the body-physician feared the

effect of any prolonged discussion, Skladkowski paints the Marshal sitting in a plain tunic at a great table heaped with papers, one pile kept in place by a big revolver. He looked well, and, as usual, the presence of his old comrade, General Rouppert, made him jocular. His lightness of heart owed something to the fact that their business was promotions in the Sanitary services of the army. For in the Marshal's eyes these services hardly ranked with those of the three principal arms, and his most strict and anxious care was always devoted to the infantry, the queen of battles.

The Sanitary promotions having been thrust aside after a cat-and-mouse conversation in which the two subordinates hardly dared to interpose, Pilsudski relaxed into anecdote. When he was in England, he said, no man would enter a railway compartment in which a woman sat alone, although it was not labelled "Ladies". Skladkowski ventured, "With us it is just the opposite", but felt himself snubbed by silence. Later, thinking of his nieces in the universities of Warsaw and Wilno, the Marshal sharply criticized the dilettantism of Polish studies and the national reluctance to specialize in a restricted field. Tired by a meeting of post-May, 1926, Premiers on the previous day, he could not be brought to speak the final word on Sanitary promotions.

A week later, four generals and a colonel attended the Marshal, but observed with alarm that he was in full uniform and greeted them with formal politeness. They were soon to hear that no more promotions were to be made that year. Pilsudski said nothing of the economic crisis or of the security of peace. He touched briefly on the misfortune of the Polish army in having been improvised in war-time, with two bad armies, the Austrian and, still worse, the Russian, as its prototypes, and with a lack of good material for high command.

After two days of hard work, the Marshal held another meeting to correct the faulty system of ranking officers, which he improved by raising the regimental commanders. He looked well, breathed freely, and avoided fits of passion, even when denouncing the multiplicity of officials. In pre-war days, he said, travellers crossing the Niemen found one customs officer and two or three policemen on the German side, while, on the Russian, the numbers were twelve and six respectively. Moscow had ten times as many postal officials as London needed to deal with fifty-two times the Moscow number of consignments.

Early in July, the generals who usually took part in determining promotions were summoned to give written advice on the choice of a First Vice-Minister of War. The President attended, but Pilsudski dominated the meeting. He bade them disregard all criteria except that of ability to manipulate the army when he himself was not in command. Next day, Kasprzycki was appointed.

During the brief remainder of Pilsudski's life, the question of his health became *par excellence* the question. Late in August, he returned to work, sunburned, but complaining of persistent fever. On Independence Day, encouraged by good weather, he reviewed the troops, but the effort overtaxed his strength. A chair was brought, and, for the first time, he was assisted to his car. During the winter, his gait became that of a tottering old man, but he steadfastly refused to be treated as an invalid, and continued to steer the State.

In the first months of 1935, Pilsudski's steersmanship was rewarded by remarkable successes. The new constitution, which was finally voted in March, admirably expressed his mature conception of Polish politics. Every man and woman retained a share of the sovereignty in the right to give an equal and secret vote for the membership of the Seym. The Senate, no longer directly elected, but nominated as to one-third of its members by the President of the Republic, brought to parliament the strength that comes from the proved merit of every individual member in some department of affairs. Parliament itself could pass bills into law and check the government by votes of want of confidence.

This restriction of its powers might rid Poland of the "partyism" which had ruined her in the eighteenth century and which threatened to ruin her in the twentieth. It was still improbable, however, that a Seym elected by the people would ever be sincerely satisfied with a secondary position in the State. And secondary it must be, so long as the government could pursue its own policy and carry on the administration without authorization by the Lower House.

The President, declared the constitution, stands at the head of the State. For its destinies, the responsibility before God and history rests on him. His supreme duty is to care for its welfare, for its readiness to meet attack, and for its position among the nations. He must co-ordinate the activities of the supreme organs of State. He appoints the Premier, with colleagues whom the Premier recommends. He calls and dismisses parliament, is the supreme head of the armed forces, and represents the State in dealings with foreign Powers. He decides on war and peace, nominates all the highest officials, and has the rights of impeachment and of pardon. He is elected for seven years, by an electoral body appointed by parliament. If the retiring President nominates one candidate, and the electoral body another, the choice between them is made by referendum. The President swears to guard the dignity of the State, to apply the constitution, to administer equal justice, and to regard as his supreme duty solicitous care for the welfare of the State.

Such was the rulership which Pilsudski might well have accepted, had it existed in the days of his strength. It forms the crown of a political structure which is neither parliamentary nor totalitarian, but Polish, and which is designed to make the Poles free citizens of a strong State. Equally Pilsudskian and Polish was the foreign policy which, in the spring of 1935, met the growing force of Hitlerism and the imperial ambition of Mussolini. Neither France nor the League might make a tool of Poland, but with both Poland wished to remain on cordial terms—such was the formula of the State which firmly refused the Eastern Pact. When, with an eye on subjugating Abyssinia and maintaining Austrian independence, Italy drew closer to France, Poland was careful not to be lured into antagonism to Germany. But she did not allow respect for Germany or resentment against Lithuania to make her an accomplice in the threatened German move on Memel. Strength, peace and independence remained to the last the watchword of him who was publicly acclaimed as the great builder of Poland.

CHAPTER XXXIX

THE FINAL SCENES (1935)

EARLY in April, 1935, the Marshal conversed at length with Mr. Anthony Eden, and on the 10th he was summoning his colleagues as usual. By this time, however, his thinness, pallor and feebleness were such as his friends could not sincerely ascribe merely to his time of life. The death of his dearly-loved sister had added to his depression, and his customary visit to Wilno, on 19 March, failed to bring him relief. Abstinence from all food, save tea and biscuits, could not relieve his pains, and at long last he consented to a medical examination. This he postponed until after Easter, which he spent with his family "in peace". Even then, his friends feared that he might recant, but, on 24 April, an experienced and kindly professor arrived from Vienna. The Marshal at first declined to see him, but Rouppert's influence prevailed, and, on 25 April, the Austrian made the examination. He found clear evidence of cancer, which had already reached the liver. He declared the disease incurable and thought the end not far off.

Pilsudski still refused to surrender to his body's weakness. He wished to see Laval, as he had seen Eden, and so well was his state of health concealed that, when he was compelled to excuse himself on the grounds of indisposition, the illness was believed to be diplomatic, a mark of aversion from the Eastern Pact. On 8 and 9 May, he had been seen to walk slowly along the terrace of the Belvedere. On the next day, Friday, he became so much worse that the professor was brought from Vienna in an aeroplane. None the less, he refused to descend below a bath-chair, and thrice received Beck on political questions raised by Laval's visit. On Saturday, he summoned General Rydz-Smigly to a long conference about the army. In the evening, however, a haemorrhage drained the last remnants of his strength, and convinced even the most incredulous of his friends that Poland must prepare to lose him.

Sunday, 12 May, the ninth anniversary of the *coup d'état*, witnessed the final scene. Towards evening, Skladkowski found Rouppert and Wieniawa in attendance at the Belvedere. Their Commandant, they said, was still conscious. He had raised his hand to bless his children, and protested when the doctor's needle pricked his arm. A priest had been sent for, and soon arrived, to give Extreme Unction. Slawek, then Prime Minister, came, and departed to inform the President and Council. At 8.45 p.m., Pilsudski's life reached its peaceful close. Wife and daughters, priest and doctor, three old Legionaries and the Commander-in-Chief, these knelt around the bed, while the adjutant on duty remained standing. In his hand the dead man clasped the medallion of the Ostra Brama Virgin, which he always bore.

From that day to the present, one continuous thread of Polish life has been a requiem for Pilsudski. All the shires and cities contend in discovering and fulfilling plans to do him honour and to display their unfading love. Statues, portraits, pyramids appear on all sides; streets, squares and institutions everywhere receive his name. In Wilno, soldiers keep endless watch over the tomb in which his heart lies at his mother's feet. In Cracow, among the tombs of kings and heroes, his remains the most honoured dust. Russia bestows on Poland his prison records; Germany, his Magdeburg cell; while the Poles decide that only a sarcophagus of pure silver can be worthy to enshrine his bones. His death-day witnesses a more intense commemoration than even the Armistice in Britain. When, in October, 1938, the Polish wrongs at Teschen were redressed, his pupil, Beck, told the crowd that something had been done to remove the causes of Pilsudski's immeasurable sufferings for slighted Poland, and to realize his dreams, nay, his wise estimates, of what her empurpled majesty should rightly be.

The funeral ceremonies of May, 1935, were worthy of a sensitive and artistic nation, long schooled in suffering, and now mourning for her greatest man. Amid immense and reverent crowds, the Marshal's body was borne with every military honour from the Belvedere to the Cathedral, where a great service was held at midnight. Thither, for a day, the people flocked to take their solemn farewell. Next day, after the funeral mass, Bishop Gawlina preached a memorable sermon, reviewing the Marshal's life and mighty deeds. Then, with every mark of family affection and of Polish and foreign reverence, the victor was borne to the parade-ground for his last review. This done, the procession escorted him to the funeral train, which set out for Cracow in a sudden storm.

Before its departure, the waiting crowd—cyclists, bareheaded women, men in ancient coats and boots, drenched by the rain—surged towards the coffin. All through the long journey, the people flocked to pay their homage and to lament in concert as the Marshal's train passed by. In Cracow, on Saturday, 18 May, official and intellectual Poland headed the vast concourse of military and civil mourners. After a four hours' march, the President of the Republic uttered a majestic and eloquent tribute at the Cathedral gates. "To Poland", he said, "he gave freedom, boundaries, power and honour. . . . The mighty lord of Polish hearts and souls, he has bequeathed to us a rich inheritance." One more great funeral service, with both Greek and Latin rites, and the highest generals bore the coffin to the Wawel crypt, where the mourners took their last farewell. Through four hours afterwards, bodies of representatives filed by. There still remained the ceremonies, no less reverent and moving, of the burial of the Marshal's heart at Wilno.

Bishop Gawlina's sermon, preached in the presence of four princes of the Church, serves in some measure to fill that gap in any great man's life which is left by silence with regard to his religion. Pilsudski, we may assume, was not the man to turn lightly from the faith of his fathers, especially when that faith was intertwined with the very being of the Polish people. The technical apostasy of his marriage in 1899 was never punished by the erasure of his name from the muster-roll of the faithful. His second marriage was celebrated with Catholic rites. Pius XI, " the godfather of Polish independence," loved and addressed him as a son. He continued to wear the medal of the Virgin, and, apparently, to regard himself as a professing Catholic. Parents by thousands prevailed on him to act as sponsor for baptismal vows. In his last hour, and after death, the Church treated him as a cherished member.

None the less, whatever devotion he may have felt, his silence on such subjects, and the lack of many observances, add to the value of the Bishop's inspiring review of his life as seen in the light of the Christian verity.

"Even unto death for justice," cried the preacher, "—by that watchword Joseph Pilsudski steered all his life. When he first encountered the invader, his noble soul demanded the truth, and stirred his arm to fight for justice. God's spirit spoke to his young soul, which, true and noble, turned with joy to the Most High. God's hand was over him, and in him the Lord delighted. He signed his head with the sign of greatness, and bade him fulfil His mission among our people. In this his mission Joseph Pilsudski believed. He believed in divine justice. He knew that peoples have not such souls as individual men, to receive reward or punishment like theirs from God, the eternal judge. He knew that, here and now, God's justice must reward each people for its virtues or punish it for its sins. Therefore he claimed the resurrection of Poland from a just God.

"He knew that the wrong done to our dearest fatherland was a crime crying to heaven for vengeance, and that every movement to erase that crime is a righteous deed tending to restitution. And from this conviction there grew in the soul of the future Leader of the People the great moral assurance, the belief in the blessedness of battle, the belief in the triumph of the Polish sword. That belief lived on from the youth of the Warrior through all the stages of his march, when he determined to arm the soul of Poland against degrading agreement with the invader, when he thirsted to deliver the ark of the fatherland from dishonour. . . .

"In 1920, the fortune of the fatherland was at stake. It was the moment of which its witness, now Pope Pius XI, declared that 'the angel of darkness is fighting a great battle with the angel of light.' All Poland stood against the enemy, and her leader was Joseph Pilsudski.

"Thou, Leader, wast the fulfiller of the righteous judgments of God for the sin and crime of Partition, for so many tears poured out, for so many families destroyed, for the persecution of the holy faith, for churches dishonoured, for suffering exiles sent to Siberia, for the low moans and despairing cries which rose to God from amid the clank of chains. At thy hands, Christian culture triumphed over barbarism. In Europe, order was regained, and the Church our Mother, freed by thee, gives thanks. With thee as Leader, our boundaries and the structure of our State took shape. Nine years ago, the government passed undivided into thy hands. Thou didst prepare the future of Poland, desiring her great and strong. On thee fell all the heat and burden of the day. And as of old thou didst prepare for war, so in late years thou hast prepared for peace.

"Marshal of Poland! May Saint Michael, God's ensign, bear thy immortal soul before the throne of the Most High God of Armies, and may God reward thee with His eternal light and boundless peace for all the good that thou hast done, for all the evil that thou hast suffered, for what thou hast accomplished on earth for His glory and for the good of our people. Amen."

Chapter XL

THE STANDPOINT OF 1939

CAN we, within four years of his death, measure Pilsudski's greatness? The Marshal himself declared that a true verdict could not be given by this generation, and some wise Poles maintain that even his thoughts and purposes cannot yet be fully understood. Comparison with Lenin, the more famous creator of a greater State, may help us to measure the stature of his conqueror in 1920. Their careers, indeed, ran strangely parallel. Both "the lordling" Pilsudski and the youth who petitioned the Tsar's ministers as "Hereditary Nobleman" were born of mothers who taught them to hate the tsardom. The lives of both were deeply influenced by the same abortive crime—that conspiracy of 1887 which brought Lenin's elder brother to the gallows and Pilsudski's to Siberia for fifteen years. Both married ardent revolutionaries, and, until their later forties, both lived for seemingly hopeless revolution. Both spent many years in poverty and exile; alike returning from Siberia to refuges in London and in Cracow.

In private life, both were kindly men, prone to the jovial laughter which prompted Italian children to nickname Lenin "Signor Drin-drin". Both were inveterate journalists, able organizers and effective speakers. Both split their party. Both passed from obscurity to the helm of a vast though chaotic State. Both towered over their associates, won the worship of their people, and remained great political forces after death.

Differences, indeed, there were, some so deep-seated as

to make comparison with Lenin an inconclusive method of even roughly measuring Pilsudski. While both possessed unbounded moral courage, Pilsudski loved adventures, while Lenin only nerved himself to endure them when necessary for the Cause. Lord d'Abernon asserted that only imminent danger raised the Marshal's pulse from 40 to a normal rate. Pilsudski could never have declared with Lenin that any idea of any God was the most vile infection. At bottom, Pilsudski was the soldier; Lenin, the civilian: Pilsudski, the patriot; Lenin, the universalist: Pilsudski, the realist; Lenin, the *doctrinaire*. Both were by nature human, but Pilsudski, with his far richer endowment, made a greater sacrifice of his humanity than did the more prosaic Lenin. It is curious that no estimate of either by the other has yet seen the light.

Lenin, it must be remembered, governed Russia for barely five years, and those full of civil war and famine. Pilsudski dominated Poland for twice as long a time, and with better human material and communications. It may be worth recording that, some seventeen years after Lenin's fatal illness began, a widespread belief prevails outside his State that it may not long endure, while Pilsudskian Poland is accounted relatively stable.

Some of the marks of greatness were Pilsudski's beyond all doubt. Courage, both physical and moral, self-sacrifice for Poland, capacity for many kinds of work, energy prodigious and long-sustained—these could not be denied him. From the boys of Wilno to von Beseler, from the first Legionaries to the foreign generals in 1920 and the British financial mission, those who met him felt that a rare being was before them. The Greek Premier likened him to those statesmen of ancient Greece and Rome who governed their people in peace, and in war led them to battle. Countless men and women were subjugated by the sheer force of his personality. A considerable man, a memorable man, an outstanding man he was, beyond all question.

From "outstanding" to "great", however, is a far cry, and many have denied Pilsudski greatness. Whatever his distant goal, he approached it, apparently, by a zigzag course. First a member of the P.P.S., then of the Fraction, then not a Socialist at all, now for the Central Powers, now for the Allies, long a bitter enemy of Powers with which he later made *ententes*, a democrat who abused the parliament until some thought him demented, and who led troops to drive the Premier from office—on the face of it, his career needs explanation. Turning from parties and alliances to persons, the student finds that a few men, Legionaries for the most part, remained Pilsudski's friends, but that he broke with many, and that some, at least, of these were patriots and men of worth. The statesman's course, indeed, cannot be straight if rocks and currents chequer the sea, and few great men have escaped disparagement and hatred. Cavil may be ignored if Pilsudski chose fitting aims for Poland and impelled her powerfully to fulfil them.

"Romanticism of ideals, realism in their pursuit"— such was Pilsudski's watchword, and to it his policy conformed. For the vague and divided Poland of 1914 to become a clear-cut and united Power was indeed a romantic ideal. When, in April, 1935, he faintly signed a true Pilsudski constitution, he might indeed admire what he and the Poles had done. Illiteracy was hastening towards extinction, and since the events of May the average tenure of the Foreign Minister had grown from five months to above six years.

Was Poland, however, stable? In 1791, the signing of a

constitution had heralded the downfall of the Polish State. Poland still lay between Great Powers who wished her ill, while at home poverty and political discontent were rife, and party spirit had not ceased to rage. The country was reborn, but hardly yet regenerate.

It may be urged, however, that even if some social earthquake or vagary of dictatorship should cause Poland to collapse, Pilsudski's title to greatness would yet remain secure. If only no crack in the foundation or structure of his building existed, he had already achieved what only a great man could do. Who in 1919 could have supposed that, after twenty years, Poland could be a progressive State of five-and-thirty millions, enjoying good-neighbourly relations with both Germany and Russia, having a parliament, a reasonably stable government, a balanced budget, a well-trained army, and the memory of eighteen years of peace? And who in 1939 can suppose that without Pilsudski her achievements would have been on such a scale as this?

Historically speaking, indeed, even the earliest of Pilsudski's decisions is of yesterday. All that can be said is, that in none of Poland's problems has his solution been proved incorrect, and that in many there are indications that he was peculiarly right. What kind of State should the Polish nation endeavour to create?—that was the foremost question when he came from Magdeburg. He answered: a State united, national but tolerant, with access to the sea, trusting for defence to its own government and army, avoiding imported institutions, but so forming its own as to ensure social justice, framing its constitution on liberal lines while guarding against the well-known evils of democracy, the patron of its weaker neighbours but never the client of the strong. Time, multiplying the Jews and

THE STANDPOINT OF 1939

peasants, developing the consciousness of the Ukrainians, and heating to boiling-point the nationalism of the Germans, has already confronted Poland with a harder world. But his friends and pupils still remain at the helm, and still proclaim and practise the principles that he bequeathed. The elections of November, 1938, proved, at least, that his policy has gained in favour with the people.

Diplomatic successes have overcome the intransigence of Lithuania and have removed the long-standing grievance with regard to Teschen. German fury against the Jews and Romanists has gilded by contrast the humane repute of Poland. Weightiest of all, since the patrimony and the life-blood of the nation are at stake, the Pilsudski solutions of the German and the Russian questions have held good and thereby gained in prescriptive force. The closer pact with Moscow late in 1938 echoed the Marshal's reply to the signs of German aggressiveness of early 1933. The first days of 1939 suggest that the sequel will be no less happy.

INDEX

(Place-names in brackets are those of the present day.)

Abyssinia, 310
Academic Legion (1918), 109
Act of 5 Nov. 1916, 87, 89
Airmen, American, 3, 4
Alexander II (Tsar 1855-81), 17, 199
Alexander III (Tsar 1881-94), 17
Allenstein, 140
America (*see* United States), 120
American Poles, 67, 180
Armistice (11 Nov. 1918), 102, 118, 161, 200, 239, 286, 313
Army, Pilsudski's system, 125, chap. xxxviii
Austria (Empire, to 1918), 2, 3, 24, 39, 45, 60, 64, 78, 79, 86, 156, 185, 191, 193, 199, 213, 267, 283, 289, 293, 303, 307
Austria (Republic 1918-38), 148, 310
Auxiliary Military Committees (1917), 85

Bacinski, Captain (Gen. Baczynski), 4
Baikal, Lake, 19
Balkan War (1912), 62, 64, 67
Baltic States, the, 119
Baranowski, Wl., diplomat and author, 80

Bartel, Prof. Casimir, thrice Premier (b. 1882), 229, 230, 233, 236-238, 245, 252-255, 257, 260, 262, 263, 272, 274
Basin, the Dombrowska, 108, 109
Beaumont Square, London, E., Revolutionary Headquarters, 30
Beck, Colonel, Foreign Minister since Nov. 1932 (b. 1894), 265, 268, 269, 275, 276, 297, 300, 306, 312, 313
Belgium, 62, 148, 289, 311-313.
Belvedere, Warsaw Palace, 92, 151, 170, 182, 193, 200, 210, 221, 227-229, 234, 238, 256
Berlin, 55, 90, 93, 99, 100, 138, 201
Bessarabia, 123
Bezdany, village, chap. x, 98, 271, 287
Bialystok, 123
Bilinski, Leon, 286, 288, 289
Birmingham, University Slavonic Department, xiii
Bismarck, Count Otto von (1815-98), 7, 263
Bloc, non-party, of collaboration with the Government (1928), 249, 250, 258, 262, 271, 275, 281, 290

322

INDEX

Bloody Wednesday (1906), 287
Bloody Sunday (Jan. 1905), 46
Boerner, Captain, 103
Bolshevists, 101, 105, 106, 108, 110, 113, 114, 117, 118, 120-144, 146, 154, 157, 161, 164, 173, 187-189, 194, 205, 210
Borderlands, Polish, 12, 76, 120, 126, 146
Bosnia, crisis of 1908, 60
Boswell, Prof. Bruce, historian, xiii
"Bottom of the Eye," article, 259-261
Brest-Litovsk (Bresc), 123, 134, 136, 137, 188
Brest - Litovsk, prisoners of (1930), 114, 277, 278, 284, 290, 295
Briand, Aristide, 295
Britain, xi, 148, 191, 209, 210, 306, 313
Brittany, 119
Broadcast, Pilsudski's, 11 Nov. 1926, 239-242
Brusilov, Russian General, 78, 79
Bucarest, 146
Budget, the Polish, 165, 259, 262, 266, 274, 294, 295
Budget for 1931-2, 280, 291
Budienny, Soviet General, 131, 133, 134, 136, 139, 140
Bug, river, 123, 134, 136, 137, 188
Bulgaria, 64
Bund, Jewish society, 25

Canterbury, 132
Capital, by Karl Marx (1867), 17
Castle, Warsaw, 227
Catherine II, the Great (1729-1796), 12, 247, 269
"Central Lithuania," 142, 146, 151, 155
Centre-Left Congress (1930), 275, 281
Cepnik, H., author, xiii
Charles VIII (last Austrian Emperor, 1916-18), 114
Charles XII of Sweden (1697-1718), 128
Chelm, 137
Chicago, 154
Christian Democrats, 225
Cieszyn. See Teschen
Citadel, Warsaw (*see* Tenth Pavilion), 227-229
Clemenceau, Georges, 117
"Colonels' party," the, 258
Colonels, Council of, 78
Commandant, the (Pilsudski), 98, 109, 238, 256, 261, 302, 312
Commissars, 136
Communism, 50, 109, 110, 250
"Comrade Victor" (Pilsudski), 28
Concordat, 147
Congress Kingdom (1815-31), 2
Constituent (1st Seym, q.v., Feb. 1919-Nov. 1922), 114, 144, 153, 156, 159

Constitution of 1791, 320
Constitution of 1921, 124, 146, 154, 162, 166
Constitution of 1935, 258, 290, 305, 306, 308-310, 319
Constitution, the " Little," 161
Constitution, Russian, of October 1905, 43
Cooper, Lt.-Col. M. C., American Airman, 4
Corridor, the Polish, 130, 275, 290, 300, 305
Cossacks, 132
Council of Regency, 94
Cracow (Krakow), 24, 40, 42, 49, 50, 62, 65, 69, 70, 72, 73, 76, 78, 86, 94, 97, 108, 111, 186, 199-201, 218, 241, 267, 312-314
Crimean War (1854-6), 7
Crisis, the economic, 266, 267, 290, 292, 299, 303, 304, 307
Crisis, Polish, of 1922, chap. xxiv
Cromwell, Oliver, 250
Currency, 89, 147, 148, 165, 166, 174, 190, 193, 194, 210, 214, 289
Czechs, Czechoslovakia, 3, 72, 113, 123, 124, 127, 133, 135, 141, 151, 157, 158, 195, 205, 305
Czeremoszno, village, 196
Czermanski, Z., artist, xiii

D'Abernon, Lord, 26, 318
Danes, 298

Danzig (Gdansk), 3, 105, 115, 117, 120, 124, 135, 136, 137, 143, 151, 156, 157, 174, 195, 257, 275, 290, 300, 301, 304
Daszynski, Ignatius (pr. Dashinski) (b. 1866), 62, 101, 105, 135, 251, 266-271, 277, 279, 285-288
Davoust, Marshal (1770-1823), 75
Dawn, newspaper, 25, 27, 29
Demblin, 72, 287
Denikin, Antony, Russian " White " General, 132, 187
D'Etchegoyen, author, xiii
Dmowski, Roman (pr. Dmoffski) (1864-1939), xiii, 22, 44, 59, 104, 112, 117, 124, 135, 138, 143, 153, 155, 182, 211
Dombrowski, *alias* Pilsudski, 35
Dorpat (Tartu), 16
Dunajec, river, 73
Dwinsk (Daugavpils), 126
Dyboski, Roman, Professor, xii, 22
" Dying World " (article), (1929), 266, 267, 278

East Prussia, province, 137, 139, 140, 143
Eastern Pact, 305, 306, 310, 311
Eden, Mr. Anthony, 311
Edwards, Sutherland, author, 6
Egypt, 294, 296, 297
Elbe, river, 93

INDEX

Elections of 1938, 321
Elections, the Polish, of 1922, 165; of 1928, 246, 249; of 1930, chap. xxxv
Estonia, 3, 7, 119, 128, 156, 205

Faithful Service Order (1916), 79
Fascism, 231, 250
Fauntleroy, Major, 3, 4
Ferdinand, King of Rumania, 164
Finland, Finns, 44, 128, 156
First Brigade, the Legionary, 76, 77, 78, 79, 177-179
Foch, Marshal (1851-1929), 106, 135, 174
Four-Power Pact, 301
"Fraction" (of P.P.S.), 50, 319
France, 2, 14, 60, 62, 123, 145, 148, 174, 176, 180, 191, 192, 195, 209, 210, 220, 251, 290, 305, 306, 310
Frederick the Great (1712-86), 128
"Funds at disposal," the, 259

Galicia, 24, 70, 72, 96, 114, 124, 127, 140, 146, 156, 164, 193
Gawlina, Bishop, 313-316
Gdynia, 174, 194, 235, 257, 275, 289, 299, 304
Geneva, 247, 248, 295, 306
Genoa Conference (April-May 1922), 156, 181

German Minority in Poland, 130, 249, 321
German Soldiers' Council, 101, 103, 200
Germany, Germans, 2, 59, 60, 78, 79, 81, 83, 84, 86, 91, 95, 98, 102, 105, 122, 124, 127, 128, 135, 138, 141, 145, 148, 149, 154, 156, 157, 159, 163, 165, 175, 182, 185, 195, 199, 200, 205, 209, 210, 220, 221, 237, 250, 257, 266, 267, 290, 296, 300, 301, 304-306, 308, 310, 312, 320, 321
Ghetto, the, 200, 201
Gillie, D. R., author, xiii, 52
Gladstone, W. E. (1809-98), 263
Gorlice, 76
Grabski, Ladislas (b. 1873), twice Premier, 191, 192, 194, 201, 205, 210, 224, 225, 289
Gramophone Records, Pilsudski's, 197, 198
Greece, 318
Greek Church, 7, 11, 48, 112, 314
Grodno, 53, 114, 123, 137, 140
Grzybowski Square, Warsaw, 45, 270, 271

Haller, Joseph, General (b. 1873), Commander, 62, 104, 124, 173, 186, 207
Haller, Stanislas, General (b. 1872), Chief of Staff, 207, 208

Harrison, E. J., author, xiii
Helsingfors (Helsinki), 12
Henri IV of France (of Navarre), 183
Hindenburg, Paul von (1847-1934), German Marshal and President, 196, 204, 205, 295, 305
Historical Bureau, 209
Historical Commission (1925), 207-209, 215
"Historical Corrections" (1931), 286-289
Hitler, Adolf, 285, 295, 300, 301, 304, 305, 310
Hohenzollerns, 3
Howard, Sir Esmé, diplomat, 120
Hungary, 122, 123, 133

I.K.C., "The Polish *Daily Mail*," 13
Illakowiczowna, Kazimierza (Mlle Illakowicz), poet, the Marshal's Private Secretary, xiii
Independence Day, Polish, 11 Nov. (1918), 239, 308
International Socialist Congress (1896), 30
Irkutsk, 19, 20, 21, 22, 61
Irtuish, river, 19
Italy, 77, 199, 250, 306, 310

January Insurrection (1863), 7, 8, 22, 24, 66, 191, 198, 199

Japan, 43, 44, 47, 157, 287, 298
Jews, 11, 25, 33, 36, 49, 71, 110, 117, 121, 140, 148, 155, 157, 165, 166, 172, 182, 189, 205, 229, 249, 305, 320, 321
Jitomir, 131
Joffre, Marshal, 293

Kalisz, 196, 246
Kama, river, 19
Kasprzycki, General T. (pr. Kaschitski) (b. 1892), succeeded the Marshal as War Minister (1935), 308
Kasztanka (chestnut), Pilsudski's mare, 241, 242
Keller, General, 196
Kellogg Pact (1928), 257
Kharkov, 16
Kielce, 70, 71, 196, 236
Kiev, 40, 52, 53, 131, 132, 207
Kirensk, 20, 21
Kluck, General von (1846-1934), 204
Koc, Adam, Colonel, 101
Kolchak, Admiral, Russian "White" General, 132
Konopczyński, Prof. Wl., 207
Korfanty, W. (b. 1873), 149, 163, 278
Korostowetz, author, xiii
Kosciuszko (1746-1817), 178
Kostiuchnowka, village, 78
Kovel, 196
Kovno, 76, 123, 172
Kukiel, General, military historian, 63

INDEX

Kwiatkowski, E. (b. 1888), Vice-Premier, 235, 263

Labour Day. *See* May Day
Lapy, 34
Latvia, 6, 119, 120, 125, 132, 156
Laval, 311, 312
Law of April 1935, 319
"League," young Pilsudski's, 13, 14
League of Nations, 149, 158, 188, 195, 205, 237, 247, 248, 266, 295, 300, 301, 305, 306, 310
Lectures, Pilsudski's (1910), 61
Legions, the Polish, 75, chap. xiii, 86, 89, 91, 92, 94, 96, 98, 99, 110, 180, 183, 184, 186, 194, 196, 197, 200, 201, 206, 236, 246, 251, 256, 275, 292, 293, 299, 301, 303, 306, 312, 318, 319
Lemberg (Lwow, q.v.), 61, 66
Lena, river, 20
Lenin (V. I. Ulianov) (1870-1924), xi, 17, 123, 126, 128, 133, 263, 317, 318
Leningrad. *See* St. Petersburg
Letts, the, 3, 6, 7, 119, 128
Leytonstone, 40
Libau (Liepaja), 120
Limanova, village, 73, 75
Lithuania, 3, 5, 6, 17, 26, 42, 74, 110, 119, 120, 122, 128, 129, 140, 141, 143, 146, 151, 152, 155, 156, 157, 159, 173, 183, 188, 195, 243-245, 247, 248, 251, 257, 290, 305, 310, 321
Lloyd George, David, 117, 123
Locarno Conference (1925), 209, 216, 305
Lodz (pr. Wooge), 28, 34, 35, 43, 51, 90, 287
Lomza, 140
London, 25, 30, 33, 35, 40, 41, 308
Lublin, 76, 78, 101, 104, 105, 126, 196, 200, 201, 288
Lubomirski, Prince, 101
Ludendorff, Erich (b. 1865), German General, 204
Lwow (*see* Lemberg), 62, 71, 76, 78, 105, 108, 110, 113, 114, 134, 136, 140, 143, 155, 173, 183-186, 216
Lwow, Prince, Russian Premier (1917), 89

Madeira, 284-289
Magdeburg, 93, 97, 99, 144, 154, 177, 184, 191, 210, 231, 256, 312, 320
Malicki, J. K., historian, xiii
Malinowski, Alex., 35, 190
March 19 (Pilsudski's name-day), 194, 285
Marienwerder, 140
Marne, battle of the (1914), 204
Marx, Karl (1818-83), 17, 21
May, 1926, events of, chap. xxxi, 237, 281, 307, 319

May Day, 33, 224
Memel (Klaipeda), 156, 247, 310
Memorandum of 26 Dec. 1916, Pilsudski's, 81, 82
Memories of the Legions, 204
Mendelson, Stanislas, 27
Mickiewicz, Adam (pr. Mitskáy-vish), (1798-1855), 31
Militants, 46, chaps. ix, x, 59, 287
Minsk, 123, 125, 133, 139, 140, 141
Modlin, 136
Moltke, Count von (1800-91), Field-Marshal, 213
Montenegro, 64
Moraczewski, A. (b. 1870), Premier, 110, 144
Moscicki, Ignatius (b. 1867), (pr. Mos-chit-ski), Professor and 3rd President, 30, 203, 235, 237, 262, 269, 272, 274, 276, 297, 304, 308
Moscow, 72, 308, 321
Mozyr Group, 137, 138
Muraviev, Count, 8, 12, 31
Murray, 1st Lieut. K. M., 3
Mussolini, Benito (b. 1883), 263, 301, 310

Name-day, Pilsudski's. *See* March 19
Napoleon III, 198
Napoleon, the Great (1769-1821), 84, 125, 128, 150, 187, 198, 220, 255, 256, 282

Narew, river, 134, 136, 137, 138
Narutowicz, Gabriel (pr. Naroot-oh-vish), 1st President (1922), 164, 170-172, 176, 181-183, 189, 193, 229, 231, 234, 246
National Assembly of December 1922, 169; of May 1926, 230, 234, 235
National Democrats (*see also* Dmowski), 22, 44, 45, 60, 63, 65, 66, 71, 104, 105, 112, 153, 166, 173, 186, 191, 200, 211, 233, 249, 266, 281, 288, 289
National Minorities, Polish, 147, 165, 249, 290
National Workers, New York, 189
Nicholas II (Tsar 1894-1917), 31
Nida, river, 76
Niemen, river, 52, 134, 139, 140, 141, 142, 196, 308
Niepodleglosc (Independence), Historical Journal, xiii
Nijni Novgorod (Gorki), 19, 22
Nivelle, General, 187
N.K.N., 70, 73, 76, 79
November ("October") Revolution, Russian, of 1917, 128
Nowak, Professor, Premier, 163, 164, 166

Ob, river, 19
Okon, priest, 154
Orawa, 114

INDEX

Ostra Brama, chapel and Virgin, at Wilno, 29, 121, 312
Ozarow, 204

Paderewski, Ignatius (b. 1860), 104, 112, 113, 120, 123, 127, 144, 154, 208
Parcellation, 124
Paris, 22, 26, 47, 67, 102, 104, 112, 145, 146
Parliament, Polish. *See* Seym
Partyism, Polish, 237, 309
Patterson, E. J., historian, xiii
Peace Conference (1919), 113, 123, 149
Peasants, 7, 166, 176
People's Will (Russian Revolutionary Society), 14, 17
Perl, Madame, 188
Perm, 19
"Pertinax," French publicist (M. André Géraud), 133
Peter the Great (Tsar 1689-1725), 11, 128, 150
Petlura, Ukrainian General, 130
Petrograd. *See* St. Petersburg
Physical Education Council, 264, 297-299
Piasts (Polish Party), 166
Pilsudska, Alexandra, the Marshal's second wife. *See* Szczerbinska, 150
Pilsudska, Jadwiga, 150, 230, 239, 264, 293, 297, 299, 312
Pilsudska, Maria (Joseph Pilsudski's first wife), 34, 40, 149, 150

Pilsudska, Maria Billewiczowna, wife of J. V. P. Pilsudski, the Marshal's mother, 7-9, 312, 317
Pilsudska, Sophia (Mme Kadenacowa), Joseph's sister, 23, 311
Pilsudska, Wanda, 150, 230, 239, 264, 297, 299, 312
Pilsudski, Bronislas, 13, 17, 18, 21, 61, 145, 317
Pilsudski, John, Finance Minister, 282, 290
Pilsudski, Joseph (Józef Klemens Pilsudski), First Marshal of Poland, *passim*
Pilsudski, Joseph Vincent Peter, father of the Marshal, 5, 8, 283, 291
Pilsudski Committee, U.S.A., 189
Pinsk, 123
Pittsburg, 155
Pius XI, Pope (1857-1939), 138, 314, 315
Plébiscites, 149
Plock, 136, 137, 139
Pobog-Malinowski, W., historian, xiii
Pogrom, 49
Poland, Poles, *passim*
Poland and the Poles (1919), xiii
Poland in January 1939, 320, 321
Polish Handbook, xiii
Polish National Committee (Paris), 102, 112, 119, 124

329

Polish Pomerania (Pomorze), 143, 157, 229
Poniatowski, Prince Joseph (1763-1813), Marshal of France, 179, 227
Poniatowski Bridge (Warsaw), 227, 231
Pope, the, 147
Populists. *See* Piasts
Posen (Poznan), 24, 93. *See* Poznan
P.O.W., 76, 77, 80, 81, 85, 87, 90, 95, 96, 97, 99, 101, 111, 186, 190, 209, 288
Poznan (*see also* Posen), 105, 112, 113, 114, 116, 125, 138, 144, 156, 157, 188, 200, 201, 228, 229, 231, 266, 267
P.P.S. (Polish Socialist Society), 22, chaps. v, vi, 38, chap. viii, 47, 64, 98, 183, 221, 222, 280, 319 .
Praga (Warsaw suburb), 138, 227
President, the Polish (*see also* Moscicki, Narutowicz, Wojciechowski), 146, 147, chap. xxv, 231-234, 252, 257, 258, 282, 284, 309
Promotions (army), 293, 294, 307, 308
Prussia, 5, 24, 283
Prystor, Alexander (b. 1875) (Premier, 1931-3), 46, 53, 57, 272, 290, 293, 294
Prystor, Madame, wife of Alexander, 54

Przemysl, xii
Pulawy, 136, 137
Radziwill family, 239
Radzymin, 138
Rapallo (Treaty of, 1922), 159
Rataj, Matthias (b. 1884), Marshal of the Seym, twice Acting President, 228, 229
Redl, Colonel, 66, 67
Regency, Council of (1917-18), 99, 101, 104, 200
Reval (Tallinn), 12, 40
Rhine, river, 93
Rifleman, The, 67
" Riflemen," Pilsudski's, chap. xi, 69, 85, 87, 98
Riga, 12, 27, 40, 120, 141, 142, 145
Riga, Treaty of (1921), 146
Roja, General B., 108
Roman Catholicism, 24, 321
Rouppert, Dr., General, 72, 294, 307, 311, 312
Ruhr, Occupation of the (1923-4), 176
Rumania, 123, 133, 145, 164, 175, 176, 251, 257, 293, 294
Russell, Sir E. J., agronomist, xiii
Russia, Russians, 2, 5, 7, 11, 17, 59, 60, 63, 77, 82, 89, 91, 95, 98, 117, 122, 128, 129, 141, 148, 156, 157, 159, 176, 190, 191, 193, 196, 199, 200, 204, 220, 221, 231, 248, 250, 262, 266, 267, 283, 293-296,

INDEX

300, 301, 304, 305, 307, 308, 312, 320, 321
Russian frontier, 32, 41
Ruthenes, 3, 89, 110, 114, 165, 185, 243
Rydz-Smigly, Edward (also Smigly-Rydz), second Marshal, 67, 79, 124, 207, 229, 297, 312

St. Nicholas (Petersburg asylum), 38
St. Peter and St. Paul fortress in St. Petersburg, 17
St. Petersburg, 5, 17, 18, 27, 38, 46, 189
Sakhalin Island, 21
Sandomierz, 86
Scotland, 119
Second Brigade, 77
Senate, the Polish. *See* Seym
Serajevo, 69
Serbia, 64
Seym, First (Constituent) (Feb. 1919-Nov. 1922), 131, 146, 147, 150, 153-155, 160, 177; Second (Nov. 1922-Nov. 1927), 165, chap. xxv, 174, 177, 184, 185, 197, 201, 208, 212, 214, 216, 222-225, 232, 233, 237, 238, 242-245; Third (March 1928-Aug. 1930), 249-256, chap. xxxiv, 272-274, 276-284, 304; Fourth (Dec. 1930-July 1935), 283, 290, 292, 306, 309
Siberia, 18, 19, 35, 125, 287, 317

Siedlce (pr. Sheddle-ce), 49
Sikorski, General Wl., Premier (War Minister 1925) (b. 1881), 63, 138, 171, 192, 202, 206, 210, 212, 213, 215, 216, 218, 222, 224, 225, 236
Silesia, 105, 113, 143, 149, 157, 159, 164, 290, 305
Sinhalese, 80, 87
Skladkowski, General, Premier since 1936, xiii, 108, 109, 237, 238, 250-252, 255, 261-263, 268, 269, 291, 294, 301, 302, 306, 307, 312
Skrzynski, Count Alex., Premier and author, 221
Slavonic Review, the, xiii
Slavs, the, xi, 6, 16, 24
Slawek, Walery, thrice Premier (b. 1879), 46, 48, 55-57, 203, 258, 274, 275, 282, 283, 290, 312
Sliwinski, Arthur, Premier, xiii
Slovaks, 3
Slowacki, J. (1809-49), poet, 246
Smigly, General, 207. *See* Rydz-Smigly
Smogorzewski, C., author, xiii
Socialism, 13, 14, 15, 22, 26, 27, 30, 32, 39, 44, 229, 249. *See also* P.P.S.
Soldiers' Government, German, 1918
Sosnkowski, General K., War Minister (b. 1885), 61, 63, 70, 72, 93, 94, 97, 99, 100, 191, 192, 287

Spa, 188
Spain, 237
Spandau, 93
Spiz, 114
Sport, Pilsudski on, 297-299
Stabilization Loan of 1927, 263
Stalin, Joseph, virtual successor to Lenin, U.S.S.R., 305
State Tribunal (1929). See Tribunal
Stochod, river, 78, 79
Strasbourg, 159
Strife, newspaper, 42
Styr, river, 78
Sulejowek, site of Pilsudski's villa given by the Army, 180, 181, 184, 189, 193, 197, 205, 210, 215, 227, 230
Sulkiewicz, A., 28, 41
Suwalki, 125, 140, 142
Swirski, 58
Switalski, K. (b. 1886), Premier 1929, 261
Switzerland, Swiss, 40, 62, 195, 243
Szczara, river (pr. Shchara), 141, 142
Szczerbinska, Alexandra, second wife of Joseph Pilsudski, 54-56, 58, 150, 312
Szeptycki, Count S. (b. 1867), General, War Minister 1923-1924, 176, 193
Szpotanski, Stan., author, 145

Tannenberg, 204
Tauroggen, near a Pilsudski estate, 23
Temporary Council of State, 1917-18, 80, 82, 85, 87, 88, 89, 90, 91, 97
Tenth Pavilion (Warsaw), 36, 37
Teschen (Cieszyn), 113, 114, 124, 140, 305, 313, 321
Tilsit, 23
Times, The, xiii, 126, 255
Tiumen, 19
Tokio, 44
Tomaszewski, J., diplomat, xiv
Tomsk, 19
Tribunal, parliamentary, 259, 264, 265
Trotsky, Leon, Soviet leader, 126, 138
Tunka, village, 21, 22
Turkey, 64, 176
Turning-point, 209
Tutachevski, Soviet Marshal, 132, 133, 135, 139, 195
Twer, 22

Ukraine, Ukrainians, 16, 105, 108, 110, 112, 113, 114, 118, 121, 124, 125, 127, 129-133, 139, 141, 143, 146, 157, 164, 208, 249, 277, 301, 305, 321
Ulina Mala, village, 94
United States, the, 231, 263
Ural Mountains, 19

INDEX

Verdun, 145
Versailles, 116, 117; treaty of, 124, 306
Vienna, 55, 75, 78, 90, 201, 311
Vienna (1814 Congress), 2; (1906 Congress), 50
Vilja, river, 134
"Vistula Provinces," 2, 24
Vistula, river, 72, 74, 135-139, 141, 156, 227, 300
Vladivostok, 21, 162
Volga, river, 19
Volhynia, 77
Von Beseler, Governor, 78, 79, 81, 89, 92, 95, 96, 101, 318

Waldemaras, Lithuanian statesman, 243-245, 247, 248
Warsaw, 12, 14, 24, 27, 31, 34, 43, 45, 46, 47, 49, 53, 69, 72, 76, 80, 85, 87, 89, 90, 95, 97, 99, 100, 101, 105, 106, 109, 111, 112, 113, 123, 126, 133-140, 144, 161, 170, 173-175, 180, 181, 184, 185, 189, 190, 193, 195, 197, 200, 205, 227-230, 234, 246, 288, 303, 306, 307
Warsaw Gazette, 189
Wasilewski, L., Foreign Minister, 119, 120
Wawel Hill (Cracow), with Castle and Cathedral, 246, 314
Wereszycki, H., historian, xiv
Wesel, 93

Weygand, General, 135, 143, 144
White Russia (region), 122, 129, 143, 146, 165, 243, 249
"Whites," Russian anti-Bolshevists, 128, 129, 132, 133, 135
Wielopolska, M. J., 180
Wieniawa, General B. (b. 1875), later Ambassador, 294, 312
Wilno (*Russ.* Vilna; *Lith.* Vilnius), 5, 10-18, 22, 26, 27, 28, 31, 34, 53, 55, 58, 64, 114, 119-125, 133, 139, 140, 142, 143, 151-156, 159, 173, 177, 180, 184, 187, 188, 192, 198, 207, 208, 229, 247, 251, 256, 262, 292, 307, 311, 312, 318
Wilson, President Woodrow, U.S.A., 89
Witos, Vincent (b. 1874), twice Premier, 112, 135, 150, 155, 160, 166, 171, 174, 176, 177, 217, 224-229, 249, 278, 289, 295
Wkra, river (pr. Fkra), 136-138
Wojciechowski, Stanislas, 2nd President (pr. Voy-che-hoff-ske), 27, 32, 33, 34, 41, 121, 171, 176, 182, 208, 210, 213, 215, 221, 224, 227-229
Workman, newspaper, 27, 28, 34, 35, 40, 44, 49, 98, 171

Wrangel, General Peter, Russian " White " Leader, 132, 141
Wrzos, K., journalist, xiii

Year 1920, The, 195, 203, 207, 208
Young, Mr. Hilton (Lord Kennet), 193

Zaleski, Aug. (b. 1883), Foreign Minister (1926-32), 263
Zamorski, deputy, 154, 155
Zamosc, 140
Zamoyski, Count, 104
Zbrucz, river, 124
Zeligowski, General (pr. Zheligoffske) (b. 1865), War Minister 1925, 111, 142, 151, 163, 173, 188, 210, 215, 216, 218, 219, 221, 224, 247, 265
" Ziuk," 12
Zloty, the (1924), 194
Zulovo, 5, 8, 10
Zulovo Pigeon, 13
Zurich, 27
Z.W.C. (League of Military Action), 52, 54, 58, 61, 63, 287

For Product Safety Concerns and Information please contact our EU representative GPSR@taylorandfrancis.com
Taylor & Francis Verlag GmbH, Kaufingerstraße 24, 80331 München, Germany